Henry Ward Beecher

Yale Lectures on Preaching

Henry Ward Beecher

Yale Lectures on Preaching

ISBN/EAN: 9783337164003

Printed in Europe, USA, Canada, Australia, Japan

Cover: Foto ©Lupo / pixelio.de

More available books at **www.hansebooks.com**

YALE

LECTURES ON PREACHING.

BY

HENRY WARD BEECHER.

DELIVERED BEFORE THE THEOLOGICAL DEPARTMENT OF YALE COLLEGE, NEW HAVEN, CONN., IN THE REGULAR COURSE OF THE "LYMAN BEECHER LECTURESHIP ON PREACHING."

FROM PHONOGRAPHIC REPORTS.

𝔖econd 𝔖eries.

NEW YORK:

J. B. FORD AND COMPANY.

1873.

CONTENTS.

LECTURES ON PREACHING.

I.

CHOOSING THE FIELD.

N returning, young gentlemen, after a year's absence, it would hardly be possible that I should not, in some parts of the several lectures which I shall give, have occasion to touch again many of the topics which came up incidentally during the first course of lectures. And yet it will be my effort to pass over an entirely different field. And, without rigidly restricting myself to it, I propose to consider the auxiliary influences which are requisite to the preacher's life; those institutions and various instruments in the church and out of the church by which he will prepare himself as a preacher, or reap and secure the fruit of his preaching.

I purpose in this introductory lecture to consider the influence upon a man's preaching of his primary choice of a place. That will involve more than seems upon the mere statement.

I apprehend that when the mind is called to the choice of a profession, it acts usually under influences

that are more sentimental — more, in the proper sense
of that term, romantic — more purely spiritual, than
when it comes afterwards to act upon the choice of a
place in which to exercise the profession. A man
perhaps considers the various avenues of life, asks
himself into which of them he shall throw his life-
forces. A great variety of influences act upon him ;
but if he is in the early stage of religious enthusiasm,
or if he has been bred in a household where all the
anticipations of father and mother have pointed in one
way, then, when he determines to be a minister, it is
oftentimes the mere ratification of a sort of vague and
general expectation.   Or, if he be late brought into the
kingdom of spiritual realities, there is a glow and an
enthusiasm upon him, under which he determines to
become a preacher of the gospel of Christ.

Now, one of the incidental evils that unfortunately
attend a laborious preparation for the ministerial work
is the toning down of that generous and enthusiastic
religious feeling ; so that when one has studied assidu-
ously for two or three years, though he may know a
great deal more, and in some respects his Christian
character may have rounded out and become more
symmetrical, he is very apt to have more consideration
of secular things. He thinks more of things as they
are, and gains or loses by the process, according to the
mode in which it is carried out. For when a man asks
himself, now near the end of his course of study,
" What shall I do ? Where shall I go ? Where shall
I settle ? " there begin to arise a multitude of considerations which did not at all affect his mind when
he chose the profession of preaching ; and considera-

tions, too, which, while they are not formally objectionable, often do very great mischief.

THE FOUNDATION PRINCIPLE.

The presumption, I think, in every case,—it will have its exceptions, but ordinarily the presumption in the case of every young man about entering the field for preaching is that he should go *where preaching is needed most,* and not where he himself will be best off. He who follows the example of Christ and the Apostles most nearly,—not in the letter but in the substance, in the spirit, — surely cannot be far from right. If there be any example which is ascertained, it is that " He who was rich for our sakes became poor, that we through his poverty might become rich." If there was any one point that Paul emphasized, it was that he would not boast of what had been done by the Spirit of God through other men's labors, — how the gospel had been preached around through extensive regions,— but would glory in that which he himself had been permitted to do, laying his own foundations, and not building on those of other men. He gloried in going where none had been before him, where the world was new, where the hardships were apparent, where other men perhaps would shrink from bearing the burdens that he had the power and the spirit to bear. And he who goes where men need him most, follows closely the example and the spirit of his Master. That is the spirit of the gospel of Christ: to take care first of those that most need care, and to do the most for them that lack the most; to care, not for those that are already well helped, but for those that are despised and ready to perish.

PARISH OR MISSION.

So that the presumption is, if the spirit of the Master is to be the guide, that men should go either into fields at home that are low down and require hard work, or into the remoter regions that may be called mission-fields. And the question may be summed up in these two words: Will you choose a *parish*, or a *mission?* And when I say "mission," I do not mean a foreign mission, necessarily. Will you take work that is fresh to your hand, where you will have to be creative, or will you take that which requires simple superintendence and already has its course, which you have to supervise merely, as an engineer runs an engine already built?

IDEAS *versus* FOLKS.

A great many considerations would incline one to go into the mission-field. But, after all, there are, I think, nine men who go to parishes where there is one that goes to a new and open field. For when a man has finished his studies he is full of ideas, — full of new ideas. "Well, ought he not to be?" Yes; but he loves his ideas. "Well, ought he not to love his ideas?" Yes, but he loves ideas more than he does folks; — and that is heresy, — flat! He has got a system, and he wants to try it. He has got some sermons, — he wants to see how they will fly! He goes out with the feeling of the theologian; but the feeling that should send every man into the field to work, is sympathy with man. That is the whole of the gospel, in a word. Divine purity, divine knowledge, divine power, have a compassion for imperfect, sinful, lost, wretched men; and he is the true minister who has that compassionate sympathy, and subordinates everything else as the instrument of it. But when young men first come out of the seminary, they are very apt to be more in sympathy with ideas than with people, and so they want to go where their ideas will have a free course. " What could I*do with all my sermons, if I were to go out into the backwoods where they won't let me *read* a sermon ? What could I do with all my arguments, my statements, my nicely put questions and answers, among a people absolutely uncultivated ? "

PLEAS FOR SOFT PLACES.

And next comes in this thought, which is the thought of ambition : " I have taken three years to prepare myself for college, and have worked hard; I have been four years in college, — that is seven ; and three years in the theological school, — that makes ten years that I·have spent. I have improved my time; and now am I going to bestow myself upon a field that is not big enough to hold the half of me ? Is it duty ? Ought not a man to put himself in a field where all his powers and all his stores of knowledge will have an opportunity of being developed ? And why should he tuck himself away in a corner ? Why should he go into a field where there will be but one part in ten that he can make any use of ? " And so the man deceives himself under the plea of conscience, — that he is bound to bestow his goods in a larger barn than he would get if he went into a poor and needy place.

Then comes in also very seductively the vanity of friends, which so easily finds a nest in our own vanity

wherein to lay its eggs. "Father has been poor, and
he has 'scrimped' himself and the whole family to
get me through my course." And the father himself
feels it. He says, "I have sacrificed everything for
this boy, and he has had a hard time. He has lived
close to the bone; now he has got through. Every one
says he is one of the most promising young men that ever
went from this county; he has seen hard times enough.
It is time he should have an easier place. He has felt
so much of poverty, he would better go up to such or
such a church, where he can have a good salary." They
want to take a turn and find a larger place, where the
boy can do good and enjoy himself. If, on the other
hand, the father be rich, he says, "But my son has
been brought up as a gentleman's son, and he is not
used to these things; it is becoming that he should
have a place in accordance with his social surround-
ings." Whether he is rich or whether he is poor, each
one wants to get a good parish.

Then again comes in with still greater force the
thought, "I have been more blest, probably, than any
man ever was in the world, in that *she* has consented; I
have now the prospect of possessing the fairest, dearest
woman that ever was created, and I don't propose to
take her into one of these rugged fields: a man ought
to have some foresight; I mean to go into a place
where I can support her." And so Love pleads for a
home parish with a good income.

And then — and I think it probably the best plea of
the whole — the young man says, "I have, in spite of
economy and suffering, run myself very deeply in debt
for my education, and if I go now into a barren field,

how can I pay my debt?" To which my reply would be: Keep school till you can pay, and then go to preaching.

THE SECRET OF SUCCESS.

I think that the question of the first field for his preaching is the transcendent question of a young minister's life. And why? Because I believe that on that, very largely, turns his disposition; and that on his moral disposition turns his success as a preacher. If you go into the field with self-seeking, and more or less under the influence of vanity or ambition, you vitiate the power of your preaching in its very source.

It is not by wisdom or philosophy, it is not by rhetoric, though these may incidentally contribute to a man's success; it is by that secret, subtle, invisible, and almost incredible power which a man derives from the Holy Ghost that he succeeds. And that power works in man with what is most generous, most disinterested, most sincere, most self-sacrificing, in him.

Now, in the determination of your life, you turn the rudder when you select your field. If you say to yourself, — however much you may veil it or c ver it, — "I will go where much prosperity shall attend my life," you make one of those great, generic choices that mark out the future, and insidiously, but all your life through, it will be a hindrance to you and a limitation of your power.

If you go into your work with heroism; if you sacrifice yourself for it, without knowing that it is a sacrifice, if you give your soul and body to the work of God among his poorest and neediest, so that you are thrown upon the necessity of living by faith, — you will find in

it ample reward, you will thrive by it, and rejoice in it.
Thus you will start your ministerial character upon a
plane out of which will come all the influences that you
need, the mightiest influences that are known in this
world. Not by might will you become a mighty laborer,
not by power, not by genius, but by that disposition in
you and in your sermons that likens you to the Lord
Jesus Christ, — that royalty of self-sacrifice, that glory
of pitying love, that intense and entire sympathy with
other men rather than with yourself, that spirit of personal plasticity by which you may wrap yourself around
circumstances, and glorify base things, and seek out low
and little things to give them all your power, and be to
men what Christ is to you, — wisdom, sanctification, justification, all!

This, then, I say, is the reason why the determination
which a man makes in respect to his sphere is likely to
have a life-long influence upon his disposition, and so
upon that which is more potent in the matter of preaching than any other thing. For I still insist that, however needful and appropriate are intellectual equipment
and all the accessories of personal bearing, culture, and
refinement, the prime condition of right preaching is
heart and soul; and that to make these right is to keep
them in accord always with the bounteous, loving, all-
sacrificing, self-denying spirit that was manifested in
the Lord Jesus Christ.

BUILDING IN A NEW FIELD.

What, then, if a man acts under these influences and
goes out into the poor fields; into fields where, for instance, there are no churches; or where, if there are,

there had better be none, — that is, where it would be better to dissolve them and crystallize again. Let us see some of the methods by which a man should build up under such circumstances, and what would be the relation of this kind of work to the office of preaching.

In the first place, no man can go into a new field and not learn very speedily — I know it to be so — how helpless one is that has been brought up in the midst of a highly organized society and is suddenly drawn out of it where society is inchoate; where it is in a forming process; where nobody loves anybody; where a man has to be pope, cardinal, bishop, parish, — everything in himself.

When a man goes into a new neighborhood, — and consider, gentlemen, consider; don't think of Connecticut while I am talking to you, for, important as the State is, it is not the continent! — consider not even the States upon the Atlantic slope; once they were something, but they have ceased to be, comparatively speaking. Consider that great three-thousand-miles stretch from ocean to ocean. Consider the great waves of population that are rolling in. Consider how, from North to South, from East to West, the whole land is now one vast missionary ground. Consider what a host of African people there is to be educated, to be built up into the Lord Jesus Christ; the vast masses of foreigners that are mingling with our people. Consider what a work there is for the Christian heart to do in all the length and breadth of the land; in the North, in the South, in the East, in the West, in every State, in every section, but particularly in the great, new empires that are growing up in our midst! The question

1 *

that is seriously asked by every thoughtful Christian mind is : How shall we supply the gospel to these vast, needy masses ?

WHAT IS A CHURCH ?

Now, in going out among such populations you will find, drifting in the mass, here and there, single families, single individuals, of trained intelligence and moral worth; but society itself, at large, is not yet formed, and certainly its institutions are not formed. One of the first experiences that a young preacher has, in going into new fields, is the necessity of gathering and forming a church. The first question that comes up, then, is this: Have you learned anything in the seminary which will enable you to gather and form a church ?

What is your idea of a church ? Suppose you were thrown down to-day in the midst of three thousand or five thousand people, along some of the new railroads, that have been gathered there in one or two months, — have you any aptitudes ? Have you any thoughts or plans ? Do you know what you would do ? You have heard the churches discussed as Protestant and Catholic; that is all very well. The notes of the church have probably been sounded in your ears through all your studies. All very fine are these theories of the churches and their claims, but they are very different things from the practical church which you have got to use when you get among poor, common people.

Here, then, is the root of the church : I hold it to be simply *the development of social influences around a central spiritual element*, to keep it warm, to keep it alive. I hold that it is impossible, in respect to the mass of men, to develop the spiritual element except by the active and the reactive influence of the domestic and social feelings. Indeed, the church itself is founded upon this philosophical principle, namely, that the higher spiritual elements in men are so weak as to need the auxiliary influence of the more common social feelings. Thus the very root idea of a church is to *get men together* in their religious life, that they may help themselves and each other by their social relations.

THE FIRST STEP.

Therefore, in going into any field, your first work will be to find out, Is there one man ? If there is, are there two, three ? Can I find six persons in this community, whom I can get together to meet me, and who will talk on the subject of religion together, and let one another know their wants, their hopes, their feelings ? Take a stick of pine and put it down here, another there, and another yonder, and set them on fire; they will all go out. If you take those different sticks and put them together, they will all burn throughout to ashes. You can keep up an inflammation when you put them together, but you cannot if you separate them and let each one burn by itself. Now, churches are made like fires, and not as the light of single candles; therefore, when a person goes into a new community, the first problem is how to draw together those that are beginning to feel the dawning of the Divine life.

THE PREACHER'S PERSONALITY.

You will probably find, in nine cases out of ten, that there is no strength, or available material, in the

church that is any great help to you. Have you in
yourself the power to be the fountain? Have you the
passion by which you can take those five, six, ten, fifteen or twenty persons, and, grouping them together,
breathe into them a common life, a sympathy, a love of
friendship and sociality? Though that is to be inspired
and carried up as far as possible; yet that is only the
beginning; for through that and by that you must
breathe into them a church life and religious feeling.
That is the first work. I have seen a great many men
in my former life in the West, who came out from New
England well equipped and well intentioned. Usually
they spent the first year of their life in bemoaning a
want of Eastern institutions. The second year was
better, but their action was awkward and ineffectual.
It was about the third year before they fell into the
spirit of their mission, so that they could improve all
their time, and begin the work that is to be done in
new fields by gathering people together.

But when you go into such a field to preach, you may
lay up all your written sermons on the shelf. People
won't come to hear them. In the first instance, you
will have to take your Bible in your hand and go to
them, go to them in their fields, their cabins, or their
houses. Preaching does not mean pulpit, thank God!
Preaching means making known the unsearchable riches
of Christ, to one, to forty, or to a hundred, as the case may
be. He who is a teacher, and who pours the inspired,
Divine truth into the hearts and consciences of men,
is preaching. That is preaching; not yet in the largest
development of it, but in its elements, in its seed-forms.
A man, therefore, who goes, I won't say to ring the bell,

because there will be none; I won't say to call the people to church, because there will be no church building; but who goes as a minister into a county where are scattered, we will say, five thousand people, goes to hunt up the lost sheep, to talk with them, man by man, household by household, to pray in their families, to make himself literally a shepherd, seeking a scattered flock, — that man is a true *preacher* of the Word, in the highest and best sense of the term.

REFLEX INFLUENCE AND EDUCATION.

And what will be the reflex influence upon you, — you that have to go out after men? If your heart is in it, if you love the work because you love God, and because you really yearn for men, it will become so delightful to you that you could scarcely be induced to leave it. There is a pleasure in the sense of having given up everything for Christ. There is a deep enjoyment in having devoted yourself, soul and body, to the welfare of your fellow-men, so that you have no thought and no care but for them. There is a pleasure in that, which is never touched by any ordinary experiences in human life. It is the highest. If it be solitary, so much the worse. If it be occasional, so much the worse. But there is in it a pleasure, I think, next allied to the raptures of heaven. And a man who has but his Bible and *knows* that; who goes searching out in these new places those that need the truth, and proclaims it to them, and then, as one and another heart is opened to him, gathers them together, organizes them into a society; calls it a church, or an assembly of God's people; begins then to fan the social feeling, bringing them more and more into friendly relations with one another, teaching them, administering the ordinances, being himself minister (that is, servant, slave of all, doing all work) — that man, I think, will have more joy in the ministry than any other.

At any rate, I look back to my own missionary days as being transcendently the happiest period of my life. I look back to the childhood of my ministry as most of you look back to the childhood of your life.   The sweetest pleasures I have ever known are not those that I have now, but those that I remember, when I was unknown, in an unknown land, among a scattered people, mostly poor, and to whom I had to go and preach the gospel, man by man, house by house, gathering them on Sundays, a few, — twenty, fifty, or a hundred, as the case might be, — and preaching the gospel more formally to them, as they were able to bear it.

ELEMENTS OF POWER GAINED— CREATIVENESS — REALITY.

Creativeness, then, is one of the elements that will be developed in you by this earnest striving of all your powers to inspire men, to draw them together, to organize them into a living, growing church. There will also be developed the element of *reality* in preaching.   A large amount of preaching has come to be upon questions that have been spun and run out by philosophical consideration into nice but not very useful discriminations — questions of theology, questions of evidence, —a thousand intellectual and moral distinctions, which are not unadapted to the higher forms of civilization, but which have no relation to the great mass of the people.

But he who goes into a new field to work, goes where everything is to be done for a purpose, and with men as they are. There is a reality about everything he does, which does not belong to older parishes; and this will make him intensely practical, intensely real. Going into a new field in this way, one has, if I may say so, an emancipation, a liberty, which the conventions of older society would scarcely allow him.

INDIVIDUALITY.

The exercise of his own primary personal humanity is invaluable to him in the whole course and career of his life. It gives him a certain strong individuality. Men in new countries walk singly, men in old countries walk in platoons, in companies, and in regiments. We do what others do. We want to know what is the custom; and that has the force of law. And so men are gradually conformed. They smooth off all individual excrescences, and adapt themselves to the notions and manners of others. Nothing of this kind can exist in new States and settlements. The consequence is, that men who are there formed have intense individuality, which gives a great deal of force.

I have seen many men in older communities, who, I think, have wasted their lives by repressing the things which are peculiar to them, and in which there would have been a signal power. They have repressed them in deference to the customs of the community; and those things in them which would otherwise have been salient and powerful die within them unknown and unused.

WORK FROM THE BOTTOM UPWARD.

In making your selection of a field, then, when you
are about to go out from study to practical work, the
principle, it seems to me, on which you should choose,
should be, not "What is best for me?" but "What is
best for the cause of God among men?"   Not "Where
can I be settled among refined and affectionate people?"
— though I do not consider that an offence, or a crime;
— not "Where can I have a stipend that shall amply
support all reasonable wants?" — though I do not consider that a vicious desire; — not " Where shall I have
an appreciative audience in which my peculiar kind of
talent, my refinement, my poetical tendencies, or my
subtle philosophical nature, would have a fair, agreeable
opportunity?"   Although there may be cases (God
knows; we don't, always) where a man would better
settle in an old community on these very accounts, — I
do not debar men from regular churches, — yet, unless a
case can be made out specially, it seems to me the presumption is that every young man should go into work
at the bottom.   And this may be either in the open
field, as it were, or in the cities.   If you go into the
open-field work, as I have already said to you, you will
have your special difficulties, such as belong to a sparse
population; but, generally speaking, you will be comparatively free from dealing with men of vicious habits.
Not that there are not rougher neighborhoods among
the new lands, where men are coarse and animal, but
that the special "criminal classes" hardly exist there.
In cities, on the other hand, men undertaking untilled
fields of labor usually find themselves in sinks of bad-

ness, more or less; and, under such circumstances, this choice implies even more self-denial than comes with the attempt to create churches in the newer settlements of the West and the South, because it necessitates dealing with natures far more perverted than the average of men who have the hardy vigor and independence to settle a new country. Therefore, in the formation of schools, mission-schools, or little praying circles, which are nascent churches, in the cities, you have still more to deal with the personal principle. You have to bring to bear on men still more directly the power of your own direct, personal influence. You are to be yourself the channel through which the Spirit of God works upon the hearts of these men; and you must do for them, in your measure, what the Spirit of God and of the Lord Jesus Christ has done for you. You must carry their sorrows. You must take, in one sense, the punishment of their sins. You must suffer with them. You must abase yourself, and go down to their condition.

AN APOSTOLIC EXEMPLAR.

We hear a great deal about the cogency of argumentative preaching, about the eloquence of preaching. When shall we hear about the power that comes from self-abnegation in preachers, — the losing of self? Do you know how many hundred, how many thousand, ministers there are in the United States to-day who have no charges, nothing to do? Do you know how many thousand churches there are that are vacant to-day in the United States; churches already formed, but without anybody to minister to them? Here are a thousand ministers; nobody wants them. Here are a thousand churches; nobody wants them, — empty, hollow.   Never such a time, never such an opening, never such a need in the world as to-day; and yet thousands of men there are — not drafted into other departments, not carrying on a part of the great collateral work — who are destitute of that peculiar spirit which should lead them to "spend and be spent," as the Apostle was willing to do and to be.

Let me read you a paragraph: "Behold, the third time I am ready to come to you, and I will not be burdensome to you; for I seek not yours, but you. For the children ought not to lay up for the parents, but the parents for the children. And I will very gladly spend and be spent for you; though the more abundantly I love you, the less I be loved."

Now, there are a great many splendid things that Paul has said; but, judging them in the moral sphere, I do not think he ever said another thing that so drank up into itself the very quintessential spirit of the gospel as that last, — that he was willing to spend and be spent for them, even though the more intensely he loved them and sacrificed himself for them, the less he should be loved of them.

We love loveliness. We love them that love us. But Paul knew he was a strong man, and has told us so on divers occasions; he knew he had power second to none; but he gave it to these people who were very dear to him, saying, "I am willing to give more; I am willing to be utterly ransacked and used up for you; I am willing to do it, though I were to find a decrease in your affection and esteem for me in the proportion in which I love you more and more." This loving against all obstacles, this all-surrendering power of love, — this is what is wanted in Christian ministers.

THE POWER OF CHRISTIAN HEROISM.

There are no difficulties to-day that are not surmountable. The gospel has not lost a particle of its power. I hear a great deal said about Christianity passing away. When Christianity has passed away out of this globe, my friends, there will be nothing of the earth left. Christianity is not the technic of theology; it is not the organ or the ordinances of the church; it is the development of Divine power, truth, equity, and love in the most noble of all conceivable forms. And the intrinsic power of such developments will never weaken or fail. It is the type of the Divine nature made manifest by Christ, and, by the Apostles, afterwards, brought as an active force into life and applied to men. Do you believe that the heroism of love, that the amplitude of a cheerful and a heroic self-denial, that tears for others and joy in others, have lost their power in this world? A man in Christ Jesus to-day is just as noble and as powerful as he ever was, and becomes more and more so, with the refinements and exaltations of life. The trouble is that ministers have become professional, have become class-men. They work for single strata in society; they work for the higher ranges of life. They are lifted above the necessity of emptying themselves. They can hardly be said to follow Him, the delineation of whose life is a perpetual lesson to us.

"Let this mind be in you which was also in Christ Jesus. He, being in the form of God, thought it not robbery to be equal with God, but made himself of no reputation, and took upon him the form of a servant, and was made in the likeness of men; and, being found in fashion as a man, he humbled himself and became obedient unto death, even the death of the cross." There was no obstacle to stop him. It was the holy, impetuous downward plunging of love till it should reach the very bottom below, where there was no sentient life. That is the example of Christ; there is the divinity of Christ; there is the example and the type which the Christian minister is to follow.

THE NEED OF TO-DAY.

So, if he go into his place of labor and preach without fruits, it is not that the gospel has lost its power; it is that he has lost his power. If men seek to do good, and find that they are so restricted and limited in our day, it is simply because they are not clothed with those moral impulses and that moral power from which originally the gospel took its impetus, and which are still just as competent to the production of like effects as they ever were. When we have a generation of men that are otherwise as amply equipped as they are in knowledge and in aptitude for using knowledge; who are willing to make themselves a little lower than the least, willing to take the humblest places, willing to abide there so long as they are needed and till they are called by the unequivocal voice of God's providence away from those spheres,— as soon as we see such a generation of ministers, just so soon shall we see more than the old Pentecostal glories upon the earth! We have need of such ministers.

You cannot lift up the ignorance in our land, you cannot go into the squalor and poverty that begrime our cities, you cannot preach the gospel to every creature, unless you are baptized into this higher Christian spirit, and are willing to spend and be spent, — loved or unloved, as the case may be, — and to continue the work of God in the salvation of souls.

MISSION-WORK THE BEST TRAINING.

And when one has wrought patiently and with the expectation, perhaps, of spending his life in such a sphere as this (and, if God so wills, he will gladly continue to serve Christ there), if afterwards he should be brought by God's providence into a higher sphere, he will be as much better qualified for that higher sphere as the work which he has gone through is a higher education than any mere intellectual training. He never will lose that love for men, he never will lose that close sympathy with them, he never will lose that earnestness, he never will lose that practicalness, which this early training gives. His sermons will glow, they will be full of power, and he will have and will exercise among men that subtle influence which comes from this development of a great Christian humanity by work under circumstances of self-denial and toil among his fellow-men.

QUESTIONS AND ANSWERS.

Q. Is not the young minister choosing his place a little like a young lady choosing her husband ?

MR. BEECHER. — Yes, sir ; I think it is a thing that is done on both sides. I think as many young ladies choose as gentlemen, only it is done in a little more delicate manner, and indirectly.

Q. How often, should you judge, has a young minister occasion to choose any more than, as you stated at the start, between a foreign or home mission on the one hand, and leaving himself at the disposal of the providence of God and the church on the other ? Can he pick out a parish for himself honestly or honorably ?

MR. BEECHER. — I think there may be circumstances in which a young man will say, " I am shut up, in my own judgment and in the judgment of wise friends, to just so much of a career. I am at liberty to do only just such things"; and where that is honestly the case, I think he is to act as fearlessly and with as little self-condemnation as in any other circumstances. What I wanted to impress upon you was, that with a class of students brought up in an old community, and surrounded by worthy and excellent churches, the general tendency will be to make themselves the carriers-on of other men's work; and that, for the purpose of gaining a higher discipline and education, it is worth every man's while to go into new fields, where he has to begin the work, a creator himself, and become the minister of an older church at a later period, with an ampler education and experience.

The gentleman who asked the preceding questions [the REV. DR. BACON] then said : " I asked that question, not as implying any mistake on the part of the lecturer, for I feel most heartily thankful for the whole current of thought in this lecture, and for the very vivid and desirable impression which I believe it has produced upon all our minds, but for the sake of intensifying this idea : that it does not become a young minister or a candidate for the ministry to be on the lookout for a place where he can get introduced ; and that he should leave himself in the hands of God's providence and of the church. And, if he is not satisfied with that, let him put himself under the care of the Methodist Conference,— there are those here who are able to give him advice in that respect, — and let them dispose of him."

MR. BEECHER. — Well, gentlemen, you may laugh at that matter, but in the West I lived right alongside of Methodists, where I was in the minority and they were in the majority, as is overwhelmingly the case in Indiana ; and I saw a great deal of the working of that system. Of course it is not perfect, nor is any other system perfect ; but I do not believe there is any other system on earth in which you can take men at the state in which they take them there, with as few aptitudes, and then work up as good ministers out of them by training, as they do. And I attribute their success to this simple fact, that they put the Bible into a man's hand and send him out among the people. It is the grinding of a man upon other men that makes him sharp. Of course, if you have men that are educated to begin with, it will be still better. But the Methodist brethren take men, literally, right from the plow, from the flail, who cannot even speak good English. I knew good "Old Sorrel," as we used to call him, of Indiana ; now a sound, well-educated, cultivated man, a man of great influence and power. But when he first went on the circuit in the Whitewater valley, he did n't know enough to tell the number of the verse of the text. He had to count off from the beginning, "one, two, three, four," in order to announce "the fourth chapter and the sixteenth verse." They take just such men, in the West, and put them into a field and set them at work ; and they *grow* all the time. They are reading as they ride ; their library is in their saddlebags; they are reading in their cabins. They unfold slowly, but the beauty of it is, that they are all the time bringing what knowledge they have, to bear upon other men. This working of men on men is the way to make men, and workers.

II.

PRAYER.

ANY an enthusiast, when he begins his career as preacher, is subject to a disenchantment of the rudest kind. He has been brought up to think of the Christian ministry as the noblest profession which can occupy and task the human mind. He has looked at it in its ideal perfection, he has thought of it as springing from the will of God through Jesus Christ, and as standing, therefore, upon the highest place of sanctity. And he loves — perhaps not altogether from selfish reasons — to surround it in his thought with Divine authority, with pre-eminence, with all that shall give him the right to stand, as the representative of the Lord in the community, to make known the law of God, and to enforce that law.

But no man will go into the field to-day and not find himself in practical experience stripped of much of this expected power. He will find the pulpit subject to the same law which acts in other institutions. The strong will be strong, the weak will be weak, the poor will be poor, the spiritually rich will be rich ; and there is many a man who expected to walk in the high places of the earth that goes pitapat, pitapat, down behind the hill, and hides himself in great disappointment. And it is worth our while to take into consideration, not how Christianity stands, but how the Christian ministry and the Christian church stand to-day, and what is their relation to the community.

CHANGED POSITION OF THE CHURCH.

Certainly the position of God's kingdom in the world is not such as it was in the beginning, before the Christian church was born, while it was carried in the loins of the Jewish church. Still less is it as it was in those ages in which the Christian church was the rival of the State itself, and dominated nations and held the universal conscience in awe and fear. That is past. It will never probably come again on earth. Few places yet remain with such ancient notions that children, looking out of the door and seeing the minister walking with all the dignity of the institution upon him, run back, afraid of him. With the old staff, and with the old buckles, and with the old three-cornered hat, has gone a great deal besides the habiliments.

GROWTH OF OTHER PROFESSIONS IN LEARNING.

There are other people in the community that have ranged up beside, in many respects overtopped, the Christian ministry. For, once the church was the main repository of learning, and the ministry were on the whole in advance of the community in solid learning. The Christian ministry still, in, I think, almost every land, may be said to be soundly educated, and to compare favorably with any of the learned professions; but it has lost the distinction of pre-eminence in this regard. It is no more looked up to as the custodian of knowledge. Not that it has lost any; not that it has not gained; but that other professions, through a larger and more liberal method of education, have also gained in knowledge, and the whole community has grown, both in intelligence and knowledge. The distance between the top and the bottom of society is growing less and less. Not so much because the top does not grow, but because the bottom is growing up all the time. The relative distance, therefore, between the preacher and the hearer is lessened continually, and will doubtless go on to be lessened.

THE SPREAD OF LETTERS.

Nor are we to forget that the pulpit, to-day, is not what it was a hundred years ago, certainly not what it was anterior to that date, as a vehicle for communicating knowledge. It was not only the encyclopedia, but it was the literature, almost. It had the function of making known to the great body of peasants, to the yeomen, to the great middle class, to the ordinary households of the community, everything they learned above the usual level of their own lives. It was from the pulpit, either on the Sabbath or by the prelections of the week, that the most knowledge was gained. The schoolmaster did well, but the minister was the teacher-in-chief.

But, to-day, there is no such thing possible. We speak once in seven days; there are newspapers with fifty thousand tongues, that speak seven times in seven days. We speak what little we can weave into our periodical sermonizings, but books are flying everywhere; magazines of every dimension and every description are penetrating the nooks and corners of society. The carman that sits down to eat his nooning meal reads as he eats. Men that travel are stuffed with pamphlets, with books, with printed matter of every sort. Science is cheap, literature is cheap, all fictions are cheap, and are serving everything from the highest to the lowest interests of society, from the most sacred to the meanest and wickedest. The pulpit cannot in celerity, certainly not in versatility and abundance, come into comparison with them.

In the work of the dispersion of thought and knowledge over the world, the machinery of general society has been augmented almost beyond conception, and the pulpit has been left far behind. It neither stands ahead of the other professions in general learning, nor does it compare, as a means of diffusing knowledge, with the other enginery which is at play all over the globe.

And therefore men say, " The pulpit has had its day." I say its day has just begun. I say that all this business of taking out the ore of knowledge and smelting it, and manufacturing it, and carrying it commercially to the nations of the earth, which has been so long performed by the ministerial profession, has been in some sense an encumbrance to them. It has not been altogether a power. It has given a distinction to the ministry and an authority to the church ; it has wrought out pride and vanity and unwarrantable claims, which the church is better without than with.

THE CHURCH ONE FORCE AMONG MANY.

It seems to me, however, that men do not take into consideration the fact, that, in any community, the church is now only one of the potentially organized influences or forces that are at work. The numerous industrial vocations of society, and the commercial vocations (for they may still be classed generically with the industrial), so widely extended and calling to their service such able men and so many of them, — these forces that thunder at the bottom of society are tremendous, and are not to be despised because they are normal. And if they follow the line of the Divine intent, they are working at fundamental morals, working in the direction of a true manhood. But they are organized, they are necessary, they are going forward with vast power. If one abstracts them, and in his imagination considers what is the force of the hammer and of the saw and of the plane, what is the power of the engine, and of the very many men that manipulate them in society, it would seem as if the globe itself had become one vast smithy, and there were more than human forces working in the shop and upon the anvil. And the pulpit has got to operate in communities that are already possessed by these intense industrial forces. Nay, there are also all the trades and avocations of every kind, the liberal professions, as they are called, and, besides these, the whole swarm of special organizations, — what may be called the skirmishers of civilization, the lyceum, the masonic lodge, the literary association, the benevolent and reformatory and temperance societies, and what not, — hundreds, multiplying with astonish-

ing fecundity every year; all these influences are at
work, together with the organized forces of government
itself. And when the young man goes into what is
called a public-spirited town, he goes into a church that
stands in the midst of what may be called a dozen other
churches, only secular instead of religious, — organized
forces in society. They belong to the Divine Providence, and they are workers together with the church,
if a man is wise to understand and use them. If a
man thinks they are antagonistic, if he looks upon them
with jealousy and calls them a part of the world, he
separates himself by just so much from the Divine
Providence and from the understanding of God's will
revealed in the events of his day. For all these great
forces have in them a certain law, that of custom; a certain ethic, an ethic that relates to a man's transactions
in so far as the business of any given circle or profession is concerned. They are all operating upon the
minds of men.

So when the Sabbath day comes, and I get into my
pulpit, do you suppose I go there now with these people
fresh before me, all virgin silver, all unwrought metal,
thinking that I am the first man that has had hold of
them and the last that will have hold of them, in respect to affairs? I tell you these men have been exercised in intellect more than I can exercise them, — these
men that have driving behind them forces which impel
them to complex, discriminating thought, to all manner
of critical inspection and judgment, to a thousand mental processes which I cannot by mere speaking equal,
— these men have all of them been touched in their
sympathies. They have been driven by a certain

law-conscience in custom; they have all been law-finders or law-breakers, — for to find and to break are almost synonymous in human life. These men are operated upon by a hundred living forces before I get a chance at them. These forces are not rhetorical, they are not merely enthusiastic; they are influences that are a part of life, that belong to the cradle, the table, the fireside, and the shop. They belong to that life which is like a stream from which, when a man is once cast into it, he cannot escape; he goes with it easily, or, if he resists it, it rolls him on in spite of himself.

THE FUNCTION OF THE PULPIT.

The pulpit, then, stands up in the midst of a great organized State, with industrial forces organized and under the supervision of the Divine Providence; and it is one force among many. Now, the question is: shall the pulpit attempt to appropriate to itself the business of all these? Why, it were worse than folly. Shall the pulpit undertake to put itself into antagonism with these? That is, as I have already said, to go into antagonism to God in his providence. What is the great duty of the ministry, in reference to these organized forces of society? It is to spiritualize them, to inspire them, to give a *soul* to the great working, thinking, throbbing world. It is to open to it and let down upon it the inspiration of the Holy Ghost, the fire of the invisible world, that higher and nobler consciousness of humanity which is struggling blindly, mutely, down below, but which gets emancipation on the Sabbath day, when men come to know what are the meanings of all those things, dimly seen or rudely felt, which they have met during the week. And the minister stands there to touch actual experiences, manly experiences, noble experiences ; to touch them as the sun touches the cloud-storm that is retiring from the field, when all colors spring out and the glory of God rests upon it.

In this light, we shall go to our preaching work under very different auspices from those which we should be likely to have if we took a *dilettante* view of the sacredness of the Christian ministry, and of the great authority of the men on whom the hands have been placed, and who have the right to say, " Do this and do that," and " Be thou here and be thou there." All that power is stripped away ; that is all gone. You cannot bring it back by tears, nor by invocations, — thank God ! It is very easy for you to stop the eagle before the egg is hatched, but no art was ever able to put the eagle back into his egg after he had been hatched.

Society is a part of God's great plan, of which the church is the servant and the minister. And society, under Divine influence, has developed these very things; and we ought to recognize that these are part of the fruits of Christianity itself, — of Christianity which is infinitely flexible and susceptible of development, so that it constantly meets the new phases and new aspects of affairs.

THE MINISTER'S POWER.

You will not, therefore, in going out into your work, disesteem intellectual preparation, as though it were a thing not necessary. Yet, remember, you are not going to dominate in the community because you are so powerful in intellect. You are going to meet on each side of you men that are fully your equals. You ought not to lose that enthusiasm for truth which, if carried a little too far, becomes authority, which takes on the "airs" of right and of rulership. Every man should have such a sense of what is becoming to truth, to virtue, to piety, and to God, as to be filled with a sacred fire of championship, with an enthusiasm for it. But, after all, you are not going to stand in this world as the old priests stood. That place is gone. Men are not going to reverence you striplings just because you are called "ministers." Boys are you now, young gentlemen. May you never forget to be boys as long as you live! But putting a "Reverend" before your name is not going to change your nature or your function. You are to stand in society according to a great allotment, a Divine allotment and reason. It is not fear of you, it is not reverence for you, it is not awe for the sanctuary, for the day, or for the usage, that is going to be the secret of your power, if you have any. It must be yours to impart to all the other great organisms of society spiritual tendencies and spiritual directions. Your genius, your consecrated intellect, all your acquirements, all your knowledge and your practical skill, will be vain, unless you succeed in opening in the hearts of your hearers individually, and in the community where you dwell, a higher conception of what life means, a higher thought of what manhood is; unless you are able to bring down the invisible life, and give it as the atmosphere of the visible.

SPIRITUAL PERSPECTIVE.

The old pre-Raphaelite painters — if you have ever

cried and laughed over their pictures — for they touch
the fountain both of admiration and of tears — painted
with exquisite coloring and profound sensibility; but
their pictures were flat, without any background, without perspective, without foreshortening, without effect
of distance, or true form, or atmosphere. So the world
is, without religion. The business of the pulpit is to
give an atmosphere to this world, and to put things
into their relative places and due proportions; to spread
out that which the sun brings over the great globe,
when it rises with healing in its beams. Your business is to accept the world, to accept mankind, the
great brotherhood, and to love them, and to have such
sacred commerce with the other life that you become a
channel, conducting the Divine grace to men. I believe, too, that ordinances are channels through which
Divine grace comes. One thinks that baptism is one
of the channels, and others think that the sacrament
of the Lord's Supper is another of the channels. I
believe that there are these side channels, but the
main conduit is the soul of man that loves God and
loves his neighbor. That is the one compendious ordi-
nance of God, and that is the artery through which
God mingles his grace and his power, to be felt among
men. And the work of the Christian minister is so
to know God, and Jesus whom he sent, so to realize
them in his own heart, that he shall be able to com-
municate them by sympathy, as well as by teaching, to
the collective body, to the individual. Yea, they are to
feed, in their distributive functions, not only the persons but all the households, all the associations, all the
industries, everything that belongs to the community

where they are placed, — thus not simply indoctrinating, which is excellent, which is a very good base from which to depart, but really imparting a Divine inspiration to all those organized forces by which society is developing itself.

The church, therefore, stands, in my thought, as one among many. Is it the highest? It may be, ought to be. It is in its real nature the highest; it is not always practically so. There is many and many a household in town a thousand times nearer heaven than the church with its minister and all its elders and deacons put together. There is many a single praying soul, there are poor women in obscurity and in poverty, that God's angels dwell with more abundantly than they do with those that stand in conspicuity of exhibitive holiness. The higher life is very low. " He that would be chief among you, let him be your slave, let him be minister of all."

PRAYER AS AN ELEMENT OF PREACHING.

Now, I have spoken already, in former lectures, of those elements that are personal to you in this work. And I shall, this year, with some latitude of treatment, speak of those auxiliary elements which are made up partly of your personality and partly of things that are not you, that are exterior to you. And I purpose, this afternoon, in order to come by and by to the subject of the prayer-meeting in the church, to speak of prayer as one of the main auxiliaries by which the minister is to perform the work for which the church is ordained among men. I do not propose to discuss the question from a philosophical stand-point. If a man should tell me that physiologists had been all wrong in the matter of hunger and digestion, and that it had been demonstrated now that hunger was an imaginary feeling, and that coffee and bread and butter acted more through the imagination than any other way; that it was very well to go through the forms of taking them, but that their effects were really through the imagination, and not through any organic relation, — I don't think he would go far to convince me. I hardly think I should be satisfied with any such reasoning as that. If a man should say to me, "It has been shown now that we have no real knowledge of external things, we have knowledge only of subjective states, the light streaming from things giving some idea of form and color and so on; and therefore, if a man would deal with himself honestly, he could sit down in a wilderness of sticks and call it a garden; it is merely subjective, and depends very much on the man himself and his states," — I don't think that would change my feeling in respect to flowers, or fruits, or anything else.

Now, I know there is in prayer a great deal more than question or answer. I know there is something beside simply those questions about which philosophers are pottering. If prayer were a mere order sent to market, expected to bring back so much in a basket every time, I then might enter into accounts and have commercial dealing on that subject. The barrenness of prayer is, I am afraid, somewhat exposed by the low state in which it too often exists.

I do not purpose, either, to enter into that other question, so profoundly interesting and exciting to thousands of men, "Is there any answer to the prayer of

faith ?" I regard it as one of the questions of the future.
It seems to me, if there be anything that is sure, it is
that Jesus believed there was a realm of power, into
which the human mind could rise up, which gave to man
not only control over himself and his own spirit, but
such a participation in the Divine nature as that his will
would positively have control over physical laws and
forces. There are powers repeatedly promised or hinted
at in the sayings of the Saviour. There is an exaltation, — not perhaps to every person, because all gifts
are not to all, — but to certain natures there are exaltations that carry with them the nascent power of Divinity itself, as I believe. And the province of answer to
prayer — or the question whether men have compelling
power with God — is one of transcendent importance.
I do not intend to discuss that now, but to look at
prayer simply in its more generic features, and as one
of the inspirational elements by which the church is to
develop in the community its higher life and humanity.

WHAT IS PRAYER?

And, looked at in this largest view, what is praying?
Dropping out, as we may say, the lower elements of it,
what is prayer but the conscious lifting of a man's soul
into the invisible realm, into the presence of the invisible Father? What is it but shutting out for the moment, with the closing of the eye, all conscious sensuousness and secularity, and rising by the effort of the
soul, through silence, up into the region where God sits,
and dwelling — though but for a moment — out of the
body, in the presence of the Eternal God? You may
say, when once there, "He doth thus and thus and

thus "; but all the details come back into this generic element, that it is taking men out of conscious sensuousness, and lifting them up into an actual spirituality. It is bringing them out of time and standing them upon the threshold of the eternal world.

The habit of prayer, looked at in this way, elevates the individual, elevates any household; it civilizes, spiritualizes, etherealizes, the community itself.

And you cannot pray so poorly — if your prayer be sincere in that one single thing, if it be the real thought that is going up, and you have the conception of God in your heart — but that the mere *soul-bath* one gets in things unseen, the mere lifting of the wings in the great beyond, is itself worth all that anybody ever claimed for prayer. And one of the very first things that the Christian Church and Ministry should do is, as the Saviour did, teach the disciples how to pray.

I shall treat, then, to-day, first of personal prayer, and second of ministerial prayer; and, to-morrow afternoon, of social prayer, or the prayer-meeting.

TEACHING MEN TO PRAY.

Inspiration of Desire. — As regards the work of the Christian ministry in teaching or inspiring men to pray, I have to say, in the first place, that one of the secret arts, — if you use the term "art" in the sense of wisdom, — one of the subtle, secret arts of the ministry is, not didactically or demonstratively to make men pray, but, by a wise knowledge of how to teach them the thought, the feeling, to inspire them with a *desire* for some such higher utterance. If a man preaches, therefore, hard matters of fact, if he all the time secularizes his sermons, if they are ethicalized to death, if they lack the savor of the something better, the something higher, the something nobler, that is for man in his communion with God, men will scarcely learn to pray except as they learn to perform any other duty. But the secret of praying is, to want to pray. The secret of wanting to pray is, to have excited in our ·souls certain aspirations, certain yearnings, certain desires. The conscience hungers and thirsts, the imagination yearns and longs, the affections rise above all the bounds of ordinary experience in life.

Prayerful Preaching. — There is the sense of wings, I think, in every soul that is touched with the least ideality, and it is desirable to so preach to men that they shall have an upward yearning. Break up base content. Infuse into men a glorious discontent with things as they are. So idealize everything, so preach it, that the necessary things, common things, — all of them, — shall have a halo about them, a suggestion of something higher and nobler, till the soul is in an exhalant state, till it shall tend to pray always, — that is to say, to have a subtle uplifting and going up of the thoughts, out of the physical and material, and the near and present, into the invisible and holy.   -

Much of this spirit of prayer can be thus infused, while you are not actually praying, through your way of dealing with men. It is whether you are aiming at the base of their brain, where lies the great workshop of life ; or whether you are aiming at the middle of their brain, where the great household and social affinities are playing; or whether you take the top, where is the holy spirit, where we touch God, if we touch him at

all, in our thought and inward life.   Now, sermons that
are constantly working upward into that, tending toward
that, although they may never discuss prayer, are all
the time tending to spiritualize men, to give activity to
that side of their nature whose expression must necessarily be invocation and ejaculation.

But let me say that, while we are laying the foundation for instruction in this way, I have felt in my own
ministry the constant need of doing a great many other
things.   To tell the truth, it was a good while after I
had come into the church that I was like the deacon
who was asked to pray by his minister and refused;
and who, on being told that he had the gift and ought
to pray, said he knew he could do it, but he always
hated to.   To tell you the truth, I hated to pray; it
used to be a most disagreeable, enforced duty, partly
from one reason and partly from another, which it is
not necessary now to specify.   I remember that it was
a long time before I could get back to the habit of my
childhood, and kneel down and pray with any comfort.
The moment I bent my knee, I also lost my thread;
and the mechanicalism of attempting to pray morning,
noon, and night would ruin my soul, I think.   If I
had to pray by the clock, if I had to have a mechanical order, it would derange all my spiritual tendencies.
I could not do it.   Little by little, I came to the feeling
of wanting to commune with my Father; and thus I
learned, after a while, that we had to go into our congregation just as the Lord did.   His disciples came to
him and said, " Lord, teach us to pray."

Unlearning Wrong Ideas. — Generally, the first step
towards teaching men to pray is to get them to unlearn

their prayers. Insensibly they have formed their idea
of what prayer is. It is the way that the minister prays,
it is the way that their mother prayed, it is the way
that holy men have prayed whose prayers are recorded.
To attempt to pray in that way is worse than to attempt to wear another man's clothes, without any regard
to size. It is worse than the attempt of a little child to
walk with a stride as long as the father's, whose hand
he holds. For, if there be anything in this world that
must be personal and absolutely genuine to you, it is the
aspiration. Suppose, when I courted my wife, I had got
down one of the letters preserved in the family, — one
of my father's to my mother, — and I had sat down and
read that to her as a letter of courtship! It was a very
good one, in its time. But I think prayer is like the
powder that a huntsman uses; he never can use it but
once.

I am speaking now of my own views, and not of the
views of everybody. There are prayers that are like
stairs, — you begin at one spot and you always land at
another spot; and persons say that they were like the
stairs that Jacob saw in his vision, on which angels
ascended and descended, and that it takes them up to
heaven. Such prayers are perfectly right for those who
want them and can use them. But to my thought
prayer is *wings*, and a man must go, not where the
stairs are put, but just where his own will wants to go,
— to the east, to the west, to the north, to the south,
higher, lower, with many or few strokes, anywhere, as
birds fly in the summer heavens above us. And you
never can fulfill the Apostle's injunctions, "Pray always," "Be instant in prayer," "Pray in season and out

of season," — those things cannot be done, if prayer is a
set act, instead of an evolution of feeling or a holy ejaculation.

THE ELEMENTS OF PRAYER.

The sources of prayer are like the beginnings of the
Ohio River, — a thousand musical springs, separate one
from the other, none of them more than a handful, first
pouring out from the rocksides, and by and by joining
together to make the great river below, on which boats
and great steamers will float. And we have the river
Prayers, the channel for accustomed usages; but the
beginning of prayer, that which is to make the great
after-channel full always, and full of good and genuine
prayer, is this solitary thought, that prayerful emotion,
this impulse of the heart. The devout soul, in all its
ten thousand moments, is of such a nature that it is all
the time exhaling heavenward in poetry, in rhapsody, in
narration, in reverie, or in speech.

For prayer is not asking for something. I have nothing to ask for, since I have known what God's Father-
hood means. I have but one petition, and that is, "Thy
will be done." It is not for me to wake the sun. It is
not for me to call the summer. It is not for me to ask
for colors in the heavens. All these things are abundantly provided. The earth is the Lord's, and the full-
ness thereof; and I am God's beloved. He died for me
by his son Jesus Christ. He thinks of me. Do I ever
forget my children? Shall a mother forget her babe,
cradled in her arms, by day or by night? And shall
God forget us, in that great rolling sea of his thoughts,
in that everlasting fecundity of his love, in the infinite

bound of the Divine tenderness and mercy for man?
Is there anything left to ask for? When I am tired,
I carry my weariness there and lay it down. If I am
in sorrow, I am glad when I think of the Sorrowing
One. The God of all comfort is my God. When my
burden is heavy, it is not so heavy as was His cross.
When the world seems circumscribed and barren, and
I a stranger and a pilgrim, the world like a coach is
swinging on its road, and soon I shall hear the horn
that tells of its arrival.

Ten thousand thoughts of this kind, that spring from
every side of human experience and touch human life
in every part,— these are elements of prayer. So that
when I pray, I rejoice; or, as the Apostle would say,
"giving thanks in prayer." Prayer is cheerful to me.
Prayer is sweet to me; it is not ascetic. I know that
I am wicked; I know that I grieve God; I know that
there are times when it is sweet to say, "God be merciful to me a sinner!" So there are times for the majesty of storms in summer;— but thunder-storms do not
march in procession all the way across the bosom of
the summer. There is more brightness than darkness;
more tranquil fruitfulness than agitation and thunder.

MAKING PRAYER ATTRACTIVE.

And now, if you are going to make the gate of prayer
strait, solemn, awe-inspiring, for the sake of making
people reverent, coming thus through their sensuousness,
and trying that kind of empirical method to excite
devotion in them, — if you attempt that, what do you
do? You make prayer unwelcome, unlovely. You make
the soul not want it. But if prayer is communion, if

it is the sweetest of all converse, if it includes in it
everything of your experiences, high and low ; if the
children in school or in the household can kneel down
with you and love to look upon your face; if you can
make them rise up from a scene of prayer feeling that,
after all, it is "as good as a play," that is, that there
is no *force*, nothing that is angular, nothing that re-
strains in it, but all that is sweet and attractive and
joy-breeding, — if you can do that, you make prayer
lovely, you make men want it.

LIBERTY IN PRAYER.

It is not necessary that men should pray a great
deal; it is not necessary that they should pray a great
while. I think this is ordinarily one of the faults of
prayer. It is one of the faults, as I shall show to-
morrow, of social and of public prayer. Prayers are
of such a kind that I do not wonder prayer-meetings
are the lumber-rooms of the church, that all the things
that are good for nothing else are stowed away there !

We must broaden, then, and enrich our conception
of what praying is, of the liberty of it, and of the naturalness that there should be in it, and of the right of
every man to make his own prayer. "What if I cannot
make one ? May I not use the forms ?" Yes, just as
sick men use crutches, — not to supersede and supplant
their legs, but to strengthen them, till they are strong
enough to walk without crutches.

But suppose a man is unfruitful? Well, your own
slender fruitfulness of prayer is better for you than an
ample fruitfulness that is somebody else's. There is a
great deal of prayer that is something like the orna-

ments I see in parties, where they bring in, in a tub, a tree to which are tied oranges and orange blossoms; for a night it looks as though it were an orange-tree in full blossom and full fruit, but to-morrow morning you will see that they were all tied on overnight. They answered a moment's purpose; but one orange were better, if it actually grew there, than a bushel under such circumstances.

But in helping your infirmity — I would not be strait-laced in that matter. Help yourself by any means, but never forego liberty, personal liberty, — never fold your wings. Never pray by proxy, when you can pray by silence in your own thoughts.

Now, to inspire this spirit of prayer, to make men enjoy it, is a supreme art. I had almost said that when a minister has the power to inspire gradually in his church a desire for praying, an enjoyment in prayer, his work is comprehensively done in the world, and he could almost say " Let me die." Because I think that out of this spirit of communion with God, out of this spirit of nearness to heaven, out of this spirit of an upper manhood, out of this spirit of the gloriousness, the joy, and the beauty, and the bounty, of the heavenly land that just overhangs us, — out of this comes almost everything in the church that has moral force in it.

EXALTATION IN PRAYER.

So much for the attempt to teach your people and to inspire them with the spirit of prayer. The other point, and the only other one that I shall deal with, this afternoon, is your own praying among your people. It is very difficult to speak on this subject, because it is

so much a matter of constitution; so much in the way
men are organized, so much in temperament, so much
in education.   I think I may say that no part of ministerial preparation is more neglected than that of singing and praying.   We are indoctrinated very thoroughly,
we are taught in the history of the church, we are
drilled in the order and discipline; but how much instruction do we need on the subject of prayer!   I do
not know that I can give you any instruction about it
except this, that I think the most sacred function of
the Christian ministry is praying.   I can bear this witness, that never in the study, in the most absorbed
moments; never on the street, in those chance inspirations that everybody is subject to, when I am lifted up
highest; never in any company, where friends are the
sweetest and dearest, — never in any circumstances in life
is there anything that is to me so touching as when I
stand, in ordinary good health, before my great congregation to pray for them.   Hundreds and hundreds of
times, as I rose to pray and glanced at the congregation, I could not keep back the tears.   There came to
my mind such a sense of their wants, there were so
many hidden sorrows, there were so many weights
and burdens, there were so many doubts, there were
so many states of weakness, there were so many
dangers, so many perils, there were such histories, —
not world histories, but eternal-world histories, — I had
such a sense of compassion for them, my soul so longed
for them, that it seemed to me as if I could scarcely
open my mouth to speak for them.   And when I
take my people and carry them before God to plead
for them, I never plead for myself as I do for them, —

I never could. Indeed, I sometimes, as I have said, hardly feel as if I had anything to ask; but oh, when I know what is going on in the heart of my people, and I am permitted to stand to lead them, to inspire their thought and feeling, and go into the presence of God, there is no time that Jesus is so crowned with glory as then! There is no time that I ever get so far into heaven. I can see my mother there; I see again my little children; I walk again, arm in arm, with those who have been my companions and co-workers. I forget the body, I live in the spirit; and it seems as if God permitted me to lay my hand on the very Tree of Life, and to shake down from it both leaves and fruit for the healing of my people! And it is better than a sermon, it is better than any exhortation. He that knows how to pray for his people, I had almost said, need not trouble himself to preach for them or to them; though that is an exaggeration, of course.

PERSONAL HABIT AND PUBLIC DUTY.

And now, my young friends, without dwelling longer upon this matter of ministerial prayer, for my hour has expired, I have only this to say, — that I think it grows principally out of the habit of prayer in your own souls. Some people have asked me, " Do you ever write your prayers ? " Why, I had rather undertake to make a diagram for every particle of my blood, what it should do all day, than to attempt to sketch out a prayer. Prayers are as flowers that scatter themselves all the hillsides over, and all the valleys through, according to the will of the shining sun that draws them up toward it. Prayer must be spontaneous, voluntary, effluent as the

atmosphere itself.   It comes to those who pray much,—
I do not mean those that spend a great deal of time in
the closet, because you can while away a great many
pleasant hours over dull books with interjectional
prayers; but those who have thoughts that rise spontaneously up to God, — for that is prayer.   I have
friends who are so dear to me that I hardly ever go
a whole day unconscious of them.   And sometimes, for
hours together, I couple very much of my personal history with theirs.   Have you never had friends that
were so dear to you that, though they were a thousand
miles away, you talked with them in the room, and, if
you had a picture, there were two pairs of eyes looking
at it, not one ?   Have you ever carried on this kind of
double existence with friends ?   Well, it seems to me
that is the attitude of the soul that loves God, — that
knows itself to be his, that expects to dwell with God,
that does not think of him as a great judge, or as a des-
pot, but as the sweetest, most genial, most affable, the
nearest, the noblest, the most beautiful, the most to be
desired, the altogether lovely; the one that made the
sense of beauty in me, and is infinitely more fond of
beauty than I am; the one that touched in me the
fountain of poetic feeling, and is himself transcendently
more poetic than all that ever sung on earth; the one
who is the fountain out of which sprang everything
that we love, or revere, or desire here !   If such be our
thought of God, and our life is hid with Christ in God
every day, it is out of that fountain that comes pulpit
prayer.

PRAYER THE SECRET OF STRENGTH.

And if you pray in the pulpit, and are dry, do not be discouraged. All streams run small at first, but grow better, grow deeper. Take more care of the inward man. Be nobler. Oh, you have to be good men, you have to be noble men, more generous, more disinterested than anybody else about you! Sermons will not do; it is *life* God wants to bless, and it is your life, if you are settled in any parish, that God will make the means of grace to men. And you have to live lives of holiness, not after the Madame Guyon sort, or any particular sort, but after *your* sort, which is the purity of heart and the simplicity of faith and the freedom of will, ascending toward God. Live in that, grow in that, deepen in that, and people will begin to say, "Our minister's prayers, it seems to me, are more nourishing than they used to be." Then, when men vex you and trouble you, instead of getting angry, pray. Then, when troubles come, instead of feeling that you have too much trouble, pray and pray. When you find that talebearers in the community are after you, and you are annoyed and vexed in your parish, and there is scandal going around you here and there, pray, pray! It is the best way to head off little troubles. It is the best way to lighten great burdens. Pray always, be instant in prayer. Pray deep, deep as your soul goes, high as your thoughts can rise, and then you need not take much more trouble about your pulpit prayers, — they will come. And when I hear a parish say, "Our minister may not preach as well as others, but oh, it is a balm and a refreshment to hear him pray!" I

congratulate them, they are not far from the gate of
heaven.

QUESTIONS AND ANSWERS.

Q. Would it not be well for the congregation to be made to feel
that they are expected to join in the prayer?

MR. BEECHER. — I suppose that when a man stands
before his congregation he feels joined to them. I am
conscious of that myself. I seem almost to pass into
my congregation. I feel as if we were all one, as if
my utterance were the utterance and the voice of all
the sympathetic souls in the congregation. A great
many say, "Let us pray," I suppose, because they have
got to open the door somehow, and that is the way it
has been customary to open it.

Q. May a person be eloquent in prayer without a vivid imagination?

MR. BEECHER. — I think that all prayer has imagination in it. I think that faith is spiritualized imagination. Faith that works by love is ideality, or the
imagination joined with affection and working in a
spiritual direction; so that all sense of God, all sense of
invisible things, means imagination. But the imagination, like every other thing, may exist in different
degrees. It may be strong enough simply to be recipient, or it may be strong enough to be both recipient
and in a small degree creative, or it may be positively
creative, or efflorescent. The last form gives the highest development of it, carries one into the very borders
of what we call genius in that matter. I think there is
a genius of prayer just as much as of poetry. I knew
a woman so illiterate that she could not talk better

than a common negro. She came from the South, though she was a white woman, and lived in one of the southern counties of Ohio. When she began to pray, after a very little her spirit came to her; she seemed to drop the mortal part, and she fell into the language of the Old Testament. I heard Judge Fishback, now gone, say that he had heard all the able men in the West, but he never heard a human being who had such power, who affected him as that poor ignorant woman did, when she got into those higher moods, and brought to her second or higher nature the use of all that sublime language of the Old Testament that seemed to be the channel to her spiritual feeling. I have heard old negroes in Indianapolis pray so as to make me wish I was in their place. There is a genius for prayer; but then it is just as it is with the element of beauty. The highest development of beauty makes you an artist; then you go along down until you come to that development in men which makes them decorators; and then lower down, to the great average mass of men who simply have a sense of what is tasteful or beautiful. A sense of beauty is distributed from the top to the bottom, though in different degrees; and the power of prayer follows the line of the gift. The gift is great in some; it belongs to all, but in varying degrees; and is susceptible, like all other gifts, of development by use.

Q. Some men do not have the power of expression, — of word expression. Now, what do you think of that yearning that there is in the Congregational Church — I do not say whether it is right or wrong — for something like a liturgy?

Mr. Beecher. — I should say that that ought to be met by hymns. I shall come to that in my lecture on

music. There are no such prayers on earth put into
form in liturgies as those that have been put into
hymns. The trouble is that nobody thinks a hymn is
a prayer. When a prayer is being made in the form of
a hymn, — in which the music gives it wings indeed, —
people think that is the time to scratch their head, the
time to stand up and look about, or to sit still and take
it easy, the time to hoist the window and get a little
more air, the time to look after their hat, the time for
the sexton to go with a whisper around the house. The
desecration of prayer in hymns is something perfectly
shocking!

The Congregational Liturgy is in the Hymn-Book, I
think. Where fifty men want a liturgy, there is no law
that I know of in heaven or on earth to prevent their
having one. It is the liberty of the Congregational
Church. But I believe there is one already made. It
is said that liturgies must grow, they cannot be built;
and this liturgy has grown. From the time of David to
the time of Wesley, and on down to our day, God has
been inspiring men; and they have given forth their
divine utterances in psalms and hymns and sacred
songs. A wise use of the Hymn-Book will develop
more liturgical effect, I think, than can be got in any
other possible way.

III.

THE PRAYER–MEETING : ITS METHODS AND BENEFITS.

 SUPPOSE there is hardly any other part of church service that is regarded with so little estimation in the community at large as the prayer-meeting. And I think facts will bear me out in saying that this feeling is participated in by the church, on the part of the greatest number of its members, nine out of ten of whom look upon it as perhaps a duty, but almost never a pleasure. It is a " means of grace " ; and they feel about it as I did when I was a boy about being washed in the morning and having my hair combed. It was better than going indecent ; but it was an exercise that I never enjoyed, and I was heartily glad when it was over. In most churches I think that is the feeling in regard to the prayer-meeting ; that it is dull ; that it is for the most part without edification ; that in some mysterious way it may be blessed to the soul's good, — but how they do not know. Persons resort to it when they cannot very well help it. Now and then the meeting blazes up ; there is a revival ; there is some novelty ; something has transpired that excites a momentary interest; but perhaps ten months in the year, on an average, the prayer-meeting is eschewed by the great body of the church, and by the community wholly.

There is another bad side to it, — children do not like it; and anything that children dislike in religious service, habitually and universally, has reason to suspect itself. There is an element in true religion that follows the example of Christ, — the children wanted to come, and the Saviour called them and put his arms around them, took them upon his knee, and laid his hands on them and blessed them. And, from that day to this, I think that where service is delivered in the true Christ-spirit it will be found that, in one place or another, there is something for children; and the children will find it out. Where the minister does not interest the children, where the meetings of the church have nothing for the children, something ought to be changed or added. Revision is needed.

THE DEMOCRATIC THEORY.

Now, it is notorious that the prayer-meeting is "below par," and therefore it may be the more striking to say that, for my part, I regard it as the very center and heart of church life, — not necessarily of preaching; although its reaction upon preaching may be made to be very great. We have thrown off hierarchical methods of worship; we have advanced — I mean the Presbyterian and Congregational Churches and their *confrères* have advanced — the theory of the equality of the church in its members; the idea that it is a family and body of believers; that it has in itself inherently the gifts of divination; that it does not derive its graces through any ministerial channel except reason and the ordinary methods of communication. This is our theory. And it behooves, therefore, all those that believe in such a constitution of the church, to see to it that the church does develop some fruit that shall sustain the theory. If, therefore, the church life is barren, if it is meager in development, we lay ourselves under a just liability of being thought to disprove, by our life, that which we attempt to prove by our philosophy or by our reasoning.

POWER OF INDIVIDUAL EXPERIENCES.

If there is anything in the world that ought to develop church life, it is the gathering together of the whole body of the brotherhood, the men and the women in the church, for mutual edification. Do you not believe that there is a constant communication of the Holy Ghost with every heart that is striving God-ward,— yea, and every one that is not? Do you not believe that every heart that has been made willing in the day of God's power, that is in a recipient state, is receiving from day to day a realization of the Divine presence, an inspiration in duties? Is there not a life going on in the hearts of God's own people, under all the varied conditions in which they are living, that is worth some record, some interpretation? And is it possible that one man, no matter how studious, no matter how gifted, — is it conformable to our idea of the constitution of the church that one man, standing in the pulpit, shall be able, simply because he devotes himself to instruction, to pour out upon a congregation such knowledge of experimental truth as inheres in the life of the congregation itself? If there were any process by which we could look inside of men's lives, their unconscious as well as their conscious religious life; if we could follow the mother in all her moods and musings and prayers and anxieties, and all the methods by which she is lifted out of and over, and carried victorious through, any discouragements and trials in the rearing of her little church, the household; if we could go with those that are discouraged and downhearted and not naturally hopeful, whom all the world seems to beat against and to crush, and see how their feebleness and weakness is from day to day helped and sustained; if we could gather out all that which the young feel in their weary moments; if we could see how men strive under temptations, against pride; how men that are borne in upon in the business of life strive against avarice; what battle is going on in the shop, in the street, and wherever men are; what the whole round of real, practical godliness is, in its weakness, its overthrow and defeat, in its matched battle or in its victories, — if we could gather out all these things and bring them into some form and lay them open, do you believe there is a single man on earth, though he were a prophet or an apostle, or both, that could equal the revelation of the truth of God as thus given in the lives and history of all the members of the church? The great and wonderful work going on in the lowest and the least is more stupendous in its relations to the Godhead and the eternal estate of the blest than the external greatness of any kingdom in the world! And it is all the time stimulated and developed. Here is the growth of passions; here is the growth of moral emotions; here is the dawn of love, waxing stronger and stronger unto the perfect day; here are the joys, the sorrows, the upliftings, the downcastings,—all the ten thousand things which not only teach us to pray, but which pray in us and through us, " with groanings which cannot be uttered." Is there any voice for these things, except as we gather up here and there a scrap from the congregation and make it known? Now, the ideal prayer is this voice of the church, telling what it has learned of God in its daily conflict, bringing out the whole of that great range of Christian work that is going on in any community where there is a true church of Christ. For, as the Apostles were called to testify that they had seen Jesus, and that he was raised from the dead, so the Church should testify that Christ is raised in them from the dead, and tell what he is doing by his work in them.

THE VOICE OF THE CHURCH.

Now, I hold, in the first place, that, according to our idea of it, there can hardly be a prayer-meeting in a hierarchical church; because there can be no such thing, as we understand it, where one man is the channel through which the church worships, and through which alone God speaks to the church. But the prayer-meeting is the voice of the church and of all its members. It belongs to our peculiar organization, and it can scarcely be in any other system. Instead of developing or encouraging it, many of our churches are asking, " Can't we help our leanness and our barrenness with a liturgy?" I do not object to a liturgy

3 *

more than I do to banners on a house, if it pleases
men ; but I would not regard it as the indispensable
method, not as something that we need, until we have
exhausted that which belongs to us, namely, the power
that inheres in the very radical idea of a church among
us, that God communicates with every heart, not me-
diatorially, — by earthly mediation, — but by direct impact, by direct soul-piercing ; that he thinks into men,
and that their thoughts are the rebound of his ; that
he pierces them with divine emotion ; and as, when the
sun pierces the earth, up spring flowers and out burst
fruits, so, when the soul feels the Divine inshining, all
that is noble in it rises efflorescent and victorious.

And when you shall have developed that in the
church, if still you complain of leanness, and want of
interest, and barrenness, then bring in a liturgy, then
bring in some other thing ; though I think the combination of a liturgy with Congregationalism is the
mingling of foreign elements that do not go well together. It is a patch on the old garment ; one or the
other tears, — and it does n't make any difference
which ; there is a hole.

This being the general idea of a prayer-meeting, you
will not have to go far to see what are some of its
advantages and what are some of its hindrances. Of
these things I shall speak to you plainly. And mostly
I speak from my own observation and experience.
The ideal of the prayer-meeting, then, is a family meeting, — a household coming together and telling, all of
them from time to time, what God hath done for them ;
helped to do it by the discriminating leadership of
whoever presides in the meeting, by questions, by vari-

ous methods, calling attention to things that otherwise escape the notice of brethren, and bringing out the full record of the dealings of God with his household, that church.

THE PRAYER—MEETING PROMOTES FELLOWSHIP.

In the first place, it produces, or tends to produce, the almost unknown quality of which so much is said in the New Testament and so little known in the church, —*fellowship;* a sort of joyful inspiration at the sense of a "fellow" by your side, that kind of relation one to another which persons have who are met as on Thanksgiving day, or on Christmas, when a family comes together. Everybody is glad, and nobody can tell why, except that It is my brother, it is my sister, it is my father or my mother, my uncle, my aunt, my grandfather. It is that feeling of heart-exultation, that overflow of gladness; and persons run around and laugh. "Why do you laugh?" "Well, because I feel so happy!" Now, gather a church together; bring them into such relations with each other that they all feel that yearning, that fraternal feeling, that gladness, that exultation in each other. Ah! you never can do this as long as you seat people apart in pews, set them up straight, and make it a sin for them to look at one another, telling them to think with awe about holiness, driving them up out of the sphere of ordinary feeling. They may come in very properly, put their hats down very properly, sit properly, and nobody speak above a whisper, but you cannot produce the feeling of fellowship so. But there is a genial and social element, a loving element, if men

know each other, — as they will come to do, — out of
which fellowship will grow.

IT DISCOURAGES CENSORIOUS JUDGMENT.

And after a little while this kills uncharitableness.
There is not a man living, with any grace in his soul,
who does not feel a yearning toward another that has
done wrong, and owns it, and endeavors to get over it.
Do you know why it is that we feel so toward that
old church-member, forty years a member, and still
so stingy and so proud, — why we all look askance
at him ?   It is because he does not feel that he
is sinful; it is because he does not feel that he is
proud or avaricious.   But if he had come into the
house of God among his brethren, and with the simplicity of a child said, " Brethren, you know my
weakness, but you do not know how I have struggled
against it"; and if you had heard him in his prayers
ask that God would deliver him from avarice; and if
he had talked with the young people in the church,
saying, " Now look at my example; I am trying to
fight against it, but don't you get into any such course
as that," — you would feel a sympathy for him.   Your
fellow-feeling for him would soften your judgment of
him.   Another man is naturally a peacock, who spreads
himself, and who is full of the glistening reflections of
other people's brilliance ; he is laughed at, and people
pick him to pieces, — for there is a vast amount of joyous cannibalism in a right Christian church, — and they
are all pulling the feathers out of him !   But suppose
that man in the gathering household, not ostentatiously,
not going around as a professional experience - teller,

should at his proper time and place, and with evident sincerity of feeling, confess, "This is my disposition; my brethren have spoken to me about it, but they do not need to; I know it; it has been revealed to me in a thousand ways; and I do not like it, I strive against it," — you that are meek should help to restore such a one. Suppose you think, "That man knows it just as well as we do." Did you ever see a brother that would point at his younger brother and say, "That fellow, you know, has got a club-foot"? We never ridicule the infirmities of our brothers and sisters, and certainly not those of our children. They appeal to our compassion, as should the constitutional moral peculiarities of men, especially if they have been developed and exaggerated in the world.

What we want more than anything else in this world is, that men who would go to the stake for the doctrine of total depravity shall admit that they have some of it themselves, and that they are making a brave fight to overcome it. It is wonderful what a grace there is in sympathy. God blesses it in a great many ways. And if in the church there were such a thing, if you could by judicious ministration here, or by gifts there, or by both, bring brethren really to speak of that which is going on in their own lives, it would be a great help to them and to others; it would create and foster the true feeling of fellowship in the church household, and allay harsh judgments and uncharitableness.

IT CHERISHES MUTUAL HELPFULNESS.

Now, when we are saying that there are a thousand sweets while we are on the journey to Canaan, we are always thinking of *poetical* sweets. But the journey lies *in* men; it lies in your pride, your laziness, your envy, your jealousy, your passions; in one or another form of human weakness, — there is where the journey is, and where the work of God is going on. Why should not men be trained to make with sufficient frankness, not indelicate disclosures, but a proper and just reference to these things among brethren for one another's sympathy and helpfulness? If you had reason to think that your brethren were manfully striving to overcome their faults, I do not believe you would ever meet them without wanting to put your arms about them. I know persons whom I never go past without feeling that I would like to lay my hand on their head and bless them. Yet they are some of them wretchedly imperfect. But they are genuine, they are sincere and earnest in their Christian endeavors.

IT DISCOVERS MUTUAL NEEDS.

Fellowship can hardly be developed by any fanciful measures, — fellowship of men as Christians. You *can* fellowship; oh yes. If ye salute those that salute you, what thank have ye? If ye do good to those who do good to you, what do ye more than the publicans or the Pharisees? If you like folks that are *likable*, why not? That is all down hill. You like this one because he is a clean, round, splendid fellow, and interests you. That is all well enough; of course you like him. But how is it with the scrawny folks? How is it about the people that do not interest you? Do you like them? Don't you go about picking up elective affinities or spiritual affinities, getting your companionship here and there? Don't you go to the table and take everything that has sugar on it, letting all the plain things go? Get hold of men because they *need* you. You should fellowship with men, not because they have intellectual treasure and genius, and make the hours so golden for you, but because, like you, they are sons of God, and fight, like you, in the same battle. Soldiers in the field have what they call battle-companions, — pledged to mutual helpfulness and ministration; if one is wounded or falls, the other assists him or cares for him. They go into the fight with these understandings. Have we any such thing in the church? Yet there never was a severer battle than that which is going on all the time in the church, where the heart is touched with Divine aspiration, and is struggling against the temptations of the world. The church should be trained to the disclosure of individual needs and trials in the prayer-meeting, so that those needs may be met. It is part of the minister's business to so train it. There are a great many books which you never have read, and, luckily, never will read; but there are other books that are written by the Holy Spirit, page after page; there are books, the reading of which would make you a thousand-fold wiser than books written by the greatest human authors, — what God is doing in silent souls. You ought to find it out, and I think the prayer-meeting is the place to find it. No man will answer the true ideal of a minister, who, having a church, does not have a prayer-meeting, and who, in the prayer-meeting, does not try to find out what is going on with his people by this kind of disclosure.

IT DEVELOPS POWER IN THE CONGREGATION.

This serves as a counterpart and a counterbalance to the pulpit itself. In most churches, the pulpit is apt to be a lectureship. The minister goes there, and what does he do? He gives out a hymn; it is sung by the choir, and the congregation hear it. He reads the Bible, and they hear it. He leads in prayer, and they hear it. He preaches, and they hear it, — those of them that are awake. He gives out another hymn, and they hear it and go home, and that is the end of it. What have they done? They have been recipients; everything has been done for them, upon them, to them. They have done nothing. There ought to be a counterbalance to this. This is putting all the power into the pulpit. But one of the things that should measure the power of the pulpit is the magnitude of the living power which it develops among the congregation. If a minister goes into a church which is all pulpit, and stays ten or twenty years, and goes out of it and it is all pulpit still, while he may have done a good many things, there is one which he has not done, — to his discredit! He has not developed the church power as distinguished from the pulpit power, — the brotherhood.

It is a good thing to have a noble father and mother; but one of the things that noble fathers and mothers must do is to bring up their children so that, as they come one after another up to manhood and are turned off, they too are noble. And it is through these minor meetings, where you get close to men, and conventionalities are broken down, and intimacies are established upon other grounds than those that rule in social life,

that this work is to be done, if it is to be done anywhere.

IT DISCLOSES GIFTS AND GRACES.

Then, the prayer-meeting does another thing; it develops the gifts that are in the church. There are
gifts that lie hidden,— the possessors themselves don't
know of their existence. There are men who have
received no culture, and yet have great good sense.
There are men who have had no opportunity for learning the art of expression, who, nevertheless, have that
discrimination, that balance, that insight, which constitute tact. They have comprehensive judgments of men
and things. They are able to manage their fellow-men
out of doors, to control business and carry it on, under a
thousand inequalities, successfully to an end. But they
are not supposed to have any gifts in the church, because they never volunteer, they do not say anything.
The idea largely prevails, that, if men speak in meeting,
they must speak expositorily, or hortatorily, both of
which things I think to be hindrances in prayer-meetings. Of hortatoriness, I shall speak in a moment. It
is the *bête noire* of prayer-meetings; it is the devil that
ought to be exorcised to begin with. But men say, "I
have nothing to say," thinking that if a man speaks he
ought in some sense to imitate a minister; that speaking in a prayer-meeting ought in some way or other to
be ministerial, and that the speaker should discuss a
point, unfold a doctrinal truth, state some discrimination; that some catechetical matter should be explained.
Now, if you get rid of that idea, there are a great many
men who have a great deal to say. As, for instance,

E

the value of patience is up, and I say, " Mr. ——, what
has been your experience in respect to that ? You
had a family of four boys ; they all died drunkards,
did n't they ? " He rises very slowly ; he is very broken
in his language ; he says, " Yes, they inherited that tendency from my ancestors." " Did you find it very easy
to bear with them ? " " Oh ! when my first boy came
home, it seemed as though I would burn the house down
over my head ; it seemed as though I would give up
everything ; it seemed as though I was all on fire ; my
brain and everything was upset." He goes on and gives
the way in which his feelings were changed. You
question him, you help him, you bring him out. " How
was it when the second one came in ? " And that man
will unfold the history of a father-heart striving and
moaning after faith and hope in God, and holding
on to those boys that are bringing disgrace on themselves and wretchedness on the household. There he
has been for, to my certain knowledge, twenty years,
carrying four boys, clinging to them, losing his own
life almost literally for their sake. There is a grand
epic of patience, wrought out in a Christian man's
heart ! Cannot I develop that by a few questions ?
And when the Spirit is working, and when men are
thus speaking, you will not make grammar an essential
grace. It is in this way that you develop gifts.

WOMEN TO TAKE PART.

I believe in women speaking and praying in meetings, as well as preaching and lecturing and voting, —
not voting in meeting, but *Voting.* I feel that the
church has lost one half of its best power in the exclu-

sion of the sisterhood from speaking in our meetings. But revivals know no law, and the consequence is, that when we have revivals and morning meetings, even the stiffest churches allow mothers to get up and ask prayers for their children. And, once get them on their feet, with a very little dexterity you can catch some very nice silver and gold fish out of them. When they open their mouths, throw in a question. In that way, I have frequently done what I could not do in any other. It is said, "Open your meetings to women, and you will get only the chaff. Only the scatter-brains will speak, and all those who are considerate and modest will be silent." Why should they not, when you sit glowering there ; and, though you throw the noose, they know you don't want to catch *them ?* There is no encouragement, no help, no temptation, nothing ; and only those speak that don't care for you or your desires. And what hope or courage is there, under such circumstances, for any-body that is self-respecting ? But presently prayers are being asked for children, and one father gets up and says, " I have a son at sea, and I ask prayers for him "; and another one gets up and says, " I have a son of whom I have heard that he is lying sick of a dangerous fever, and I ask prayers of the brethren for him." "Are there any other requests to be made ? " An elderly woman, rising, says, " My son and daughter are dead, and I have five of their children to take care of, and I strive with poverty, according to my best endeavors; I ask the sympathy and the prayers of the brethren for these five." "How many are there, madam, did you say ? " "Five." "How old are they ? " "Well, the oldest is now seventeen, and he is the strongest one among us, and then —" "What are the ages of the others, madam ? What is the disposition of this eldest son, and has he ever shown any inclination toward religious things ?" "Yes, sir; he has, at times, shown a good deal of feeling." I can get a good speech out of her before she knows it, and you know it will be substance, every bit of it; it will be meat. And so you can get a well-regulated woman talking in prayer-meeting, without anybody being shocked or hurt. In that sly way, young gentlemen, you can circumvent the old fogies and have the women talk in meeting without offence.

If I have any remembrance of my own mother; if I have a remembrance of the other, the second mother, that brought me up; if I have any remembrance of my sisters and of those aunts that were more than Virgin Marys to me, and who dedicated themselves to virginity that they might give their lives to charity; if I remember the prayers that they uttered over us little children, the instruction they gave us out of the Word of God, the conversations that they held, — I know that I have derived the deepest, the sweetest, and the truest religious impressions of my life from the utterances of woman. And if woman has these gifts, and can speak to children in the household, I say that she has no right to put her light under the bushel of the family, but that she should set it on a candlestick, where it shall light all that are in the house. And the church has a right to the gifts of these women, — the mothers and the sisters that are doing the great work of life. It is gold too precious to be lost, and we are dying for want of just such material; and yet, on a mere quiddity, on a mere punctilio, we are excluding from the

church elements that would make us incomparably rich.
And so we have our beanpoles of propriety, but not a
morning-glory twining round about them and blossoming to the glory of God.

I will not in this indirect way attempt to make a
lecture on women's rights. I simply bring this in as
an illustration, — and it will also suggest a way in
which you can bring in unpalatable subjects merely as
illustrations.

(I was speaking about the way in which the prayer-
meeting develops the gifts of the members of the church,
and all these remarks, therefore, you will set down
under that head.)

THE PRAYER-MEETING MAKES TRUTH PERSONAL.

Then, meetings for prayer, properly managed, take
truth from its generic condition and bring it home to
men as a personal thing. It becomes casuistry. You
develop cases of conscience; you develop grades of
disposition; you develop truth in its relations, as you
cannot in any other way.

One of the troubles which every minister of any standing and experience has found, has been how to fashion
sermons so that a great truth could, after all, be made
to branch till it reached out and touched all the individual cases. He has had the feeling come over him,
" Well, they are simply infinite !" And a sermon may
begin like the handle of a splint broom, but it will end
with as many different points as there are in the end of
the broom. So you feel that you cannot do it. True, you
cannot so well do it in the pulpit. But, if you have a
living church, — and it depends upon yourself whether

you have or not,— if you make your prayer-meetings
so social, so genial, so elastic, so open-mouthed and
open-hearted, that you can ask anybody questions and
they are not ashamed to talk, and talk goes backward
and forward among them,— and almost every man sees
things a little differently from his neighbor,— and one
and another asks, "What shall I do in such and such a
case?"— you will find that a truth which you state
generically instantly becomes specific,— that it is multitudinous. I am continually struck with this, that
when I introduce a topic in prayer-meeting, and open it
as it runs in my mind, I hardly get through presenting
it — I am hopeful, I look at things in the light of courage
and hope — before a brother on my left hand, who always
has a kind of melancholy caution, brings me up with,
"Don't you think, Brother Beecher, that if persons were
to follow that out in such and such relations it would
be liable to such and such perversions?" "Oh yes, I
never thought to stop up that hole"; so then I give it
a little plaster in that direction. And so it goes all
around, and men look at the subject from some experience of their own, from some habitude of their own
minds, from some new, different philosophy of their own.
They put questions which result in the end in bringing
this truth home, from its generic state, to a personal
truth, to black and white, to each particular person.
He gets it as he wants it.

So truth, when you bring it into a congregation, is
like a roll of cloth, which may be cut and fitted to all
the different sizes of men. It comes in cloth, it goes
out garments. When you come to see how truth stands
in its relations to the individual man; the infinity of

it, the universality of it, the multitudinousness of it, the richness, the wonderful power in it, — this is one of the most convincing evidences of its divinity. The truth, when you come to study it in relation to men's wants, is like nature itself, when you come to study it in all its infinite diversities and minute differences. This is the work of the prayer-meeting. Don't you begin to feel ashamed that you have done so little with the prayer-meeting? Don't you begin to think that the prayer-meeting is the long-lost art, and that the church ought, more than on anything else, to pivot on that? I think a church is more likely to live a great while that pivots on the prayer-meeting, than those are that pivot on the pulpit.

IT ATTRACTS OUTSIDERS.

There is also in this matter an application of the prayer-meeting to which I wish to call your attention, — the effect which a prayer-meeting of this kind has, from time to time, upon outsiders, upon spectators. In the first place, the freshness, the liveliness, and the reality of it bring men to it. Your meeting will be crowded in a little while. It will grow; and by and by you will make chords vibrate in men's hearts, as you bring out the power that is wrought by the Holy Ghost in the personal experience of individuals, — filling the whole air with a new sense of Providence and Divinity, sending men home enlightened and strengthened in the midst of their struggles, and enriched by the conscious presence of God in a thousand ways. People will come to the meeting; and you cannot get a room big enough to hold them under such circumstances.

THE EFFECT ON SPECTATORS.

I call your attention to the effect which it produces upon spectators who are not Christians. Take them into an ordinary prayer-meeting, and it is the most dangerous place you can bring them to. It produces on them very much a sense of imprisonment. It is galley-work, and they don't like it. The idea of going to the trouble of being convicted and converted in order to get into a prayer-meeting is rather discouraging to them; and I must say I don't blame them. But let a man going by step into a *real* prayer-meeting. He hears singing in there, and rousing good singing too. He rather likes hymns, and he slips inside of the door and sits down. A man gets up, after the meeting has advanced, and says, "Brethren, our pastor has been opening up the subject of Sincerity, and it came pretty near to me. I try to be sincere, but I must confess that in conducting my business I slide sometimes, before I think. Now, yesterday I went into a transaction something like this,"— and he gives an account of an affair in which he had been a little too quick for the other man, and rather got the best end of the bargain; and he says, " Well, I did n't feel particularly happy all the way back to the store. My conscience rather accused me, and I made up my mind that I should go and rectify that thing." The man who slipped in is the very man with whom he had that dealing, and who had said of him, " Damn him ! he is a member of the church." That is what he said immediately after the business transaction, but what does he say now ? " Bless his heart! The old fellow has some

feeling, has n't he?" Now, any man that can change
a "damn" into a "bless" is doing a good work. But
here is a man who judges men by no charitable standard, who sees things as they are in business. He comes
in and sees a man who had all his life had faults. He
finds out that that man knows them, and is trying to
get over them. He knows that that man tried sharp
practice over him, and sees that he feels sorry for it.
He is speaking about it, though in an impersonal way.
"Really," says the new-comer, "I guess there is some
sincerity, after all, in religion." When he goes home,
he says to his wife, "Where do you suppose I have
been?" "Well, I don't know. I suppose around to
Fox's, to see Humpty Dumpty." "No, guess again.
Where do you suppose I have been?" "Well, I don't
know. Some theater." "No, guess once more." "I
give it up." "I have been around to the prayer-meeting." That is a surprise to her. Says he, "I tell you
what; it was really a good meeting. I positively
enjoyed it." He has to tell it all. When the time for
the next meeting comes round, he says, "Put on your
shawl, my dear, and let us go around to the prayer-
meeting and see what we will get." They go around,
and find that it is fresh, and means business. He may
not believe all he hears there, but, after all, there are
many truths. Men come together, and they take hold
of the very roots of subjects and discuss them. They
try to be honest. That man cannot help himself. He
is already convicted. He has not a Mount Sinai conviction, perhaps, but he may have a little haycock
conviction. He has got a consciousness of faults. He
has got the preliminary tentative states that, under

ordinary, suitable, fair instruction, will develop in him.
Manly sympathy, really humane feeling toward him,
will bring that man right along. Ask him, " Don't you
think you have faults ? Don't you commit sins ? Are
you not guilty of derelictions both to God and man ?
Is n't it time for you to begin to think about this
thing ? "

Other men come in there. They are exhilarated,
they are lifted up. Don't let a prayer-meeting know
that there is anybody there but the " brethren." Don't
say a word to "sinners." I would shut up a man's
mouth who began to talk in that way, as quick as I
would turn the faucet of a wine-cask if the wine were
leaking away. It is the actual sight of what we mean
by piety, it is the sight of imperfection, it is the hearing of groans, it is the sight of tears, it is the recital
of joys, it is faith, it is hope, it is love, it is fellowship,
it is helpfulness, — not in any of their grander poetical
forms, but as they exist in actual men and women, —
it is the battle of life going on before men's eyes,
that make the most imperative and impersonal of all
ways of preaching the truth to many men. There is
many a man that can stand the great fifteen-inch gun
of the pulpit, that cannot stand this *mitrailleuse*, this
multitudinous fire of the whole church.

I have been accustomed in times of revivals of religion to say to persons awakened and coming slowly
along in their steps toward the light, " Come to the
morning prayer-meeting." The most converting agency
I have known in my whole ministry has been the morning prayer-meeting, when I could keep the hounds off
of men, so that they should not be exhorting them and

telling them how sinful they were. Let them alone;
let them see what the grace of God is in the brotherhood.

QUESTIONS AND ANSWERS.

Q. How would you stop those exhorters?

Mr. Beecher. — Well, you cannot always stop them.
You have got to drive prayer-meetings just as you do
horses. You cannot keep flies from biting them, nor
them from whisking their tails, in a summer's day.
You have got to make the best of your annoyances.
The absurd saints that I have had, the ridiculous crea-
tures that have come in, the interruptions that we have
had! Meetings brought to a blessed point, — like a
cow that has given a good bucket of milk only to put
her foot in it, — to be entirely ruined! There is a kind
of spiritual *bummers* that run around to prayer-meetings. I will tell you more about that, however, next
week.

Q. What about the length of prayers in prayer-meetings?

Mr. Beecher. — Short, generally, but long when you
can't help it. I wouldn't want the Ohio to overflow
its banks, or the Miami to run over, but once a year.
We used to let them when the snows melted on the
mountains, — we couldn't help ourselves. Down came
the torrents; and I have seen the biggest boats navi-
gating the streets of Lawrenceburg. I liked once a
year to have a good freshet; but I didn't want any
more.

That matter, I think, may almost always be controlled
with a very little drill.

Q. I would like to hear a word further, if you are not going to take it up hereafter, as to how the leader of the meeting shall open the subject. There is danger of his so opening it that people will say, "Well, I can't say anything after that!" What is the way in which a leader shall open a meeting so that everybody shall feel free to speak after it?

MR. BEECHER. — Yes, that is a very important consideration. One of the things that every minister ought to have implanted in him is, that he is not going to do well every time, and that he is not going to do well at first, always, and that he has got to take up his cross and to carry it in just such things as these. He has got to learn his trade while he is practicing it for a living. In opening a prayer-meeting, very likely no directions can be given. Practice will teach. With any considerable *gumption* to begin with, you will very soon see when you make your opening too good. Avoid making too good speeches at the beginning of a meeting; do not say all that you have to say on a subject. On the other hand, avoid any such magisterial manner, any such jealousy of the cloth, that nobody will feel disposed to come forward. Then, if they will not come up when you have opened a subject, question them, call them up. "Mr. ——, what do you think of that idea?" Well, Mr. —— has to say something, and the moment he does, you tackle him, because he won't say much unless you dispute him, and you will have a little bit of an argument. But, the moment anybody begins to talk, somebody else puts in a word, and you ask some other one for his views. Then it will go around. There are a thousand arts of that kind that are perfectly innocent and allowable, which a man must learn.

Why, young gentlemen, being a minister means being busy, I can tell you, from one end to the other of your life; either busy in your study, busy on the street, or busy in your meetings. If anybody has got to be observant, fruitful, wise, full of tact and inspiration, it is the man that undertakes to lead a congregation in prayer-meetings.

I may still further answer to that question, that a wise pastor, who is conducting meetings, will be conducting meetings all the week long. There will be an undertone in his mind. All manner of feelings and thoughts are running through your mind, and you may just as well have something which will be of value to you. You see a man. You say to yourself, " I wonder how I can get at that man; I wonder how his sensibilities are." You will survey him, and look at him, as an engineer looks at a fort. You say, " How can I attack that man ?" General Sherman never rides through a country, I believe, without looking at the topography of it. He says, " There is a good place for a battery; how finely my flanks would be protected over there!" He is engaged in noting the military advantages of the country.

A minister has got to be busy all the while. Whenever you see a man, eat him. Whenever you see a man, dissect him. Think how you would approach this one; how you would get at his conscience, whether by going down through the scuttle of pride and vanity, whether by coming up through the cellar of shame and fear. You see children doing things; you see bees, — a thousand things that are full of analogies. If need be, put them down in your note-book. But keep collecting them all the while, — let your thighs be yellow.   —

Q. What is the value of the young people's prayer-meeting?

MR. BEECHER. — I think it to be very great. It is, of course, subject to all those infelicities that belong to youth, which young people do not believe in, but old people do. It is subject to a great many crudenesses, but the average result is admirable. It brings out and gives form in young Christians to obscure feelings. It gives them courage and definiteness of commitment. It teaches them how to use their implements in a Christian warfare at an early period. It knits them together, one to another. In a thousand ways it is beneficial.

Q. What would you say about the long prayer, so called, before the sermon? Old Dr. Ely, of Munson, used to pray thirty and forty minutes. Is such a prayer a means of grace?

MR. BEECHER. — I should say it was. A man brought up under such circumstances, who was not patient, might think his was a hopeless case. . So of long family prayers. A man entering a house after the prayer was begun, and waiting a long time, asked a boy how long before his father would be done. The boy replied, " Has he come to the Jews yet ? " "No," was the answer. "Then it will be half an hour more." Of course, such stories are to be taken with allowance; they are exaggerations. But exaggerations are in rhetoric what magnifying a flower or a beetle is in natural history. We cannot see them so well unless we do magnify them.

Long prayers are, as a general rule, nuisances. It is not often that a man is so wound up in feeling that nature compels the feeling to iterate and reiterate itself. A great loss or bereavement, if it does not put

one to silence, leads one in few words to repeat, and repeat, and repeat. I have seen mothers that, like the
King of Israel, walked about the room moaning, "My
son! my son! my son! my son!" a hundred times.
Others I have heard say, "O my God! O my God! O
my God!" It was mute prayer, — ejaculatory prayer,
running on as long as the wounded heart had blood to
bleed. But for men in cold blood to come into a meeting and, without any great feeling in themselves or any
great feeling round about them, to open up Euphrates
or the Mississippi, — it is abominable! And if they
should do it a few times in my meeting, I would stop
them, or I would cut them in two.

Q. Do you not think the objection of formality can be brought
against asking a blessing at table three times a day? What can you
say about the origin and desirableness of this custom?

Mr. Beecher. — Well, I can say that there is no obligation in the custom, and its formality depends entirely
on who does it and how he does it. I dined with an
English clergyman in London, and we had got about
through the main dinner and were coming to the fruit,
— Dr. Raymond and I were sitting on opposite sides
of the table. We were in the full tide of conversation, and there was no other company except the clergyman and his wife. After the cloth had been re-
moved, — I was in the midst of a story, I think, —
they both rose, and I heard, "Blb-lb-lb-lb!" and they
sat down again. "What, sir?" said I. I found out,
afterwards, that he had said, "Lord, make us thankful
for these blessings!" Well, now, I consider any such
thing as that absurd, — worse than useless. But to

see the children gathered at the table, the old father, venerable and sincere, and the mother, reverend and matronly, sweet-hearted as a saint, the children all in their places, hungry but yet waiting; and to see the old man bow his head and recognize the hand of God in all those bounties, in a short and appropriate thanks-giving, — I don't know how that is to others, but it makes *my* bread sweet. I like it! If anybody don't, he is perfectly at liberty to let it alone.

Q. Is there any more objection to that kind of formalism than there is to the shaking of hands when you meet?

MR. BEECHER. — Or saying good bye; which is, "God be with you." Nobody thinks of it, but it expresses this, — good-will. Even my English friend, I suppose, regarded his returning thanks as being a general indication that he had yet remaining a sense of the Divine favor in his dinner. If they are formal, the remedy does not seem to me to consist in abolishing them, but in making them sincere.

IV.

THE PRAYER-MEETING: ITS HELPS AND HINDRANCES.

 SHALL resume the subject of prayer-meetings under the general head of its Helps and Hindrances. Let me premise that you may be in danger, from the variety of statements and from the incitements to the ideal of the power and admirableness of the prayer-meeting which I continually attempt to develop, of going to your work in such a state of mind that when you do not succeed at once, or well, you will be thrown back in discouragement.

HARD WORK FOR THE MINISTER.

There are two very important and very difficult things to do, namely, to maintain a lofty ideal, and yet not be disgusted with ill success under it; to keep on trying; not to content yourself with poor results, but not to give over because you cannot reach the mark which you have in your mind. This will be particularly true of your ministerial life. And it may be some comfort to you by and by, though of course you will not feel it now, to know that the most difficult thing that you will have to do in your ministry is to maintain a live prayer-meeting. It is about the hardest work you will ever know. It will tax your ingenuity the most; it will tax your resources, your power over men and over yourself, your administrative faculty. He who can take a parish and develop in it a good prayer-meeting, carry it on through years and still have it fruitful, various, spiritual, — he is a general. It may be that he will not excel in the pulpit; the prayer-meeting, under such circumstances, is his pulpit.

If you go into your work, therefore, with some discouragement, remember what I tell you, that as " he that bridleth his tongue is perfect," — that is, he who has grace enough to do that has grace enough to do anything, — so the minister who knows how to make a good prayer-meeting is perfect, in a sense. It is true that there will be many times when the meeting will develop itself like a geyser, with vast volume and stones up-springing and filling the air as well as shaking the earth under your feet; but, like the geyser, it will gurgle back again, and leave mud and smoke behind. It is not difficult in times of revival, in times when the whole community are developed in the direction of moral excitement, to arouse feeling; it is difficult then to keep it down, to give it anything like moderation. The meeting then takes the bits into its mouth and runs away with you.

But when there is no general excitement, in summer months, in winter months; when there is no feeling anywhere; to maintain the heart of the church which beats in the prayer-meeting, warm, genial, crescent, — in this is labor, I may say in this is genius, if you succeed.

DIFFICULTY OF GATHERING THE PEOPLE.

It is very difficult, in some places, to draw the people together for a weekly prayer-meeting. There is that hindrance to overcome, and every man must overcome it in the particular way indicated by the circumstances of the field in which he is working, — for it is impossible to give a general rule. Then, where the population is large, there is an indifference to contend with. I have already alluded to the fact that prayer-meetings are the least popular of all meetings in the church, whether with the members of the congregation or the members of the church itself. And it is for a very good reason, — they are generally the driest of meetings. So that you will often find, when you come into a large congregation, that the weakest place in it, the leanest part of the service, will be the prayer-meeting. You are to hold yourself in the main responsible for this state of things, after you are well established in your work.

THE FOLLY· OF SCOLDING.

Above all things, do not scold your people because they do not attend. I do not believe that any amount of whips or of skill could drive a swarm of bees into a field where there were not a dozen flowers. They won't go. And to get them into a field where there are a thousand flowers, there is no need of whips or of driving. Now, it is for you to kindle such an interest there as will draw men. Generally, in your ministry, do as Paul did; encourage, praise, never blame until you have with consummate enginery prepared the way to blame. When Paul wished to rebuke people, he first stated all the good he knew about them, and all the pleasant things he had heard about them, and how near and dear they were to him. "Nevertheless, brethren," he would say, "I have somewhat —" and then comes in the other thing! In general, to scold your people because they do not come to church on Sunday is to hit those that do come and miss those that do not. To scold or to blame your people in any way because they do not come to meeting, or because they have no feeling, is not wise. It is your business to produce the feeling that will make their attendance voluntary and cheerful, that will make it impossible for them to keep away.

HOW TO START PRAYER-MEETINGS.

In the beginning of a prayer-meeting of this kind, there are both physical and moral elements that enter into it. I have here a question as to the best way to start a prayer-meeting in a place where there is none. Well, the way to start a prayer-meeting is the way you would start a fire. If it is an old church, it is like a fire-place where there has been something raked up over-night; in the morning, there is not a coal there as big as a thimble. But you get together the few that there are. You never think of bringing in a whole armful of wood and whanging it all down into the embers. You lay the wood aside, selecting the driest pieces you can find, and whittle up shavings; and, having gathered the few little coals, you put a few shavings upon them; then you blow the little pile gently at first, and up springs a light blaze. Then you lay on a few more shavings, dealing with it all the time as carefully and tenderly as a mother does with a baby; then, by and by, you put on a dry stick, picking out the fittest and the best, and soon the flame will get power; and at last, when the whole fire is kindled, you can put on what you please, green wood or dry, it will consume the strongest and toughest materials.

In the beginning, remember that the prayer-meeting turns on this fact: it is the development of the *social element in the religious direction.* Suppose, in an old church, in a great state of deadness, one or two brethren feel that they cannot live so, and there are two ways proposed. One is, to get the minister to preach a big sermon on that subject, and then to ring the bell, and call everybody to come down into the conference-room or lecture-room, and try to have a prayer-meeting. That will fail, nine times in ten. Suppose, instead of that, you look around to find some one who feels as you feel. Ask him to come to your house for prayer. Both of you look around for a third who shall be congenial, susceptible, warm. Get three together. Three are very powerful on the fourth, and four on the fifth. When you have got a praying center that begins to whirl with some degree of power, it will suck in materials just as fast as you ought to have them come. Begin at the bottom, begin low, begin and work the principle of affiliation, — of the moral affinities. Work it patiently, and in faith that there is a principle there, and you will succeed. And you will not be apt to succeed in any other way.

So, then, the first step in a prayer-meeting where the interest has died out is to go back to the very first elements; make it perfectly simple, perfectly natural,

be yourself fervent; and fervency creates fervor, as
sparks lead to sparks.

POVERTY OF MATERIAL.

Another of the hindrances which we find in our
prayer-meetings arises from the poverty of the material which is developed in them. My observation
teaches me that there are very few men who think
enough to have anything to spare for their neighbors.
In books, meditation abounds. There is a good deal
of talk about it, but I have never seen much of it that
people had to hand out for small change on occasions.
There is a great deal of philosophy in the world, but
it expends itself mostly and is absorbed in practical
things. And when you take men who have always
been accustomed to work out all that they have in
them toward the concrete, toward visible things, and
bring them together in a meeting, and expect them to
rise up in their places and develop that which their
whole life has been a training not to develop (namely,
abstract meditation or anything of that kind), you will
find very soon, that, whether it be devotion or meditation, there is but very little of it grown, and much
less brought to market.

So, then, you will find a great poverty in the materials
which you work. There will be good Christian men
and women, and yet it will be very hard to make much
out of them in a prayer-meeting. Remember this;
don't let your expectations be too high. Keep your
expectations down and your will up. Determine that
you *will* have meetings, first or last, if it takes years.
Don't be impatient on the way. You are working at

tough material. You are doing the best work that can
be done, but it is necessarily low. Then, the worst of
all difficulties is not that people are barren; it is that
they are blind, and naked, and sick, and do not know it.

NEED OF WISE LEADERSHIP.

Prayer-meetings usually fall into the hands of a few
hackneyed leaders, if the pastor is not himself present.
Now, deacons and elders may be excellent men as
elders and as deacons, and yet not be gifted either in
spiritual fervor for devotional purposes, or in the tact
that is requisite to lead a meeting. I have seen
deacon-smothered churches and elder-smothered prayer-
meetings, any number of them, where men went into
the leadership of the meeting who made everybody
afraid. The young people did n't dare to speak, nobody
dared to speak. There was a sort of " *order* " in the
meeting. To be sure, worship is something, edification
is something, freedom is something, but oh, " Order !
order ! order ! Let everything be done decently and in
order." And so they were as orderly as a pyramid of
mummies.

STALE SPEAKERS AND SPEECHES.

Then, too, you have the hackneyed speeches and
hackneyed prayers. There is one man in every prayer-
meeting who has to get up and confess that he don't
live up to his privileges and to his light, and he tells
you that every week, or it may be every month,
through the whole year. He never gets a great way
beyond that. There is another man who is always
confessing his sins, and confessing and confessing, in a

general way, — never the special sins that his neighbors
see in him, but always the doctrine of sin, and not the
practice.   So a few men of this kind run right around
in that same barren path, the regulation address and
remarks.

Worst of all, come the exhorters, or men who are
always urging folks up to their duty. This I shall
speak about a little farther on. But these hackneyed
speakers in prayer-meetings take the life out of them.
Frequently they are the best men in the community in
other respects, but they are not adapted to that place.
Young men, how are you going to get along with these
old gray-heads? Well, you cannot at first; but there
is a good deal that can be done by good sense and
patience, and real kind, humble feeling. Many of these
men have in them better springs than have yet been
tapped. There are many of them that can do a great
deal better than they think they can, and you can *help*
a good deal out of them. They are to be revered, if
they are venerable; they are to be respected for their
work, if they have been useful; they are to be treated
as fathers, and not with contempt. They are to be
treated, especially by a young pastor, with the greatest
affection and kindness. Nevertheless, it is always
fair to have a design on a man for his own good; and
it is always fair for a pastor, seeing these men in the
way, to do two things, — first, to attempt to get more
out of them, to talk with them, to lead their thoughts
to other things, to get them to express other things when
they speak, and to shorten their prayers when they
pray; secondly, to develop another center. Bring in
new material; get hold of the young, and put new life,

new blood, into the meeting. This is a kind of co-operative antagonism. It is taking the meeting gradually out of the hands of those who have ridden it to death, and putting it into the hands of those that have come up under better auspices. The change will be gradual, little by little. An old church is very much like an old building. You have the quarrels, which may be represented by the rats and mice in the walls. You have all the difficulties, which are the leaks, the weather-boarding and shingles off here and there. You have the smoky chimneys, the squeaking doors, the ill-adjusted steps, — a hundred things that are to be remedied. You begin to patch in here and there, — to revamp; working on the house little by little, till, by and by, you get into a state that is whole-some and comfortable again. An old church has to be worked very much in this way. I have sometimes thought it would not be bad to disband old churches. Dr. Payson used to say that if he could have his own way he would scatter his church entirely; and then all that wanted to come back he would n't take in, and all that did n't want to come back he would draw to-gether; indicating that the forward ones were the spiritually conceited, and that the retiring ones were the modest and the humble. And although this is, of course, an extravagance, it marks a thought.

The difficulty of combating in churches the old heredi-tary troubles, coming out in meetings and other social relations, oftentimes occupies the mind of the young pastor fully as much as all the rest of his work put together. Old churches will go down from generation to generation and have something very noble, even

grand, in them; and, except in special cases, you are not
to think of getting rid of the difficulties as you might
burn a barn to get rid of the rats. But you have got a
work of this kind to do, when you take a church, that
will require your patience, your assiduity, your tact,
your knowledge of human nature, your grace, the control of your own temper, the richness and depth of
your spiritual feelings.

THE MINISTER TO TRAIN HIMSELF.

There is another element of which I would speak, —
the estimate which you yourself, and those of your
members who are under your influence, put upon the
prayer-meeting. If you prepare your sermon labori-
ously, if you make Sunday your idol, and spend all your
available force in that direction, and count your little
social meetings during the week as " only prayer-meetings, — nothing to do to-day but my prayer-meeting," —
if you put that kind of emphasis on it, you certainly will
not make much out of it. Although training for the
pulpit is one thing, and training for the prayer-meeting
is another, I think that the man who is to excel in
prayer-meetings must train more for them, though differently, than for the pulpit. I should be very sorry
to be forced into the conduct of a prayer-meeting without having anticipated it during the day; not so much
that I might think what I was going to say, but, as it
were, to *beat up* my nature, to get into a higher mood,
to rise into a thought more of the Infinite; to get some
such relation to men as I think God has, of sympathy,
pity, tenderness, and sweetness; to get my heart all
right, so that everything in me should work sympatheti-

cally toward certain devotional ends. Get yourself trained.

Never, therefore, regret your prayer-meetings; the harder they are, the more you need to be strong in them, the more you need to feel responsible for their right conduct, to have full-heartedness in going into them. Train for them, then; not so much by preparing the way for what you shall say,—though that at times may be wise and useful,—as by having the right moral forces, the right sympathies, in yourself.

LET EVERY MEETING TAKE ITS OWN SHAPE.

In conducting prayer-meetings, I have noticed one mistake which is constantly and naturally made, and that is, when you have had one good one, to have the next a very poor one. Just as young ministers, when they have preached one good sermon, think, "There, now I will preach another next Sunday that will just be the mate to this." And when on the next Sunday they come to preach it, it is stale, it "all flats out" in their hands, and they do not know what the difficulty is. My father once said to me, "Henry, never try to run a race with yourself." If you have preached a good sermon, do not try to preach another just like it; do not try to fill up the same measure that you have filled. The probability is, that while there may have been much labor and preparation for that good sermon, there was also much of that volunteer force, much of that native, that unexpected help, which you cannot get again by mere volition. Time and again I have seen a prayer-meeting that rose and culminated, full of sweetness, of freshness, of Divine spirit, full of the best fruit of the Spirit in man. Everybody went away edified, happy, and joyful. And when they came together the next time, they came saying, "Now let us have just such another." There never was and never will be just such another. You may turn a kaleidoscope a million times, and the rays never will fall twice alike. And so meetings, since they spring not from prescribed forms and definite rules, but are the unfolding of the voluntary conditions of feeling in hundreds of persons, can never be just alike.

Therefore, in the conduct of a prayer-meeting, while you may have some theme or topic, while you may have in your mind some idea how it shall shape itself, and run, always be vigilant to see if there is not a germ in the meeting itself, and be sagacious to discern and catch it. Frequently you will go thinking, "I will spend to-night on the subject of prayer," and you make some attempt on that subject. But some one will get up and bring in another theme, and he will feel it so much that you will find everybody else feels it. Seize that; do not go back to the old topic, you have got the real meeting there. And with a little nourishing, blowing, catching all the sparks and bringing them together, you will very soon have a meeting that opens up in nobleness and beauty. Let every meeting develop the vitality that is in its own core; let it unfold its own germ. There is a germ, if men only know how to develop it.

FEELING CANNOT BE FORCED.

Let me say a word on the subject of attempting to force feeling. It is true that feeling begets feeling by sympathy, but it is also true that persons may be so much beyond their neighbors in any given direction of feeling that the chasm between them cannot be filled up. Then, feeling acts just the other way.

I recall scenes in the West. I recollect being at a city on the Ohio River, and a brother who had been laboring for nearly four weeks in camp-meeting revivals was sent over in advance of Synod, which was to meet there, to prepare the church for it. He went with all the nervous fervor that there was in the labor he had just been going through, and commenced pouring himself out upon the church, bringing them together, telling them of their dead condition, setting their sins in order before them. But he was in such a state of excitement, so far above them, that nobody caught the spirit. They rather took his exhortations as the negro slaves across the river in Kentucky took kicks, — they only crouched and looked sullen, and went on. And when Synod came together, that was the state of the church. They had been on the anvil, and with small hammer and trip-hammer they had been pounded unmercifully.

I recall very well one Sunday night. Brother Snead had had the general care of the meetings, and I was appointed to preach on Sunday evening. That was a sermon born out of the extremity of desire. I had preached several times, and with no special effect; but there was one person whose conversion had lingered, and for whom my whole soul had gone out. And in the strong desire that I had, I struck out a plain and quiet sermon on the parable of the Prodigal Son. I went with that sermon into the pulpit on that Sunday night, and began preaching it. It was of the love of God, and the way in which he looked upon sinners,— his yearning. And, without any attempt to produce feeling, I drew picture after picture and scene after scene, until about the middle of the sermon the audience broke down, and it was like a rain on the mountains. It was the beginning of a great and glorious revival of religion there. When I came out of the pulpit, Brother Snead said, "My dear brother, you have given them sugar when you ought to have given them tartar!"

Now, this attempting to enforce the strong feeling of conviction and dread of the wrath to come might have been wise under some circumstances; but here was a case in which it was manifestly unwise, and was defeating itself, and where a much lower tone of feeling stood connected with the production of that which was needed. As an illustration, take the old-fashioned way of lighting a candle. If you have a coal of fire and blow gently, there will always come a little flame on the coal, and you can light your candle with it; but if a man should take the coal and give a sudden and violent puff, he would blow out the light of the coal and the candle too. Gentle feeling will often stand more nearly connected with the inception of deep emotion than more intense and overpowering agitation will.

Another thing: You can never make people feel by scolding them because they don't feel. You can never move anybody by saying, "Feel!" Feeling is just as much a product of cause as anything else in the world. I could sit down before a piano and say, "A, come forth"; and it won't. But if I put my finger on

the key it will, and that is the only way to make it.
The human soul is like a harp; one has but to put his
hand to a chord and it will vibrate to his touch, according as he knows how. It is the knowing how that you
are to acquire. It is the very business that you are
going out into the world for; it is to understand human
nature so that you can touch the chords of feeling.

HOW FEELING IS DEVELOPED.

In general, feeling results from the presentation of
some fact or truth that has a relation to the particular
feeling you wish to produce. If I wanted to make
you weep, I would not tell you an amusing story; I
would, if I wanted to make you laugh, and that story
had a relation to laughing. If I wished to make you
weep, I would tell you some pathetic incident, the
truth embodied in which had some sympathetic relation to feeling. Charge yourself with this: "If these
people are to feel, I, as the minister of the Holy
Ghost, am to be the cause of it by applying to their
minds such treatment, such thoughts, as stand connected with the production of feeling." If they do not
feel, it is because you do not play well. If they do
feel, it is because you are a master of your business, —
quoad hoc.

USELESSNESS OF MERE EXHORTATION.

So, then, here is where you come to the folly of exhortation, — men exhorting each other day after day,
continually, to "feeling," to "duty," without presenting any new expression, without filling the mind or the
imagination, without laying in fuel which is to kindle

into light and warmth. Mere exhortation is as if a
man should go down the street saying, "O money,
money, money, come to me, come to me!" No, it will
not come to him thus. Or as if a man should go to
his studies and invoke mathematics; that does not
come by invocation. As you gain other things by
playing the keys that produce the desired effects, so
you must do with every step that you gain in a meeting.
Men are so many instruments, and you are a skillful
player; and you will have success just as the Spirit of
God dwelling in you kindles your soul to that power,
to that perception of truth, to that sympathy with it,
to that knowledge of men; for the sense of God brings
the sense of human nature. They both lie in the same
plane, and he that has one will be very apt to have the
other. They train together. And if you have the
power of producing the sympathetic feeling, it will be
simply by applying the known causes of that effect.
Nothing is so barren, nothing so unprofitable, as *urging*
men to feel, when the shorter way is to *make* them feel.

FLIES IN THE OINTMENT.

Among the hindrances, I must mention the moths
and millers that will be sure to fly around your candle
just as soon as you have it lighted. It is almost impossible that a meeting should have any life or power
in it, or any degree of freedom, without producing
some very disagreeable results. I have had my cross
to bear in this matter. It seemed as though I never
was to be left without a thorn in the flesh, without
somebody to disturb almost every prayer-meeting. Well,
I don't know why a prayer-meeting should be an excep-

tion to every other part of life. Perfection does n't belong
here. Everything is mixed. Everything sweet has its
bitter, every rose its thorn, and every prayer-meeting its
"bummer." And you must make up your mind to it.
You must not be too fastidious, or too easily thrown off
your guard. To give you a biographical sketch of all the
illustrious persons who have spoiled prayer-meetings for
me would keep you here till midnight. I have one now
in my mind who used occasionally to utter as brilliant and
apposite sentences as I ever heard, and yet I never heard
him make an address in the world that he did not mar
and injure the meeting. It was the occasional flash that
was good, but the ordinary statements that he made
were inconceivably bad. I recollect once a meeting
seemed almost spoiled, — if anything could spoil it ; a
good meeting you never can spoil, when it has real
heart and stamina to it. But I recollect one of my sons
of vexation, when a meeting had turned on the love of
Christ, and especially the sympathy of Christ with
those that are feeble and striving to come to a higher
life under manifold difficulties, and upon the great consolation and encouragement there is in persevering, in
the knowledge that the whole atmosphere above you is
sympathetic in Christ Jesus. Just at the end, after I
had taken my hymn-book to give out the closing hymn,
thinking I had got that meeting safe out of the reach of
everybody, — this man gets up and says, "Why, brethren," — he had very red hair, — "I sometimes feel that
I could put even my red head in Jesus' bosom !" Well,
what could you do ? Nobody after that could take up
the thread of discourse, and you could not go back and
mold the meeting over again, — what could you do ?

By the grace of God, nothing; a very patient, a very meek *nothing*.

It is a good idea, therefore, to build your meetings out of such manful stuff, and to have such a spirit of courage inspired in your people that they won't be thrown off their guard by infelicities of this kind; to have your meetings so tough that they won't be hurt by any such little infliction as that. I had an old white-headed man, — I never knew his name, nor cared to, — but whenever there was a little fervor he came in. I remember a horse which my father bought, and which ran away the first day he was put in the chaise. The next day he was sold to a stage-company, and I rode behind him down to Bethlehem the first time he was put on the wheel. He carried the whole stage that day; he carried it out of the road once in a while, and from one side to the other, with such a burst that it seemed as though he would sweep everything before him. He carried the stage all the way down. This white-haired old man was like that horse; he would take the meeting in his teeth, and rush away with it in this direction and in that direction, and you never knew where you were! He had fervor, and his prayers had a perfect Gulf Stream in them both for speed and heat. For a few meetings I thought I had got a great auxiliary; but, after a few more, I found that I had a shark in the net, and that it was anything but edifying.

I had another of these men to whom is committed the cultivation of the perseverance of the saints; he would talk half an hour, and not get out a dozen sentences. He would get up and exhort young men in a most painfully slow manner, and you can imagine the precious time of the meeting going. Then I had another man who used to assume a most oratorical position, and, introducing a little narrative, have everybody on the tip-toe of expectation. But it all went out in puff; there was nothing of it, no *nub* to it, no anything. He would do that at almost every meeting, and sit down with an air, and wipe his mouth, as if he had been Demosthenes.

Now, what are you going to do with such men? You must do exactly as we boys used to do when we were fishing off Cragie's Bridge in Boston. We couldn't help it, — in spite of everything we could do, the little perch would steal the bait, and the big fish would n't get a chance at the hook. We fished through thick and thin; we renewed the bait and kept fishing, and caught what big ones we could, and let the little perch bite. You must do the same, in the main. You must bear it; but you must have your meeting tempered to survive such things.

DO NOT BE FASTIDIOUS.

This I may say also in regard to another point, — fastidiousness with respect to the form of that which is said by men who have good sense and good feeling at the bottom, but not the art of polite delivery. People may say, "Oh, I wish nobody would speak but the pastor; there is some comfort in hearing him speak; but when Mr. So-and-so gets up, what he says is well enough, but, dear me! what grammar!" Now, fastidiousness is one of the devil's imps that he sends to preside in prayer-meetings. The moment your grammar and your literature are a stronger relish to you than the substance of the thought or the feeling of an honest man, that very moment there is mischief in the room; you will shut off the unpracticed. Brethren, a man may get up, and what he says may be said in the most oratorical manner, and may come home to your heart and imagination, and comfort you, and yet it will not do the church one half so much good as to hear a new man that never spoke, a young man, who shakes on his feet, to whom it is a great effort to rise, and who makes a stammering speech, in which, however, appears his adhesion to Christ, or his love for the cause, or some feature in his history. The speaking of that new man, who speaks so poorly, is worth more to the church than the finest effort ever made by an old member. You have found another man, you have got some more material. It is more important to rescue a man from outside, and bring him in, and build him up in the church, than it is to have gifts exercised by those that are already in it. You are sure of them; they are safe. But the church *grows* by the addition of just such new men.

THE NEED OF CATHOLICITY.

Prayer-meetings, too, are apt to run in particular lines. You must make them catholic and broad. No prayer-meeting is truly Christian in the largest sense, that is not broad enough to have any theme discussed or alluded to in it, which, under God's providence, exercises the hearts of any of his people. There are persons that come to my prayer-meeting to talk perfectionism. I believe in it, though I think it is adjourned until after the present sphere. But I am never afraid that my folks are going to get too perfect.

There are some thoughts lying in that direction that are worthy of our hearing; for, if that subject does not rest on a philosophical basis, still it is on a side where we certainly need to hear much. I let them talk. I encourage them to come. There are some persons who do not believe in falling from grace; but if there is a brother who does, and who thinks he has fallen from grace, and wants to talk about it, I just let him bring it out. If there is any joy, any sorrow, any doubt or any scepticism; if there is any disbelieving what you said last Sunday in your sermon; if there is any disposition, not combative, but really manly and kind, to traverse any of your positions, — get it out. Young men, become very much attached to those who do not like you. Those who do, will be your worst enemies generally; they won't tell you your faults. They will let you grow up into a little god; they will let you be the lump of sugar which all the brothers and sisters will stir around in the sweet cup of their meetings; and " our beloved pastor," and " what our dear brother has said," and all those little endearing phrases, will pass around, that do not do you half as much good as the rough-hewing of some old man or young man given to plain speaking. It may be hard to take; but manliness, broadness, versatility, largeness, all-sidedness, — these are in the meeting; get them out! When, therefore, things are brought in that seem inchoate, — they may be so, and yet may answer a purpose. Anything in the world but regulation dullness in a prayer-meeting. Have life! Mistakes? Meetings can bear mistakes. Misproportions? Meetings can bear misproportions. In the statement of views, it is not necessary that everything should always be orthodox. Men forget in ten minutes. As whales take in vast volumes of water and spurt it out, but keep the animalculæ in it for their food, so four fifths of our preaching is all squirted out again! But there are a few things that remain with everybody. In a Christian community and a trained church there is a kind of appropriating instinct; and the carefulness, the excessive caution, that men employ, it seems to me, is on the side of effeminacy, not on the side of large, manly strength, which has in itself safety and power and godliness.

BEGIN AND END PROMPTLY.

I have spoken thus far of the Hindrances; now a few words on the Helps.

Let all prayer-meetings begin with very great promptness. No matter if there is not another person in the room; begin and sing yourself. I should say that among the mechanical helps in prayer-meetings are brevity, and prompt beginning and ending at the time appointed. In general, short meetings, half-hour prayer-meetings, are better than those an hour long. An hour meeting is incomparably better than one of an hour and a half, except in very extraordinary circumstances. An hour is the average length. I am very particular to begin at the moment appointed, and to end within the hour. It is not once in ten times that I will suffer it to go over that period, and then only because there is something special or unusual. Do not let a meeting *drag*.

CULTIVATE THE SOCIAL ELEMENT.

Next, no prayer-meeting is good that has not a current to it, that has not momentum. Keep the people doing something. Suppose that every time you go into a prayer-meeting you walk up in a very solemn way, looking at nobody and speaking to nobody. You sit down in your chair, and open the Bible, and read a whole chapter that may have twenty different thoughts and subjects in it, with no earthly reason of adaptation except that chapters are generally read before meetings. Then you make a prayer, which is good enough in its way, but nothing special; then you sing a hymn, and then you call on Deacon So-and-so to make a prayer, and then you sing another hymn, and then say, "Brethren, the meeting is thrown open; if anybody has anything to say, let him speak on." Then comes the great pause, and as the brethren have nothing more to say, "We will close with such a hymn," and that is the end of the prayer-meeting. Now, suppose instead of that, when a minister comes into his prayer-meeting, he speaks to the folks at the door, shakes hands with the little children that are there, shows himself among the people, and goes naturally about, familiarly, genially, without a bit of the priest about him, the "awful responsibility" air all gone, — why, people's minds are limber! they spring up! When you come into a prayer-meeting room, you are all exhorted to feel that you are coming into the presence of God. Well, is God a scarecrow? Is God a devouring fire to the Christian? Was that the effect that Christ's presence produced when he came into a crowd? As I read it, when he came anywhere, there was sunshine. Everybody dropped everything else and rushed to him. There was an almost audacious familiarity with him. Everybody seemed to have a new impetus in life; people's blood went tingling through their bodies at the very sight of him. His was a joy-inspiring, as well as a conscience-piercing, presence and nature. When you put a pressure of the kind I have just mentioned upon people, you do not inspire veneration, but you do repress all those genial, tender, and sympathetic feelings out of which a social meeting is to derive its forces. So, in coming into your meeting, make it as social as you possibly can.

SMALL ROOMS THE BEST.

In general, meetings are held in rooms too large for them. A chamber prayer-meeting is better than a prayer-meeting in a large room, by reason of the very force of contiguity. But if only a large room can be had, and only a few people come, gather the few together in clusters so that they are near to each other; then, in opening the meeting, have it arranged in your own mind in such a way that service shall follow service with rapidity, — short prayers, short hymns, and *movement*, momentum. Never let there be a moment's pause; be yourself ready to fill the gap if others do not; push the meeting right through, from beginning to end. There is a great deal arising from the momentum which a meeting generates.

LET THERE BE VARIETY.

There is no earthly reason why prayer-meetings should be twice alike, — I mean in form. Suppose that one week it is a prayer and conference meeting; that is to say, prayer predominating, and conference taking the minor part. The next week let it be just the reverse, — conference predominating, and prayer being comparatively in the minority. Then, the next week, let it be a praise meeting. What is that? A meeting in which most of the time is filled up with singing, and not with either prayer .or conference. Make the most of your materials in their diversity. Sometimes you will draw out one side of your congregation, and sometimes another side. Study to have ever something different; not necessarily marked out and prescribed with authority, so that it must inevitably be just that, without any spontaneity in the meeting; but be prepared to make the meeting, unless the meeting makes itself.

IMPORTANCE OF SINGING.

In doing this, singing is of transcendent importance. Persons say, "What shall I do in a prayer-meeting if I have nobody that knows how to speak?" Sing a hymn. "Well, suppose I have nobody that knows how to pray, how shall I get along with that?" Sing a hymn.. "Well, but suppose I have no persons that have any of the gifts of sympathy, how shall I touch them?" Through hymns. "Suppose I am myself slow of speech?" Give out hymns. There is not a single feeling from the top to the bottom of human nature that has not been struck a thousand times by

5 *

singing hymns. Hymns have this peculiarity, that they are the most glowing inspirations which God gives to his people in these later days, crystallized and preserved, so that they may by sympathy impart the feeling which they express. As long as a man has a good hymn-book and knowledge how to use it, there is no reason why a meeting should not be thoroughly edifying and good.

SUMMING UP.

One word in closing. All these multitudinous details that I have mentioned, you perhaps may not carry away with you in your memory; but when you go into your respective fields of labor, and one difficulty after another comes up, you may then possibly remember these suggestions. I would sum them all up in this: Do not be discouraged because your field is hard and the people scattered, because the caliber of your people is small, because the meetings are dull and hard, because the work is severe. Your reward will be in proportion to your skill and your endurance. Remember, a prayer-meeting develops piety under the influence of *social enthusiasm*, and there is in social enthusiasm a power that no man can imagine who has not tried it.

Oh, what waste there is! What unused power there is in the social relations of men in churches that is hardly suspected, and that never comes out except in times of revival! And then it is set down to the credit of "the Divine Spirit"; as if that did not abide in men ever and always! Why is it that, when I use guano, I get good crops? "Why, that is the Divine

Providence," men say. Divine Providence! Yes; and every time you use guano, Divine Providence will do the same thing. And when there is a revival, that is, when you are awake, and when your life is real and full and joyous, and you have liberty of expression, then you will know that meetings may mount up into rapture. You have such power and blessedness in them that you get the testimony of God to a secret power which you may develop all the year round. The mainspring of the prayer-meeting must always be the *social element*, the subtle power of sympathy. Work for that, and by God's blessing you will work a right end.

QUESTIONS AND ANSWERS.

Q. Suppose you give out a hymn, and there is nobody to sing it?

MR. BEECHER. — Sing yourself.

Q. But suppose you cannot?

MR. BEECHER. — That is a point on which I ought to have spoken. Every minister who is ordained in the Roman Catholic Church is obliged to know music. It is a part of the qualification of the priesthood in that church, and it ought to be so in our churches. When you have got through examining a man on all didactic theology, let him sing. It is far more important with us than it is in the hierarchical church, for there the minister intones, and does not sing; but *you* have to sing. When you get to the point where bad rhetoric and bad music meet, there is intoning. Now, in all new settlements, in visiting the sick you will be expected to sing; in your prayer-meetings you will have to "set the tune." If you haven't learned how to sing, and are going West, or into new settlements, let one of the first things you learn be how to "raise" a tune. And, if you can't sing, "make a joyful noise."

Q. How as to attitudes in prayer, whether in the pulpit or the prayer-meeting ?

MR. BEECHER. — It is purely a matter of choice. Some persons in the pulpit are trained to pray standing, — I have been. I find it is natural to me. Others — and almost always in the Methodist Church — kneel for prayers ; but it would be very awkward for me. I do not know that there is any advantage in one attitude over the other. The best prayer-meetings I ever had in my early parishes were those that came along after I had got through with the main one. That is, when we had finished the regulation prayer-meeting, and there was something that interested the folks, and we got around the stove, a dozen or fifteen of us, and fell to talking about something. Some of those who were not so much interested stood off on the edge, and were looking over the hymn-book and humming a tune. Then we all joined, and sang the tune, and thus we had a meeting. Time and again they have said, "*Now* we have had our meeting." The simple reason of it was, we had had the real, free, spontaneous, social elements, kindling religious fervor and feeling.

Now, in prayer, if a man wants to stand, let him stand, if that be natural to him. I suspect that the difference between kneeling and standing is not so great but that good prayers get up there about alike.

Q. What about the choice of subjects for remarks ?

MR. BEECHER.— Of course, there are all those subjects

that belong to the foundation of Christian experience and Christian character; but then, the providence of God is choosing subjects for you all the while, in your village, in your town,—the festivities in this family, the funeral ceremonies in that family, the misfortunes of this brother, the success of that one, the going out of a young man to preach or to college, the children and the mortality among them, the losses of men. For instance, if I had a prayer-meeting here in certain circles, I would make the failure of a banking-house the subject of a prayer-meeting, and the text, "Lay up your treasures in heaven, where moth or rust cannot corrupt, nor thieves break through and steal." Such themes, things that people were feeling before they came into meeting, things that they really want some comfort or some light about,—those are the things from which you can get a religious influence. Sometimes they will take you out of the sphere of strictly religious themes, but they will not be less profitable on that account. It is said, we ought not to introduce secular topics into the church. I say, take any secular topic you can find, and bring it into the church, and make it redolent of Christian ethics, and then carry it out again into its place. If you bring a thing into the church, and then turn it out of doors again, it goes out with a new coat on.

Q. What do you say in reference to the three-minute rule for prayers in prayer-meeting?

MR. BEECHER.—It is like all mere mechanical rules; it answers a good purpose to begin with, but I should slack off all such rules just as soon as the people got the idea in their heads. You must remember you have

got an intelligent people. Do not despise common
folks. You can manage an average American audience ;
you can make them learn to do almost anything. Just
throw yourself upon them ; give them to understand that
you expect good judgment of them. I remember at a
camp-meeting in Logansport, Indiana, on a Sunday,
there were five thousand people present, and no police.
The rule out there is to have camp-meetings amply
policed. I got up in the desk and said, " Friends, there
are five thousand of you here to-day ; it is very hot
and dusty, there is very little water, the children will
be fretful, mothers may be tired, it is feared that there
may be trouble. Now we have n't a single watchman
or policeman on this ground. If there is good order
here to-day, you will have to keep it." I had no occasion to say another word. Everybody took care of himself. In a prayer-meeting it is pretty easy to let them
understand that they must be short ; a little management will bring them around, and they will be short,
and fervent, and to the point.

When you go into a new field, — a Sunday-school
convention, for instance, — and have to start with raw
material, then it is that you need rules for three-minute
prayers and speeches, and sometimes they will be
shorter than three minutes. I don't think it took the
publican three minutes to say, " God be merciful to me
a sinner ! " and yet it was an admirable prayer.

Q. Would you advise the ladies to speak and pray ?

MR. BEECHER. — I would.

Q. Suppose they would n't do it ?

MR. BEECHER. — That is just my case exactly. I bear
their silence.

Q. What do you think of the custom of announcing subjects beforehand ?

MR. BEECHER. — I don't like it. I think there may be exceptional cases. During all my ministry I have refused with the utmost obstinacy to tell what I was going to preach on, even when it was going to be a very important subject. If you advertise when you are going to preach something that is worth hearing, people will take it for granted that, when you do not advertise, your preaching is to be all filling up. It will be well to make a few rules like this : If it is a wet day, do your very best ; make your wet-day sermons better than any other, even if it kills you. And never repeat them, no matter how much those who were not there may want to hear them. If you have an important subject, never advertise it ; and the result will be that people will say, "If you get those fine sermons, you must go all the time, and take what he gives you." It will produce the tendency to go always.

The gentleman who asked the last question said : "My question was misunderstood. It was with reference to announcing a subject in the prayer-meeting, so that people may have an opportunity to think about it."

MR. BEECHER. — I beg pardon. Sometimes I should do it, and sometimes I should not. I should never do twice alike if I could help it.

Q. You speak about filling up the gaps and having no pauses. Might not sometimes silent prayers of a minute or two have a good effect ?

MR. BEECHER. — O yes, if you do it on purpose. This makes a great difference. When Randolph was asked by a man, "Mr. Randolph, how is it that you con-

trive such pauses in your discourses ? They are tremen-
dously effective." " Pauses ?" said Mr. Randolph ; " I
pause because I have nothing to say." The difficulty
in prayer-meetings is, that those pauses are because
people have nothing to say, and the effect is tremendous, — but in the wrong direction.

Q. Would you always read a passage from the Scriptures in
opening a prayer-meeting ?

MR. BEECHER. — No, I should not. I very seldom
open my prayer-meetings in that way. I had far
rather bring it in from time to time. The Scripture,
you know, is an encyclopedia. If a man should sit
down and read an encyclopedia page by page, without
any regard to subject or occasion, he would do what is
often done in reading the Bible. If I have any theme
that I want to speak upon, I make up my mind just
about what group of passages bear on the matter I am
to take in hand. I find my place, and lay the Bible
down close by, and don't let the folks know I am
going to use it. I start the meeting and throw out
that topic ; and if it takes, and is congenial, and the
audience open here and there and express themselves,
and the prayers run in that channel, I can take up my
Bible, and say, " Brethren, here, see what is said here " ;
and I read those passages I had selected, and let them
observe how they illustrate, corroborate, or refute, as
the case may be.

Q. Would you call upon the young people of your meeting
who may want to speak, but are diffident ?

MR. BEECHER. — I would. It is a good thing for them
to have an exercise-meeting of their own where, among

themselves, they can break down bashfulness and build up confidence, familiarity ; and then, in easy and gentle methods, let them also exercise their gifts in the larger meetings.

Q. Would you generally lead your own prayer-meeting, as pastor ?

MR. BEECHER. — I think that every pastor ought to lead one prayer-meeting a week in his church, no matter how many others there are.   It is his drill-meeting. It is the time when he goes into the very Holy of Holies, among his people.   It is the time above all others when he lays his hand on the very palpitating heart of his people.   He cannot afford, for his own sake as a preacher, nor for that of the work in the church, not to be present every week, and be in the very heart of it.   .

Q. Do you speak generally before the meetings, or during them ?

MR. BEECHER. — Sometimes one, sometimes the other. If people come in and seem to have no spirit or fire, I usually open with the first prayer myself, especially when my heart is full, and bring them into kindling sympathy with me, and through me with God.   Or, at other times, if I see signs of interest and feeling, I let them lead off, sometimes let them introduce the topic ; and, if there is occasion, I close the meeting myself with prayer, so as to sum up all the facts and give them the last direction.   The rule should be, never use any one method all the time.

H

V.

RELATIONS OF MUSIC TO WORSHIP.

USIC is one of the most important auxiliaries of the preacher. I do not hold those things alone to be auxiliary which have an apparent and an immediate bearing on the sermon as such; but, as I have before explained to you, the sermon is only one element of the whole movement, and the preacher should develop the course in a kind of unity, the sermon being a constituent part, and perhaps the central and the grand element. Music comes, I think, in its capacity of doing good, next to preaching. Its power is as yet a thing undeveloped. Consider, for instance, what our impressions were as to the availability of music in the Sunday-school twenty-five or thirty years ago, and compare the Sunday-schools of to-day with those of that period. What would our schools be, if you should drop out of them bodily the music of the schools ? They would almost dissolve and vanish. It is the invisible chain which holds them together and animates them ; and there is a power in music to reach, to direct, to comfort the feelings of the Christian's heart, which is, comparatively speaking, yet undreamed of. In the churches where liturgical forms prevail, it becomes necessary that the minister, as an administrator, should have some degree of consideration for music, without which it is almost impossible to render the liturgical service; but in those churches which disallow a service and make everything extemporaneous, how seldom do we find a man who is able in preaching, and at the same time considerate and earnest and zealous on the subject of music! The complaint which I hear from conductors of music is, that there is no person in the congregation so indifferent to the cultivation of music as the minister. Now and then there is an exception; but generally the minister is glad to have a conductor who will take the whole responsibility from his shoulders; and then, so that there be quiet in the choir and no disturbance in the congregation, he does not trouble himself any more about the matter.

THE MINISTER'S DUTY.

Now, every minister not only should be able upon occasion to conduct musical service, but he should make it a part of his cure, his anxiety in the development of the religious life of his congregation, to have music not only good, but increasingly good; and he should devote his time and energy to it, just as he would to the development of any topic for discourse. Music is itself an agent in affecting, not so much the understanding, as that part of man's nature which the sermon usually leaves comparatively barren. Now, it is true of the Roman service, and to a great extent of the Episcopal service, that it touches the devout imagination; that it reaches toward, if it does not actually inspire, veneration and awe; that it does feel for the chords whose response is worship. Nothing is more frequent, therefore, than to see persons who have been brought up in the Quaker faith, or the plain faith of our fathers, and their plainer worship, their barren worship almost, going over to those churches, and explaining it not on doctrinal grounds, or grounds of ecclesiastical affinity, but simply that they feel the need of a worshiping element, which is provided for them there, and not with us. Indeed, if I were to say what was the marked, the characteristic, fault of congregational churches, whether Baptist, or Presbyterian, or Congregational, I should say it was the almost entire non-provision for the element of worship. There is nothing in their economy that provides for it to any considerable extent. It depends upon good fortune whether you have a pastor who has a natural genius for devotion. If you have not, there is no other provision for it; nor is there any source within our reach from which it can be derived, aside from the mere emotion of the man who conducts the public worship.

MUSIC, THE PREACHER'S PRIME MINISTER.

There is no instrumentality that I know of, except that of music. It is the function of music to begin at the point at which the sermon ends. That instructs, that incites to emotion through the reason. Now comes music, following it up and inciting to emotion through the imagination, through the taste, through the feelings; and it takes the same truths which may have been expressed dogmatically. The truths which have taken on intellectual forms, and satisfied all that part of the mind, are now rendered substantial by song, and fill up and satisfy all the other demands of the mind, making a round and complete work. It is very rare that, in any one discourse or in any day's discoursing, a man is so gifted as to be able to reach through the reason to the great foundation chords of feeling in the human soul. It is very rare that a man gets through a day in giving out well-selected hymns, without reaching those chords through the spiritual songs, if they are rightly administered. And in our churches, above all others, this is necessary, in order to mend that barrenness, that want of provision for the æsthetic feeling, the fancy and the imagination and the more facile emotions, which are not provided for by any framework furnished to the preacher, and which, according to his various abilities and endowments or moods, circumstances may or may not have partially provided for in him. But, if he were a Shakespeare, it is impossible for any man living, twice a day for fifty-two Sabbaths of the year, to stand with such plenary power and originality as to meet all those wants of men himself, unsuccored and unhelped. And his auxiliary, if he knows the provision made for him, his grand auxiliary, the prime minister of the preacher, is music.

CHURCH MUSIC, — THE ORGAN.

I shall speak, then, of music in the church, in social relations, in the prayer-meeting. As to church music, there first arises the question of instrumental music. Where instrumental music is introduced for the purpose, for instance, of giving tone and time, — where it is a mere auxiliary of that kind, it is not without its uses. Even so poor as are the country provisions of flute, violin, and bass-viol, they are not to be despised. There is great help in them.   But now, in the growing intelligence and taste and wealth of our country, the old prejudices against instrumental music having for the most part quite died out, the organ is distinctively the instrument which is employed in all our churches. And, happily, we now have so many organ-builders, and the competition is such, that the church must be very poor that cannot provide for itself an organ in some degree commensurate with its actual wants.   I would not be thought unduly enthusiastic in speaking of this instrument, which I look upon as an historian looks upon a great nation that through a thousand years has been developed by providential events and eductions, until it has reached a place in which it stands manifestly a prime, a divine power in the world.   I look upon the history and the development of the organ for Christian uses as a sublime instance of the guiding hand of God's providence.   It is the most complex of all instruments, it is the most harmonious of all, it is the grandest of all.   Beginning far back, growing as things grow which have great and final uses, growing little by little, it has come now to stand, I think, immeasurably, transcendently, above every other instrument, and not only that, but above every combination of instruments : for, although you may obtain certain effects, certain movements, and a kind of lifelike elasticity from orchestral performances ; although there are sinuous and arrowy elements in them, and there

is a certain spirit of personal enthusiasm inspired by
them, where they are carried to a very high extent of
culture, as in those foreign bands that visited us last
season for the Boston Jubilee, or in our own Thomas's
orchestra; although, in rare exceptions, you can combine
instruments in such a way as to do some things which
the organ cannot do, — yet the finest orchestra that
ever stood on earth, compared on the whole with the
organ, is manifestly its inferior. No orchestra that ever
existed had the breadth, the majesty, the grandeur, that
belong to this prince of instruments. It is true that
now, by reason of comparatively recent improvements
in the construction of the organ, it can be played as
rapidly as the piano can, but only its upper or what
are called its "fancy" stops will bear any such hand-
ling as that. For the organ means majesty; it means
grandeur. It means sweetness, to be sure, but it is
sweetness in power, like the bubbling crests of waves
on the ocean. Whatever it has of sweetness, of fine-
ness, or of delicacy, there is, moreover, an under-power
that is like the sea itself. And I thank God a thousand times a year, when I see how many things taste
and the social elements have stolen from religion, and
I turn to this one solitary exception and know that
there is left to religion, as peculiarly its own, at least
the organ, — the grandest thing that ever was thought
of or combined in human ingenuity. Running through
all the various qualities of tone, as soft and as sweet
as the song-sparrow (which is the sweetest bird
that sings), and in its complexity rising through all
gradations, imitating almost everything that is known
of sounds on earth, it expresses at last the very thun-

der and the earthquake, and almost the final trumpet itself!

FUNCTION OF THE ORGAN, — THE OPENING.

What, then, has the organ to do in the church? Usually, when we enter churches, we are greeted at once with the sound of the organ. What is the first thing ideally? Under the hand of a master who is in sympathy with the ends and the economy of the church, what is the prime function of the organ? A great many of you will say, " I don't know exactly what. It is the custom always to play when the people are coming into church, or to begin the service with the organ." What for? Why do they begin the service with the organ? What uses do you yourselves conceive in it? I will tell you what I think about it. I think that when the family comes to church, having been hurried and flurried in getting the children ready, — when the little brood have been looked after, and the five or the six are combed and curled and hooked and shoed, and all got in order, the house shut up and secure, and the little throng safely housed in the pew, — the mind all fluttered with those sweet domestic cares, — it is a great relief if something can quietly, imperceptibly, smooth those cares away. Some come from their houses, heavy with the lassitude of oversleeping on Saturday night and Sunday morning. Having been excessively pressed during the week, they get up drowsy and sleepy, eat their nine o'clock or ten o'clock breakfast, come away to church, and are spent. There is nothing in them. Others come in, frivolous and gay and genial.

If there were any such thing possible as that, the moment they passed the threshold, you could roll down a curtain behind them, so that all the world should disappear and be forgotten, and so that care should fall behind, and dullness and weariness and sorrow, and all doubts and all fears, should vanish, — if it were possible to make the door of the cathedral or of the church a screen through which should come the fresh, living, immortal soul, but none of its drudgeries or cares, how blessed would that be!

Now, that is what the organ undertakes, or should undertake, to do. It should take up the congregation and wash them clean in sound. It should disperse all these secular and worldly impressions, associations, thoughts, and feelings, and lift them up into the æsthetic, — the imaginative. "Very well; but is that worship? is that religion?" No, but it is that state of mind out of which comes, more easily than from any other, the next stage, of positive religious feeling. When a congregation are set free from the entanglements and burdens of the world, and brought into the higher realms of imagination, fancy, and feeling, they are ready for the plastic touch, they are ready to listen, to take part indeed. If an organ be well played in the beginning, as soon as its tones cease, the congregation is reasonably prepared to join with the choir in the singing of the opening hymn or anthem.

THE HYMN ACCOMPANIMENT.

Next to this is its accompanying power. I am accustomed to think of a congregation with an organ as of a fleet of boats in the harbor, or on the waters.

The organ is the flood, and the people are the boats ;
and they are buoyed up and carried along upon its current as boats are borne upon the depths of the sea. So,
aside from mere musical reasons, there is this *power*
that comes upon people, that encircles them, that fills
them, — this great, mighty ocean-tone; and that helps
them to sing.

Then, besides, comes the interlude.   Now, the interlude is an echo, or a prophecy, or both.   If it be an
echo, it attempts to render in pure musical sound
the dominant thought of the stanza that went before.
If it be a prophecy, it sees what is coming, and prepares
the way for it, and brings the devotional congregation
to the next stanza.*   And if it be in the hands of a
Christian man, and a man of musical genius, it may
help much.   Otherwise, it is a mere noisy gap between
two verses, a sprawl sometimes, an awful racket of
chords, a sort of running up stairs and tumbling down
again.   Not one organist in ten seems to have the
slightest idea why an interlude should be played.
John Zundel † knows. I wish John Zundel had a hundred thousand children, and every one was another
John Zundel.   I speak thus, not to have his name go

---

* As to the class of music suitable for the organ, Mr. Beecher said
that there was an ample supply of ecclesiastical music, that had been
accumulating for four or five hundred years, and was sufficient for all
church requirements.   But there is no objection to what is called
"secular" music, if it be in its nature devotion-breathing.   For example, much of the music of Mendelssohn and of Mozart, almost all
that of Von Weber and of Beethoven, can be adapted to the church.
But music which is frivolous, which recalls the waltz and the opera,
is a desecration.

† The able, and now venerable, organist of Plymouth Church.

out; but to him music means worship, and the organ means religion. He is the man who told me, when he was converted, that he "prayed just as other people did now." "Why," said I, "what do you mean?" Said he, "I speak my prayers out to God." "Well, how did you always do?" "I always played them on the piano before," said he. Such was his habit. So long had he been trained, that what words are to us notes were to him; and he expressed every thought and every feeling that he had upon the instrument. And you would think he did it yet, if you heard him in his inspired moments upon the organ. It has brought tears to my eyes a hundred times; I have gone in jaded and unhearted, and have been caught up by him and lifted so that I saw the flash of the gates! I have been comforted; I have been helped. And if I have preached to him and helped him, — and I know I have, — he has preached to me and helped me; and he knows not, and never will know, how much.

THE CLOSING VOLUNTARY.

If a person has been listening to a discourse which has stirred up the conscience, and awakened fear, and left the soul in a distressed state, there is a way of giving relief without discharging the feeling. There is in music a power of lifting the soul towards the great music-land. If persons in the congregation are going out in a state of stricture, — or of rapture of mind, even, — whichever way, the organ, by sympathy or by contrast, can dismiss them into the world, having, as it were, liquified the sermon, and poured it out into the very atmosphere.

ORGANISTS.

Now, the pity of this matter is that ministers care so little about it, and persons in the church know so little about it, that organists do pretty much as they have a mind to. Nobody criticises them, nobody teaches them. There is no organ school; there are no masters who are held in such respect that their word is law. There are admirable men presiding at the organ, few and far between; but, intermediately, we are overrun with a vast number of persons who play without reason, without heart, without soul, and with no sort of religious foundation. The only thing they think of is that they have to play so many pieces and at such points in the service, for that is the way the thing is arranged. And so they play; and this magnificent instrument, that has in it such power, such impassioned eloquence, such soul-stirring influences, is too often neglected and abused in the hands of miserable musical miscreants.

First come mere musicians. They play for science, for reputation, and that is all. They think no more about it. That would be as if the minister were thinking of grammar and rhetoric and personal popularity, and nothing else. For preaching is simply a means to an end, and the sermon is a mere tool, an instrument, and the preacher but a servant. God's work is the thing to be done. I care not if the player be Beethoven and the organ be the most magnificent that ever was constructed; they are both servants, and their glory is subordination. They are to serve God in the thoughts, the feelings, the fancies, and the affections of his poor little children, of his servants, of all that are in the congregation. How many are inspired with any such conception as this? And here come in the musical monkeys, dancing on their organ, playing up and playing down, rattling all sorts of waltzes, with a long leg stretched out here and there to make it sound like Sunday music.

TRUE ORGAN MUSIC.

This leads me to speak a word in reference to the proper music for the organ. There need be no recourse to any other than ecclesiastical music, because the treasury of organ music is very rich. There has been a line of masters for four or five hundred years, who have been contributing to the riches of the world in the music adapted to this noblest of all instruments. There are yet a great many contributors to it. No man need lack preludes, no man need lack afterpieces, or even interludes. Not only themes, but methods of treatment, abound. The world is rich in them for every young musician. Still, there is no objection to the introduction into the church services of much of that which is called secular music, provided it be, in its nature, devotion-breathing. There is very little that Von Weber ever wrote that is not fit, in its nature and spirit, for the church. Much of Mendelssohn's music, although written for secular occasions, is also spiritual. And I think you could find nothing in Beethoven, from beginning to end, that would not befit the church, if it were re-adapted. So with much of Mozart's music, some of Rossini's, and many others.

But there is a great deal of music that is not simply gay, it is frisky. It is even frivolous. The introduc-

tion of such music into church, just because it happens
to be in vogue; the trick of beginning with a broad
musical opening and then letting people hear, tinkling
and trickling along down, some air from an opera, —
just a little of it, to tickle the fancy, — all covered
up, as they imagine, by the bass or by the other parts;
the foolery of playing in the house of God the waltzes
that the young folks danced to, perhaps, but a night or
two ago, or the things which they have heard in opera
during the week, or any other fashionable music of
the day, — this is a desecration; it is dishonoring a
man's own profession; it is dishonoring the house of
God, and a minister ought to be able to know it and
to stop it. One of the miseries of a ministry un-
educated in music is, that ministers frequently do
not know enough to discern when the music is good
and when it is bad. They do not know enough to be
the bishop of the organ and the organist, as well as of
the congregation.

When, in addition to that library of Lowell Mason's,
which I understand has been presented to your library,
— and a very noble musical library it is for America,
— when you shall have a lectureship founded upon
it, so that you shall annually hear lectures upon music,
and be properly drilled in it, then, I believe, there will
come out from this a generation of men who will understand what music was meant for, whether in the
choir, in the organ, in the family, or in the lecture-room.

THE CHOIR.

This leads me to speak of the choir as an assistant
in music. The first question that naturally comes up

is, "Is it best to have a choir, or congregational singing?" My reply is, It is best to have a choir *and* congregational singing, — both! When Mr. Zundel once went to play at a little church, he had the whole matter put into his hands, and was requested to develop congregational singing. After a few months, I asked him how he was getting along. "Oh," said he, "there is one element necessary to congregational singing, and that is that you should have a congregation. There are not so many persons in the pews as I have up in my choir, and so you cannot have congregational singing." Now, where that is the case, if you are to have any singing at all, you must have it in the choir.

Then, there is a class of music that may be very edifying, and yet beyond the reach of the congregation; though I have great faith in the capacity of a congregation to learn singing. The choir may edify the congregation with music, certainly on special occasions. Then, in the next place, a choir becomes a kind of multiplex leader. It takes its time and movement from the director or the organist, and gives them out vocally, and the whole congregation tend to follow it. So the choir acts as a leader.

I know it is often said that there is always a quarrel in the choir, and always trouble. Well, there is always a quarrel somewhere in the world. Sometimes it is between the pulpit and the pews, sometimes it is in the pews, or between them, sometimes it is in the choir. It flies about from one place to another. There is always more or less of a disturbance going on, but there does not need to be any quarrel in the choir, if you

will only do one thing, — infuse into the heart of the
minister, and get him to infuse into the heart of the
congregation, and get the choir itself to understand,
that *musical service is religious service.*

Lowell Mason used always to open his choir-meet-
ings with prayer, and to talk to the young men and
the young women who were with him, as though they
had come to prepare themselves to take part in rendering the service of God in the sanctuary. And he so
impressed them with this thought, he made them so
feel it, that there was never any trouble in his choir;
religion crowded it out. There have been in my own
choir little "tiffs," occasionally, such as all of you have
in your families, but there never has been a quarrel or
a serious difficulty. So far from that, I always expect
that the persons who come into my choir will, in the
course of a year, come also into the church. The feeling of the choir is a ripening feeling, a religious feeling,
and almost every member, if not so in the beginning,
eventually becomes a communicant at the table of the
Lord. Where this is the case, when choirs are leavened
with religion and made to feel that their work is religious work, there is no more danger of their quarreling,
while thus consciously serving God, than there is of
deacons and elders quarreling while performing the service of the Lord in his house.

CONGREGATIONAL SINGING.

Now, gentlemen, I am a fanatic about congregational
singing, and I should be glad to make you enthusiasts, —
as near as that to fanaticism. I hold that a man ought
always to be an enthusiast, and that no man is a good

one who has not the capacity of being fanatical in places and on occasions. The whole church ought to sing, because the whole church ought to worship, and there is no other worship provided in our churches but this. To listen to the prayer of him that is most gifted is certainly a help, and a long way toward worshiping; but, after all, no man worships in spirit and in truth who does not take a voluntary and personal part, such as is necessary in singing. I do not believe it is possible for a person to sing our hymns and not worship. I will read you a single hymn. I would like to see the man that could sing this hymn and not feel that he had worshiped. I will call your attention to another thing. A want of proper culture has permitted such irreverence to grow up, that, in the singing or the reading of such a hymn as this, one will be tucking his hat under the seat, or fixing his cane, or placing his umbrella in the corner; or the mother will be arranging the neglected curls or pulling at the collar of her little one; or the sexton will be running around and whispering to this or that deacon to know whether he had better open this window a little more or shut that one a little more. This is all wrong. Hymns are worship, and should be respected as such.

This hymn is one of the closest, most endearing, clinging, yearning prayers to Christ:—

> " Thou, O my Jesus, thou didst me
>   Upon the cross embrace ;
> For me didst bear the nails and spear,
>   And manifold disgrace,
>
> " And griefs and torments numberless,
>   And sweats of agony, —

6 *   I

Yea, death itself, and all for one
Who was thine enemy.

" Then why, O blessed Jesus Christ,
Should I not love thee well ?
Not for the hope of winning heaven,
Nor of escaping hell ;

" Not with the hope of gaining aught,
Nor seeking a reward ;
But as thyself hast loved me,
O ever-loving Lord !

" E'en so I love thee, and will love,
And in thy praise will sing ;
Solely because thou art my God,
And my eternal King."

Now, if you can sing that, and not cry, — I am sorry
for your eyes.

PLYMOUTH CHURCH.

People often wonder why folks come to Plymouth
Church so much. I will tell you; it is the singing
that brings them there. It is the atmosphere there
is in the loving, cheerful, hopeful courage of that
congregation in the singing. They get a sermon too,
but then it is more the singing, I think, that accounts
for the throng. It comforts their souls. I have seen
men come into that congregation, — and there are
at least twenty-five hundred out of the twenty-
seven hundred there that sing,— I have seen them
come into that congregation exactly as they would
go to Barnum's; because, you know, it is the trick of
the papers to represent it as a kind of theatre, or
what-not. They would sit down and look all around,
watching to see what was going to be done next.

When I arose, they would stare as though they really thought I was going to throw a somersault. I would give out a hymn, and they would still be watching for something that had not come yet, but was coming. The organ would give out the tune, and the congregation begin to sing. These men would rise, and stand in their places, and when the great volume of sound, like the voice of many waters, would break on them, I have seen them first, in a kind of bewilderment, looking all around, up in the galleries, on a sea of books opened, and everybody busy singing. And when they heard such a sound as there was rolling down upon them, or rolling up towards God, I have seen them stand, and, by the second verse, away would go the tears down their cheeks. The hymn fairly overcame them. Better than a sermon, better than any exhortation, — why should it not affect them thus ?

HOW TO PROMOTE GENERAL SINGING.

Now, in order to promote congregational singing, you must be in earnest about it. Among the things that you say to yourself must be this: " I will give my whole strength, first to preaching to these people ; next, to their social development, by visiting them man by man ; and always to the cultivation of devotion and worship among them by sacred song." How shall it be done ? Well, preach about it often. Secure the best leadership you can ; encourage your people to sing in the family, to sing in all social meetings ; let them sing the same hymns often and everywhere. That is to say, when men come into church to sing hymns, they do not want to sing many of the church hymns now used,

— there is very little perfume in them. They may be very beautiful, but they are like the japonica, which is exquisite in form and color, but has no fragrance. Now, hymns that do people good may not be beautiful in construction, and yet they may be full of the associations and experiences of the heart. The tunes that the man heard as a child, around the family altar, the hymns that were sung on Sabbath evenings at home, and that carry with them a part of his own past history, that have treasured up in them sacred memorials of the best part of his life, — those hymns, and the hymns that are sung in the Sunday-schools, should be sung in church. There ought to be but one book in every congregation. Or, if there be two, the second should be but a part of the loaf of the first one broken off, so that the same thing should be sung at home, in the lecture-room, in the Sunday-school, and in the great congregation. Then you will have hymns that come to people, touching them all around ; living hymns, filled with their own life. Sing much at home, encourage singing in the day schools, in the household, in the Sunday-school, in the lecture-room. Sing on your way rejoicing ; make everybody sing that you can, and keep them singing.

Then, there will be many hesitations and many retrocessions. That is the place for your efforts. Whenever things do not go right, draw up the buckle one hole more and go at them again, and that not only in music, but in everything else. You were put into a church, not to be overcome, but to conquer, to carry your own way, — that is, when your way and God's ways are consentaneous. The difficulties ought to be nothing but whetstones to a man, making him sharper and sharper.

FELLOWSHIP AND SONG HELP EACH OTHER.

Let me say one thing more: You never will have congregational singing as long as you have no congregational feeling. Congregational singing will certainly break down the stiffness, the formality, and the exclusive habits of your people, or else the stiffness, and the coldness, and the exclusive habits of your people will prevent or destroy congregational singing. You cannot sing throughout· the church, and not develop, subtly, that element of fellowship that gives elasticity and freedom in social intercourse. Now, a congregation that have been trained to go into church and sit down and not look at one another, to go home and not speak to one another, I don't believe can be trained to congregational singing, unless by an extraordinary pressure and process. Fellowship and song are but different developments of the same spirit; and therefore, where you have quarrels unreconciled and persons who do not care for each other, people sitting apart separately, you never will make them sing together, they never will pray together, they never will mingle in any way. And, mark my word, if you wish to make congregational singing easy, everything that you do to bring people together socially, genially, in Christian sympathy, will facilitate it. And if you wish to bring people together genially and socially, teach them to sing, and that will facilitate your purpose. Thus singing and sociality act and react upon each other, in a mutual relation of cause and effect.

THE CHOICE OF HYMNS.

I may speak a word on the subject of the selection of hymns for use in church and in the lecture-room. On what principle should we choose ? or is there any principle which should dictate the selection of hymns ? None that does not admit of infinite variations. But there are certain general principles. For example, I have always pursued what may be called a psychological plan, and have selected hymns sometimes because they were automatic; they volunteered themselves, and I knew that under such circumstances there was a reason for such hymns, there was something in the air that would make them acceptable, even though I did not know why. I take all such intimations as that; but still there is a general plan, and it is this : If I can bring the congregation, before I come personally to handle them, into a triumphant, jubilant state, a cheerful, hopeful, genial state, my work among them will be made easier by one half than if they were in a very depressed, sad state.

I believe that confession, and self-condemnation, and all that, should be like the whippings we give to our children, — sharp and quick, and soon over. I do not believe in yokes and cloaks and long-continued burdens of depression. I believe that it is a malarial poison to the soul for a man to go long bowed down with a sense of sinfulness, and that it is a vicious method of teaching that brings people into such a state of mind. It is remedial, and therefore medicinal; and to give a man medicine all the time is bad for him. The mind in the natural condition is hopeful, cheerful, trusting, loving. That is the relation which we sustain to God. We are sons. "Henceforth I call you not servants, but friends. The servant knoweth not what his Lord doeth. I admit you to that intimate relation by which I counsel with you and you with me. You know all the secrets of the household; you are my children." And it is a shame for the children of God to go always with downcast heads. When the storm comes, then the grass and the flowers and everything bow down with the weight; but when the sun comes out again, they shake off the raindrops and lift themselves up, and are stronger by reason of the storm. And so it should be with Christian men.

I think, therefore, if you begin with a doleful hymn, supposing that you are going to get your people down, you will get them down so low that you won't get them up again. You will mire them. Therefore all those hymns of depression and of sadness are to be prescribed as a physician prescribes medicine, — in broken doses, and, I think, mostly homœopathic at that. On the other hand, the true Christian state is one of a holy hilarity, a holy courage, a holy familiarity with God. It is the soul lifting itself into its natural, native air, not afraid to look at God with the veil, Christ, between; able now to see him face to face, and yet live. Therefore I strike for that feeling. I give out hymns on the principle of producing a certain feeling that I want to use.

When, therefore, I open Sunday service, it is almost always with something cheerful, something hopeful; something that celebrates the Sabbath morning and its blessed associations; the triumph of God; the triumph of the church; exultant praise. These are very wholesome elements to begin with. Then, as to the other hymns. It is a great deal better for you not to give out your sermon in your hymn, or to follow your sermon in your hymn, unless it be one of those rare hymns which will distill your sermon, and give it to them in another form. If, for instance, I wish to rebuke my congregation in the sermon for anything, I say to myself, "Now, if I give them a monitory hymn, and a monitory chapter, and then a scourging sermon, I shall overdo the whole thing. It will be without lights and shadows, and it will therefore be without elasticity, without rebound ; it is not wise. I will do this rather. The state of mind in which a person takes rebuke and profits by it, is a state of comfort and of upliftedness, and I will raise them to that if I can. I will bring them up into true Christian states of mind by my hymns and my prayer; and when I get them into that state, I can say anything to them that ought to be said to anybody." So I will sing them up and pray them up, and then I will take them down a little. And not only will they bear it, but they will digest it. The rebuke will not be powerless ; it will work out in their after lives.

The idea, therefore, that I wish to leave in your minds, is simply this, — that a man may be apparently working with his hymns in a different direction from his sermon, and yet really co-operating with it. If you want to bring any subject before the congregation, it is sometimes well to introduce it by some statement which, while very different from the subject itself, yet will be very fit for them to hear, and to be in sympathy with ; and hymns are the instruments by which

you may best do this. This will require practice ; and
it will come to every man that gets the idea and attempts to put it in practice. He will at first, perhaps,
not succeed well ; but in time he will grow skillful in
such administration of hymns.

PRAYER-MEETING MUSIC.

It only remains that I should say a word as to singing in prayer-meeting. I meant to have had some one
present, who, with facile touch and in sympathy with
me, should give out some hymns and give specimens
of dealing with an audience, to show how much can
be actually done with the hymn-book. For I feel that
with a Bible and a hymn-book a man has a whole
library ; and if he knows how to use those two things,
he knows enough to be a missionary, or to be a minister anywhere, so far as mere dealing with people is
concerned. But that I cannot do to-day. Therefore I
have only to say in a few cold and formal words what
otherwise I could have rendered in a more lifelike
form.

In speaking of the prayer-meeting, I omitted very
much that I should have said on the subject of music.
In the prayer-meeting, music ought to be a grand sub-
stratum. They are called prayer-meetings, but two
prayers are often enough for a meeting, — about two
prayers to six hymns. " Why ? " Because out of every
six people that pray, there are not two that can pray as
a hymn can. It is not probable that you will find one
person in an average congregation of two hundred that
can express so admirably, with such subtle lines, the
dealing of God with men, as Cowper did. It is not

once in a hundred times that a man can preach so much sound gospel in verse as old John Newton did. You have very few men like Wesley and Watts, who are the two wings of hymnody. Those two men soar as few can soar. We might say,

" Descend, immortal dove !
Take us upon thy wings."

When these men are invoked, they take the whole congregation on their wings, and lift them up.

Now, in singing, be familiar. For instance, if a prayer-meeting is opened with a hymn, that clears away the cobwebs. But suppose the people drawl it. As soon as they get through, you say, "Brethren, that won't do ; we can't get along with that; let us take another hymn, and see what we can make of it. Take this next hymn, so and so." It wakes them all up, and every man smiles, and they go at the next with a good will. By that time, they begin to know what they are about. Take a little of this hymn, or the whole of that hymn ; but for heaven's sake, gentlemen, don't emasculate hymns in order to meet the wants of those persons in the congregation who think they have served God enough when they come once a day and stay half an hour in the church, and then are impatient to get home ! Of those who want short hymns and short prayers, you will never make a man out of ten thousand fit for the kingdom of God. We want religion to be so important, so earnest, that men shall demand broad, deep sermons, and, in order to have them, will give the workmen time. We want men that shall drink so deep of devotion

that they will need a deep well.   Seven or eight verses
are not too much, if they are the right kind of verses ;
and, in good hymns, two verses are often enough when
you want to make a glancing shot.   Or, if you will, take
four or six.   Do not count.   Never sing by arithmetic,
but make a business of it.   Sing for the love of it.
Your prayer-meetings are real work; and the man that
is with his little congregation, molding them, inspiring
them with a common feeling, carrying them off from
the shoals where he knows they have run aground,
with the instrument of prayer, with the instrument of
singing (which is but another form of vocal prayer),
his own soul filled with the Holy Ghost, in the full
fellowship and love of men, — what can he not accomplish under such circumstances ?

To bring the inspiration of the Holy Ghost on living
men, from the days of Pentecost down to this hour, is a
grand and noble way to deal with them; and ministers
that understand their function, and know what their
powers and instruments are, ought to be able to develop out of the prayer-meeting and out of the church
an influence of Divine truth, and a feeling divinely
inspired in the human soul, that shall carry men far
along on their journey godward.   And among the
most active, subtle, effective instruments which the
minister has to work with, music, studiously and skillfully used, in the household, the social meeting, the
prayer-meeting, and the church service, stands eminent
and highly blessed of God.

QUESTIONS AND ANSWERS.

Q. What do you think of the Fulton Street prayer-meeting,
— of its receiving requests for prayers from all parts of the
world ?

MR. BEECHER. — I think very well of the Fulton Street prayer-meeting ; and I have no objection to their receiving requests for prayer from all parts of the world.

Q. What about interludes, as they are commonly employed now ?

MR. BEECHER. — I think the music would be better without them than with them. If you consider an interlude merely as a pause for taking breath, I think that is an unworthy use for the organ ; and, if it has any justification whatever, it is in this, that it extends one thought, or anticipates another, or connects the two, between two stanzas. There have been books of interludes written, which, like all things of that kind, are helps, and not substitutes.

Q. In what end of the church would you have the organ ?

MR. BEECHER. — Either end. It makes very little difference where you put the instrument. It is a very great help, in speaking anywhere, to stand encompassed by the people ; and if you wish to throw the minister forward from the rear wall, you must economize the room behind him by placing the organ and choir there. Then the minister will be the only one who will not see them ; and the whole congregation, when they rise in their pews, will see the organ and the choir, and go naturally with them. If the leader marks time, the whole congregation, without any disturbance, can easily follow his hand. On the other hand, there may be occasions in which you are required to put the organ at the other end of the church. I should say, place it behind the minister, if I were to choose. But sometimes it is put off on one side, and I know no reason why it should not be. Generally the organ fills the whole church, from whatever point it sounds.

Q. What do you think of such playing of organists as we sometimes hear when the congregation is going out after a solemn sermon and worship ?

MR. BEECHER. — Such playing as we sometimes hear in our churches is, I think, detestable. To use the organ as a mere cover of noise, under any circumstances whatever, is a defilement and an abomination. As an opposite instance, — at the close of the sermon on a communion Sabbath morning, I invite all that wish to commune to remain. A great many go out. At once Mr. Zundel takes some very tender and loving theme, and with a sweet combination of stops it fills the air. Now, those who are going out may not profit; but, as I sit in my chair and shut my eyes, it comforts me. It is so with others all through the congregation. I often wonder that people go out so long as the organ is playing, — and yet sometimes I have wondered that they stay in when they hear it.

Q. Would you make use of an instrument at a social prayer-meeting ?

MR. BEECHER. — Yes ; I would have a piano in a lecture-room, because it better marks the time, and there the time needs to be brought up. In many of our Sunday-schools we have organs, but the children are brought up to time by the staccato voice and manner of imperative teachers.

Q. In some churches we find many hymns sung to a great variety of tunes. What do you think of that ?

MR. BEECHER. — I would not be in bondage to *any*

practice. There are some hymns that I should always want sung to a particular tune, — "Jesus, lover of my soul," for instance. That is a very marked hymn. It is one of the praying hymns. There are a thousand of them, but this is one of the exquisite ones; a hymn that I should love to hear sung if I were dying. And I should like to have it to a tune that was married to it, and sung to that only. But then, in the majority of cases, I do not feel the least objection to singing a hymn to a dozen different tunes. That is to say, I do not believe in the German method. I think that originated in the feeling that the common people were so uncultured that they could not carry more than one hymn to one tune, which should be as simple as possible. From that source, I think, comes the idea that in congregational singing all ought to sing the air and let the organ carry the harmony. I say a congregation can carry all the four parts just as well as the choir can.

Q. As a matter of fact, do not people that cannot read learn a hymn more easily if it is always associated with the same tune, — children, for instance?

MR. BEECHER. — Very likely they do. That may be a reason why, in certain congregations and in certain parts of the country, for a time at least, the wedding of a hymn and tune should be without divorce. But, as a general system, applying to all congregations, I should not advise it; I would only apply it in special cases.

Q. Would you employ chanting in the services?

MR. BEECHER. — I would, and I would employ responsive reading. I am going to, — and have been

going to for ten years in my church, — but I have n't
got to it yet.

Q. Would you have the ordinary Sabbath-school music discarded from church music ?

MR. BEECHER. — I would make no distinction. I
would discard a good deal of church music. Some
hymn-tunes have crept into our books lately, which a
man might sing to all eternity, and then, if he waited
one minute, he would forget what they were, so thin
and so miserable are they ! A great many Sunday-
school tunes are like the Sunday-school hymns, — they
are sentimentalism gone drunk. I feel a righteous in-
dignation when I think of the stalwart stanzas of old
Watts, and of John and Charles Wesley, and of Dod-
dridge, of Montgomery's hymns, of Barton's hymns, and
of many others of modern date, — noble recitations of
the history of Christ and of the gospel, most magnificent delineations of the other life and of all the experiences of a Christian, — and see our children brought up
on such miserable trash and garbage as they too often
are in our Sunday-schools ! It is a sin and a shame to
bring them up in that way. I know that children are
old enough at the age of five years to feel the grandeur
of some of those old hymns. And they are being
cheated out of them.

Now, I do not say that all the Sunday-school hymns
are to be rejected; but we are overrun with them, and
there ought to be a winnowing that should separate the
vast amount of chaff from the handful of wheat. A
good deal of other music is subject, I think, to the same
criticism. There is much that it will be well to preserve, but much more that ought to be burned.

Q. What is your idea of a praise-meeting ?

MR. BEECHER. — A praise-meeting I understand to be one in which the whole congregation so associate together, that whatever they say is an argument of praise and thanksgiving. The chord is, *Give thanks !* " With all prayer, with thanksgiving," says the Apostle. You will be struck, if you look through your concordance of the New Testament, to see how much thanksgiving is insisted upon. Now, by thanksgiving I do not understand a cold "thank you." I understand by it an exultant state of mind, — cheerful, hopeful, loving, yearning, upspringing, all running in the direction of joy and gratitude and praise. A praise-meeting is one that confines itself to that, and gives utterance to it, in prayer, in conversation, and in hymns. You might also have confessional meetings ; though these, I think, should be short and very rare. It is better to have mixed meetings for such purposes, that one thing may supplement another. But praise is always wholesome.

Q. Would you always read the hymn before singing ?

MR. BEECHER. — No, I would not, — I *do* not always, I mean. I would ; but I never do read a hymn, first, when I do not feel like it, and, secondly, when I am pressed for time and must abbreviate the services. I often omit the reading of hymns, — and am very much blamed for it.

Q. Don't you think that the sermon is a part of worship as much as singing ?

MR. BEECHER. — Well, if you extend the term " worship" so as to mean by it anything that has relation to the divine life, — yes. But we discriminate between worship as an emotion, and as the indoctrination and instruction upon which a sermon is based. Many sermons are worship, as many sermons are poetry. Some sermons are dramas, some poems, some descriptions; but, after all, taking it comprehensively in a pastor's life, we consider the sermon as the element of instruction.

Q. Ought not all the elements of our nature to enter into worship? And does not the sermon represent the intellectual nature?

MR. BEECHER. — The sermon represents the intellectual nature. That is the foundation from which you start. Now, I do not think that the hymn does, nor the prayer. They commence at once with feeling as something already generated, and, as I have just said, represent and develop the emotional element of worship.

VI.

DEVELOPMENT OF SOCIAL ELEMENTS.

 PURPOSE, this afternoon, to speak upon some of the social forces that are to be developed and employed in church life and activity.

PASTORAL VISITING.

This brings me naturally, first, to speak upon the matter of pastoral visitation more directly than I did last year, when I touched it only as collateral to something else. Many reasons which once made pastoral visitations important no longer exist. There was a time when there were no schools, few books, no papers, little discussion, and when popular intelligence was very low; when even the ministers, the main body of them, were not as well instructed in religious things as the average citizens now are; when religious truth, if conveyed at all, must be conveyed by the professional teachers of religion. Under such circumstances, it behooved the pastor to go from house to house, indoctrinating and catechising the children. There were peculiar reasons, also, when men believed that the ordinances were special channels of grace which the ministry alone possessed and controlled, why the administrators of those ordinances should be among their people, not only in sickness and in death, but also in various familiar relations in life. Our churches — I mean the non-hierarchical churches — have parted with these beliefs; and all those reasons that inhered in the superiority of the ministry over the great brotherhood have passed away.

MODERN REASONS FOR IT.

But there are other reasons which justify the continuance of an assiduous visitation on the part of pastors. In the first place, because a man wants, for his own sake, to know intimately those to whom he is to preach. Paul said, "Ye are our epistles, known and read of all men." He might have said, "Ye are our texts," for he derived much, especially of the argumentative portions of his epistles, from the known feelings, prejudices, beliefs, or non-beliefs of those people to whom he came; so much so that, upon a close reading, one almost thinks he can see the color of the churches in the tenor of the Pauline epistles.

In our day, the style of theology has changed. You will be compelled to change with it. There are great causes at work, quite independent of mere individual volition. Men tell us we must go back again and pursue the old sound doctrinal systems; but you cannot get back. The sun and the moon and the stars are against you. There is a movement, there is an aerial gulf-stream, and you are swept away from that which was appropriate to the anterior state. That which fitted the condition of men earlier than our time does not fit our time, and has been, or is being, sloughed off. Preaching has become a great deal more natural and less artificial. It has more of life-form and life-force, and less of the abstract and metaphysical. Not that it will ever disavow metaphysics or abstractions, not that it will ever be concrete, absolutely, — that is not possible, — but it has largely assumed a form in which personal elements and personal sympathies mingle.

Now, this style of preaching, above all others, demands that one should reinvigorate himself by contact with life and with men. You will find that, in dealing with all those themes which go to the source of motive, which touch sympathy, which affect the hearts of men, you will be very superficial, you will be very poor in power, unless you are intimately mixed up with the life of those to whom you preach, and to whom you bring the gospel. A man may, for instance, have his pastorate in a country village, and, mingling with his people, he may write a series of discourses, which, if he were elected pastor of Yale College, would be absolutely absurd to be preached here; and yet they may be effective sermons of the gospel. They may take on so much color, they may have such form and shape, such modes of application to the unstudied village life, that if they were preached to young men of entirely scholastic habits, they would have little relation to them.

It would be very likely to be so, too, if ministers in general should make their sermons for the college. I can conceive of one making exceedingly able sermons for college classes, which, when taken out into the country, would put the parish to sleep. And for this reason, that preaching has to be vital and effective, it should derive a great deal of its element from the known life and want of the men for whom the sermon is a medical prescription.

IMPORTANCE OF KNOWING THE PEOPLE.

Now, in ordinary pastoral life, a man must get acquainted with his people. This is hard for some; it grows · easier by practice. Men may come to such a knowledge of their people that they have less and less need to visit them for their own sake, for the sake of their preparation. And, lastly, a man who has a natural aptitude for it, and has had large experience and been long in the field, may come to that state that, so far as he himself is concerned, he feels almost what is in the air, he knows what ails people without hearing, or almost without talking with them. But this is not the ordinary experience.

So, then, for the sake of a man's own freshness, vitality, directness, humanity, — that is, preaching to that which is human in men, — for all these reasons, visitation is desirable.

FREEDOM FROM CLASS INFLUENCES.

Then we should maintain visitation for our own sakes on still another ground, and that is to keep ourselves aloof from class or professional influences. It is very desirable that any class of men following the same general pursuit — physicians, lawyers, ministers — should see much of each other. The *esprit de corps* is not only a source of refreshment, but there is great instruction in it. But then, men are very strongly inclined to become selfish, to be absorbed in their class, to think and to sympathize after the manner of their kind. Now, for the minister, above all men, it is a necessity that he should sympathize with humanity from the top to the bottom; with all men, not with one class of men; not with the best men, not with men of purest thought alone, because that unfits him to deal familiarly and easily with men who have no such habit of thought. As the steward and the cook must know the tastes of those for whom they are preparing the table from day to day, so the minister must know the taste and the wants of those for whom he spreads food in the pulpit from Sunday to Sunday; and if you get into class habits, you will be a minister for ministers, but not for the people. And visitation tends largely to break that up; especially if you visit not the select families, not the places where it is pleasant to go, but everybody. Take your own pleasure along with you, and be glad to see everybody and anybody. The minister should cut the loaf of society, not horizontally, but vertically, and take it with all there is in it, from top to bottom. And you will find — as it is in the housewife's cake sometimes — that the raisins are pretty much all at the bottom.

GAINING THE CONFIDENCE OF PEOPLE.

Then, it is very desirable that the minister should have the confidence and the sympathy of his people, that he should be warmed and upheld by them. Nothing contributes so much to this as personal acquaintance with them, man by man, child by child, all through the parish. If a man has naturally ge-

nial manners, and is a man of genius, and delights
people on Sunday, they gather around him for that
reason. He gets their sympathy somewhat in that
way. But ordinarily we ought to begin with the presumption that we are not men of genius. They who
think they are geniuses when they begin, seldom have
reason to think so when they end; and if you are
one, you will find it out farther on. You would better
begin as though you were simply persons of fair average
intelligence, whose life-facts are to be developed by industry and close adherence to all the known paths of
experience. In going among your people, to draw
them to you and to open their hearts and their sympathies by pastoral visitation, you prepare the ground.
A minister who does not visit very much, in an ordinary
parish, is like a man that sows his seed in the spring
before he has plowed the ground. If you visit, that
plows them; then preach, as you have your furrows
already open where the seed may fall; then harrow
them, and, in due time, we may hope to see the result.

TWO SPECIAL CONDITIONS FOR VISITING.

There are two conditions of society in which visiting
should abound. First, it should become pre-eminently
conspicuous and mainly instrumental in your ministry,
where you are thrown among people who do not care
about going to church. And, secondly, it should
abound in those conditions where people, when they
do go, are little interested; in other words, where they
are barren and you are barren. In many communities
the church is a very small thing; there is very little
of it; and yet the population is large. Now, the people

are all yours. A genuine fisherman being told that
the stream above the dam is full of trout, only nobody
can catch them, — why, his blood is all on fire! He
says, "I cannot catch them? You will see whether
I can't!" And he will meditate about those trout night
and day, and he *will* catch them, for his ambition is
inspired. A minister going into a community where
there are but few that come to church ought to have
his whole soul stirred within him. "Not come to
church! They *shall* come to church. If they do not,
the church shall go to them." You go into a community
not to be snubbed. Let no man despise your youth or
your inefficiency. That is a genuine field for pride.

HARD FIELDS.

When you go into a community, make up your mind,
" I don't back out of this community. I have been
sent here, and, after due consideration and investigation,
here am I. I did not come to be defeated, and I shall
conquer; standing, or stooping, or kneeling, I am going
to have my way in this community, and these people
shall have the gospel." If they are pirates, gamblers,
smugglers, drunkards, racers, sporting-men, no matter,
they are *men;* and if you believe that the gospel is the
power of God for salvation, you have got it. Do
you mean to stand and let any community overbear
you, or drive you out? With all manner of zeal and
patience, with all manner of enthusiasm and affection,
and by such measures as are necessary, — if one thing
won't do, try another; if that won't do, try another;
but maintain yourself there, secure a lodgment and
gain the victory. In going into such a community, I

do not care how well you preach, they won't for a year or two find that out; but you should go among them, go to those that do not expect you, go to those that do not like you. I heard old Dr. Humphrey say that where he was first settled there was a man very much opposed to him, a farmer; and the Doctor, who had been brought up on a farm and counted himself something in the harvest-field, went out to visit the old man in his field, where he was reaping. It was before the time even of cradles, much more that of mowing-machines. The man proposed to go back to the house and entertain the Doctor respectfully. "No, no," said Dr. Humphreys; and he threw off his coat. "Give me a sickle; we can talk as we work." So he took hold, and beat the man all out of his own field, sickling. With that went all the old fellow's prejudice; he was one of the Doctor's right-hand men after that. There lived over on the other side of the street in Lawrenceburg, where first I had my settlement, a very profane man, who was counted ugly. I understood that he had said some very bitter things of me. I went right over into his store, and sat down on the counter to talk with him. I happened in often, — day in and day out. My errand was to make him like me. I did make him like me, — and all the children too; and when I left, two or three years afterward, it was his house that was open to take me and all my family for the week after I gave up my rooms. And to the day of his death I do not believe the old man could mention my name without crying. It was my good fortune to meet his daughter, or daughter-in-law, in the cars during my latest trip in the West, and it brought back this scene, which I had quite for-

gotten, and of which I give you now the benefit by way
of illustration.

HEART-WORK INSTEAD OF HEAD-WORK.

Another point : there seem to be in the ministry
men of very considerable force, men of a good deal of
one kind of tact and genius, but they do not run to
ideas.   There are a great many churches whose force is
supposed to lie in the pulpit; but it does not.   And
yet they hold together a congregation; it grows, it
mellows, it becomes liberal.   That is the case in which
a man must apply the power that is in him personally
by visitation, — making up for the barrenness of his
sermons by the richness of his own heart.   If it has
not been given to him to have a lighthouse in the
head, if the lighthouse is in the heart, let him go
personally where its light can shine often amongst the
people.   I have heard persons say, when a brilliant
preacher came into town, and there was every reason
why they should leave their parish and go to hear
the new-comer, " Still, I don't know; we have had
our own minister so long, and he is so good, and we all
love him so much, and our children have all been
brought up under his preaching, so that he has meshed
them, he has spun himself all around them, — it is
almost like a bereavement to go out of his church; and
that in spite of his sermons too."

When people won't come to hear you preach, do you
go and talk to them; and when they do come to hear
you, and you have hardly anything to preach about,
then go to them all the more.   There are hundreds of
men that talk well and preach badly.   There are a

great many that I meet on the street who talk well to me, and who, as ministers, are genial, whose faces are full of inspiration; they make points, and they have an incident or a story to tell, and besides all that they have a smile that rewards me, and I like to meet them dearly.   But oh, I *don't* like to go and hear them preach !

So then, for either of these reasons, and for those that went before, — pastoral visitation !

GENERAL SOCIAL AMENITY AMONG CHURCH-MEMBERS.

I wish now to speak upon something which is coming into vogue, but which is comparatively recent, and has not yet received that attention in the development of church and Christian life that it ought to have; I mean the social sympathy of the people, that feeling of interest in each other which belongs to church communion. That part of the community that is given to your charge ought to be made really to love each other. We read about that, and hear about it; think about it! What is, on the whole, the vital sympathy of church-members with each other?   Now I shall not be thought personal, because I know scarcely a soul in New Haven; but take the three churches which stand on the Common.   Take them family by family, and ask: What is the real sympathy, the electric thrill, the gladness that they have at meeting each other when they go to church on Sunday, or after they come out of church? How is it that, in traveling, or upon the street, or anywhere, you feel the fact that a man is a member of the same church with yourself to be a bond of sympathy?   If a man who has married your sister, but

whom you have never seen before, comes into the
house after a distant journey, and you meet him for the
first time, his relationship with the family is a reason
for gladness over and above anything you may find in
him.   He is himself and your sister too; he represents
both to you.

Every Christian is supposed to represent to every
other one the Christ that loved him out of sin and into
redemption.   There ought to be a genuine thrill of joy
on meeting.   What is the fact?

IMPERFECT KINDS.

Well, there is this: highly organized churches have
a spurious kind of sympathy.   It is the sympathy of
ecclesiastical or theological selfishness.   In times of
high controversy, when one church is orthodox and
another is heterodox, — and sometimes, you know, orthodoxy and heterodoxy are interchangeable terms, and
they shift about promiscuously, all the orthodox people
feel an intense interest in each other, for the battle
has come to be hot.   The lines are drawn.   People
are glad you belong to "our church."   They say,
"Did n't our minister give it to them last Sunday?"
A little combativeness quickens sympathy very much.
So, on the other hand, there is a kind of *esprit de corps*
in a church which represents itself as the only church,
or, if not the only church, then the best of the lot.   In
Methodist class-meetings, I have often heard men thank
God that they ever came into the Methodist Church.
But it is the Methodist Church they love; it is not the
Christ that is behind all men.   I hear men congratulate
themselves that they are in the Baptist Church, — often-

times I congratulate them too.   I know men who feel
that, being in the Episcopal Church, they are high and
dry above all others.   But it is one thing to like a man
because he belongs to the same church that you do, and
another to like him because he is a man, and a man
whom Christ has loved, and whom he is redeeming by
the power of his blood.   Ecclesiastical sympathies are
not to go for nothing, but they are of the lowest value.
They are too often put in the very highest place.   I
would not put them on a low plane ; but, after all, the
deepest feeling of sympathy between man and man
should not be in respect to mere ecclesiastical or theological peculiarities.

Then there is a spiritual or religious sympathy ex-
isting in churches.   By this I mean that where men
are genuinely converted and truly spiritually minded,
they have a sort of vague and general regard and
sympathy for the body of Christ.   I think that, for the
most part, our New England Orthodox churches get
very little further than that (I may perhaps be too un-
measured in the statement, but that is my impression).

Now, there is another kind of sympathy than that ;
namely, the sympathy which men may have with
each other on the highest spiritual grounds.   I admit
that to be the highest ; I admit that if the development of the highest form of spiritual experience
were so prevalent as to dominate other forms, and all
men could come together and touch each other on
that ground, that would be in every sense the best.
But, as a matter of fact, it is only the twentieth, or
the thirtieth, or the fortieth individual that is competent to that highest form.

THE TRUE PRACTICAL PLANE.

There are comparatively few who can feel a large, intelligent, generous sympathy with men on the highest spiritual and religious grounds. And in regard to the great mass of men, if we come into sympathy with them, we must do it on the intermediate plane, namely, where their humanity is, and on those grounds which are common to mankind; on grounds of generosity, of simple common kindness, of ordinary intercourse. There is where the play of sympathy is to be. Every church ought to bring its members together in such a way that they shall like each other, — not because they are perfect (for then how many would there be in fellowship?), not because they are of this grade or of that church; but from a feeling of generous, glowing, joyous, glorious *fellowship;* fellowship which, while it may begin or terminate in the very highest moral experiences, takes in all forms of mutual kindliness, clear down to the lowest physical conditions. Thus, to every member in the church there should be the assurance that he is welcome to all the others, or, at all events, to the great body of the Christian church. Now, is this the case? Do men get together on Sunday in that way? Do they go away from church on Sunday with any such glow as this? As a general rule, I think not. The point I wish to make is, that, in the administration of the social affairs of the church, provision should be made by which the members would see each other, not only as church-members, but in their ordinary relations, — as neighbors, as friends, as citizens, as business men, as common folks.

PROVISION FOR SOCIAL GATHERINGS.

Over and above the sympathy which you beget by Sunday services and week-day lectures and prayer-meetings, there ought to be meetings where people gather simply because they like each other; not to talk formally and stiffly about moral things, but to talk just as they would at home. This can be done in a variety of ways. In the first place, I think our churches are being built more and more with large social accommodations; parlors to the church are becoming quite as indispensable as pews and pulpits. This is a sign of the gradual change which is going on in this direction; and it is a very admirable change. No church ought to be built after this, in city or country, that has not in connection with it either a place set apart as a parlor, or a room which by some little change of seats could be made into a parlor. There ought to be, from week to week, or every other week, during the largest part of the year, such little gatherings as shall mingle the people together and make them like one another. There are few persons that you do not like better, in a certain measure, if you meet them often, provided that you are at all charitable yourself; and there are few that you will like as well, if you meet them too often and carry the intimacy too far. But up to a certain point — and you will never be likely to transcend it in these church gatherings — you will like everybody better. You find this man is not so stingy as you thought he was; that man not so cold-hearted as he seemed to be; this woman not so sharp-tongued as she had the name of being; and there are a great many other qualities of

heart and head that come out. Why! that old dul-
lard never laughed at a joke, and you thought it was
not in the power of man to make him laugh in that
way. You find there is something in him. There is a
great deal in everybody; but everybody does not always know how to get it out. Society, intercourse,
fellowship in church life, develops these things. Men
respect each other, they get over their little difficulties
more easily, they fall into quarrels less easily. There
are a thousand ways in which church life, by being developed in this manner, socially thrives as it otherwise
would not. This is not to be considered as a substitute
for meetings; it is supplementary and auxiliary.

PICNICS.

Then I am in favor of multiplying picnics as much
as possible, and all sorts of little out-of-doors observ-
ances for the summer. In Boston, they used once a
year to go down the Bay for a chowder-party; all the
concomitants of that were agreeable, and the people
who went were, to be sure, the more select part of the
congregation, but it did much to help them in their
social life. It did much to mix the people together
and make the church more harmonious and homo-
geneous. It is very desirable, too, for another reason,
— especially in cities, — namely, that our people are
of all sorts. They are from the top, the middle, and
the bottom of society. The gradations are infinite, and
it very desirable that rich people should mingle with
poor people, that persons of culture and refinement
should be kindly and intimately associated with persons of less refinement.

THE CHURCH SHOULD BE A HOUSEHOLD.

It is very desirable that you should temper the body of Christ together, so that every one of the members of the church shall have a pride in the gifts of every other one. Do you think that in a household where the oldest daughter is an artist, and paints; and the second girl is a musical genius, who, though she cannot paint, is brilliant in playing the piano; and the third girl is the housekeeper, eminent in economy and tact, who likes entertaining and likes management, and that is her forte; and the boys are, respectively, one a merchant, another a lawyer, and the other a physician, and they all excel, — do you suppose that when they come together they envy each other? Don't you suppose that the boys are all proud of the sisters, and the sisters of the brothers? — of this one, because she has a genius for painting, and of that one, because she has a genius for music, and of the other, because she has those fine domestic traits; of this one, because he is a successful merchant, and that one, because he is an able lawyer, and of the young doctor, because his last thesis was published in the "Surgical Review"? They all glory in each other. They sit around and look with glowing eyes upon one another. The gifts of each belong to all.

Now, according to the theory of Paul, — or the theory of Christ, from whom Paul got everything, (the Jews say, "Where would Christianity have been if it had not been for Paul?" and I say, Where would Paul have been, if it had not been for Christ?) so, according to the theory of Paul *and*

K

Christ, the church is a body, and you are members one of another, and what stirs one stirs all, and the gifts of every one in the church belong to all, and the feebler members ought to be proud of the gifts of the more eminent members. Is it so ? is that the feeling of fellowship, oneness, fraternity, unity in the church ; or are not men envying each other's gifts and opportunities ? Is there not infinite friction in the movement of the wheels, because the passions of envy and jealousy and selfishness are permitted to mix so much in church life ? You must get rid of those things. You cannot preach them out of the church. You cannot legislate them out of the church. You cannot get them out of the church so long as the Devil is alive ; but then you can go a great ways toward it, if you knead the church together. You never saw a good batch of bread in your life that was not kneaded a good deal ; and you never saw a church that was really good which was not a good deal kneaded.

THE RIGHT USE OF THEOLOGY.

I think that this idea of working in the church towards personal fellowship and personal unity and sympathy is far more prevalent in the New Testament than in theology. It must be, of course. Theology is osteology, and a skeleton is a poor thing to live with. But that which makes a man handsome is not being without bones. Some people say occasionally, because we hit theology a slap, that we do not believe in it. Indeed, we do believe in it ; but we believe in something else besides. Theology ought to be inside ; it is the frame on which you build everything. We believe in the succulency and the elasticity of the nerve, and the bloom and beauty of the skin that overlays it all. But what would all these things be if there were not any bones there to lay them upon, and by which they could stand up and be operated ? Men would all be gelatinous; no better than so many jelly-fish. So theology has its own sphere and function. But, more than this, even ethical preaching does not ordinarily aim at that ideal fellowship and unity which were sought after by the Apostles and the Lord Jesus Christ. That is a spiritual kingdom.

THE SUPREMACY OF SPIRITUAL QUALITIES.

I think men preach a great deal more in the line of the seventh of Romans, — then they are Calvinists, — or the eighth of Romans, — and then they are apt to be Universalists or Arminians, — a great deal more, in short, in the line of the deep doctrinal experiences, than they do in that of the thirteenth chapter of First Corinthians: "Though I speak with the tongues of men and of angels, and have not love, I am become as sounding brass or a tinkling cymbal." And then Paul goes on to say, "Though I have all zeal and all faith and all knowledge, and though I have everything, if I have not love, I have nothing." Then comes that magnificent chant, than which there never was a nobler since the angels sang the coming of Christ, that marvelous description of love that does not linger or grow weary, but rushes through; every stroke is like the stroke of Michael Angelo's brush that brings out the glowing traits ! And then that still more profound, mysterious, and marvelous passage in which it is said that

all the things that men know, and think, and believe,
are relative to time. Knowledge shall pass away,
theology, philosophy, mysteries, prophecies, shall all
cease, but there are some things that will not pass
away, — and what are these ? Faith, hope, love. These
abide. Death, by the great principle of relativity, will
wipe out thousands of experiences and things that are
important to us while we are here, and they will not go
beyond the grave. But there are some things that will
go beyond it, and are a part of immortality; and these
are faith, hope, and love.

Now, the power of preaching should be to develop
in men by the social life the affinities and affections that
are in these great qualities, and that carry them through
life and out of the present into the eternal life.

SUNDAY-SCHOOLS.

The next topic of which I will speak under the head
of the social forces is the Sunday-school; a subject so
familiar to you that I shall, perhaps, be relieved from
saying much. I think that Sunday-schools are the
young people's church. Although the minister ought
to preach so that the young people shall have their portion in his sermons, yet, for a variety of reasons, going
to church is not a very pleasant thing to little children.
They are full of life and motion, and our habits of going to church are not like those of the Orientals; they
are not like the habits that existed upon the borders,
where mothers went to church with their children, and
where all the household duties were performed in the
church, or by just stepping out of the door, and everything went on as usual. The minister preached through

the squalls and storms of discipline, and all manner of domestic infelicities, and what not ? We have ordered things so that there is a method in our churches, but it is a method to which old people can better conform than little children. They nestle. I am always glad to see a child go to sleep in church. It is one of the beatitudes. There ought to be provision made for children. The Sunday-school is their part of Sunday service, provided it is properly conducted, and is in a place which is comfortable for children, and keyed to their necessities.

HOW CHILDREN SHOULD BE TAUGHT.

Let me say generally, without pausing to discuss the whole question of Sunday-schools, that it seems to me the fundamental idea in teaching children is not the same as that in teaching grown people. Grown people need to be taught not so much ideas at first, as affections. The world has educated them, in respect to intelligence, in a certain way, and the relative deficiency in adults is in right affections. But in little children affections are pre-eminent, and feeling is their weakness,— that is, their strength ; for when a thing is too strong we always call it a weakness. So the prime purpose in Sunday-school work should be to teach ideas to children, and indoctrinate them,— to give instruction. Not that we are to omit appeals to their conscience and their affections. But it is so easy to beat the Sunday-school up into a foam, if we only have a zealot as a superintendent, and to have all the children crying, and all of them full of experiences which you know they cannot have. You might, with as much propriety, take a bucket of water and swing it around, and call it an ocean, as to bring a little child to me and say that he has these experiences which imply growth, width, and a sense of infinity.   Therefore I say that, in instructing children, whether by descriptive, or didactic, or historical means, we should do it always through the imagination, — God has ordained that children should learn through the imagination; the Reason is Chief Justice, but that which brings the case before the court is Imagination.

Children in Sunday-school are to receive *instruction*, for a variety of reasons.   First, because the children need it; and secondly, because it prevents the bringing in of those ten thousand little clap-trap things that interest children, and do nothing else.   There is nothing that interests a child so much as real knowledge, wholesome instruction, — nothing!   When I was a child, my dear aunt Esther used to promise that if I would be a good boy she would read to me on a Sunday afternoon about the ten plagues of Pharaoh; and I was enough of a Christian to like to see a fellow thrashed, so I always wanted to hear about Pharaoh!   So, too, it was with all the inimitable stories of Joseph's life, of Ruth, and the other histories of the Old Testament, and the parables of the New.

Children love knowledge.   Their inquiries are often as salutary for you as they are natural to them.

In adapting, therefore, the Sunday-school to the wants of children, treat them as rational human beings.   Believe that the foundation element in them is curiosity, as you call it, — that is, the nascent forms of philosophical feeling, the knowing states of mind that are to be developed in them.   In connection with that, but without keeping it uppermost, or rather keeping it undermost as the foundation, make moderate appeal to the feelings of children. I am opposed, heartily opposed, to the impositions that I see practiced on children by attempting to make them, at nine, ten, eleven, or twelve years old, do things and feel things that belong to adult life, and do not belong to children. The idea that you can organize them and bring them to pledges, and get them to make promises, and put them on platforms that are pre-eminently out of their reach, it seems to me, is absolutely unfair to them.

MAKE RELIGION JOYFUL TO CHILDREN.

Our Sunday-schools ought also to be so conducted that all the associations of children with the church shall be pleasant. I feel an intense desire, which grows stronger as I grow older, that religion shall be to men that beautiful thing which it really is. It is not a gaunt skeleton; it is not a scarecrow; it is not a prison, nor a bondage; it is not a chain, nor a shackle; it is the brightness, the beauty, the joy, the triumph of sun-shine. It is liberty gained by those that have been endungeoned. It is light revealing the world in wonder to men that have been blind. It is all sweet sounds coming in concord to ears long since closed, or that never heard. It is liberty, power. It is all sweetness in the soul, and ecstatic hope. I hate asceticism; I hate the bondage and the gloom which are so often thought to be necessary as medicines for depravity. Light sweeps away the visions of the midnight. Morning is the best cure for midnight, and I long to have the children feel that there is nothing in this world more attractive, more earnestly to be desired, than manhood in Christ Jesus. But ah ! I cannot preach to little children the clouded brow ; I cannot preach the eye of fire, nor the hand that carries the iron scepter. I must preach him who said, " Suffer them to come unto me," and said it with such sweetness that children spontaneously rushed to his arms. Think of what Christ must have been, when his disciples had to interfere between him and children that were running to him, or brought by their mothers. That Christ I preach ; and I love to see my children — for they are my children — gather around about the knees of Jesus with the same feelings that they have toward father and toward mother, and look upon their companions and the members of the church as though looking upon brothers and sisters. Thus gradually the thought is etherealized and lifted up to the higher sphere, as their young imaginations and the glories of heavenly relations are added to the natural affinities of the earthly state.

So, in our Sunday-schools, all precision and rigidity, except so far as is necessary for organic purposes, all tasking and all government that is painfully oppressive, should be omitted. While the Sunday-school should not be a mere amusement-shop, while the picnics and various excursions should not predominate over the moral ends, yet there should be such a proportion of them that children should love their Sunday-school better than anything else. I believe my own Sunday-school children do. In the providence of God we have about twenty-five hundred or three thousand children under my general care, and I think they are proud of their school, and love it. When the new Bethel building was in danger of taking fire from a neighboring building that was burning, I heard of it and rushed down Hicks Street, — for it is a little bit of an idol to me too, — and I saw the children sitting on the thresholds of their houses, and on the streets, and holding each other's hands and crying as though their little hearts would break. I said to one of the little girls, "What is the matter?" "Oh," said she, "our Bethel is burning! our Bethel is burning!" The children really grieved as though it were their father's house. They love the place, they love everything about it, and they love each other. Sunday-schools should inspire in children this feeling of love for religion, and for the church, and for all the offices of religion.

I insist upon this the more, because as a child I never did love Sunday-schools. The first one I went to was in the southwest pen — or pew, as they called it — in my father's old Litchfield church. I think there were three other wretches there. I had sat out my father's sermon, and this was the nooning; and while my little stomach cried "Gingerbread!" they said "Catechism." I remember swinging my little legs from those high seats. I could not reach half-way down to the ground. It was, of all things, grim and disconsolate; for I had to have catechism just as much at home,— it was not a substitute at all. The next time I went to Sunday-school, it was in the Bennett Street schoolhouse in Boston, after we moved there. I think I went there two Sundays. The first Sunday I got along well, I suppose, for it is obliterated from my mind, — I suppose I was profited. On the second Sunday some little question came up between me and the teacher, and he cuffed me, I think, and I kicked him, under the seat. I did not go any more to that school. So my personal experience in Sunday-schools has not been particularly auspicious.

But in my present charge, my own church, I think the happier spirit I have described belongs to our Sunday-schools. I speak, therefore, of what I have seen, and testify that which I do know, that it is in the power of teachers and of a church to make a school profoundly interesting; to crowd it full of children and keep it full; to teach them the fundamental truths of Christianity without neglecting their spiritual affections and religious feelings; and to make them love each other and love the church, and associate with the whole round of religion the most joyous thoughts and feelings.

QUESTIONS AND ANSWERS.

Q. Would you advise parents to compel their children to go to church, for the sake of forming the habit, against their inclination?

MR. BEECHER. — Yes; mournfully, yes. I think that where children do not wish to go to church, as a general thing it is largely the result of cause, and that that cause does not always lie in the depravity of human nature — in the child. Now, I was a minister's son, and I had to go to meeting, and I knew it. Therefore I hardly ever tried to get away. Once in a while I escaped; but I do not remember that I ever understood a single thing my father preached about till I was ten years old; and my father certainly was a good preacher. He seldom preached descriptive or historical sermons;

they were almost always structural; they had a very strong body of argument, united with appeal. He was settled in Litchfield, where there was a law school and a female seminary; and he had for a congregation, not only astute farmers and able mechanics, but also many lawyers, and the daughters of many of the most cultivated families in the land at that time. And his style of preaching, unconsciously to himself, was fitted to the more intellectual part of the congregation. And I,— poor little curmudgeon! — sat down in the pew, — and, by the by, the minister's pew was right under the side of the pulpit; the pulpit was — less than twenty-five feet high, and we were so concealed that I could n't see my father, and should never have known who he was if I had not seen him at home. I sat in that high-backed and high-sided pew, and the only light or comfort that I had, the only consolation of the gospel administered to me, was the privilege of squeaking one of those little rounds that turned in the open woodwork of the pew. Now, my mother was not a cruel woman, but she did some things that I think she has always been sorry for, since she has gone to her rest. When I would fall asleep, and really was out of the way and no trouble to anybody, she would rap my head and wake me up. That is treating children not according to their nature; it is not motherly; it is not right. Now, if children are brought up where, however much food there may be in the church for adults, there is none at all for them, why should they want to go? In the Episcopal and the Roman Catholic churches there is something for children. In that regard those churches are far beyond us. A child can follow the service in

the book, can make responses, can read, can sing, — and
there is very much of song service in the Episcopal
Church. In ours, how little is there which is fitted to
the thought of the children! While we take care of
adults, and provide for their edification, we are in danger of letting God's little ones take care of themselves.

Q. What position would you have the minister occupy in the
Sunday-school?

Mr. Beecher. — If he has nobody else that can do
it, and if he is as strong as Samson, he should be superintendent. But, as a general rule, young gentlemen,
if you can do so, shift upon other people just as much
work as you can; there will always be enough left for
you. Make others visit, if you can; make others take
care of the Sunday-school, if you can; make them
preside in meetings, if you can; send men to this,
that, and the other station. You are gaining all the
time by drilling them, and you will have just as much
as you can do yourself. In my first parish I was superintendent of my Sunday-school, and also taught a class
at the same time, so that I served from the very bottom, and went up. But after I went to Indianapolis, I
had men that could do it. In my first parish I had
only two men, — no, I had but one, and I did not want
him. I had to be superintendent, or else there would
be no school. In respect to all those things, do the
best you can. If you can get somebody that will do
about half-way, with you as his auxiliary, take him.
If you cannot find anybody, do it yourself, and all the
rest of the work besides. You will notice that in ny
community where you have to attend to so many of

these details, there is not so much intelligence as to make very strong draughts on your preaching power. But if you go into a community where there is more culture, and knowledge is greater, and where you have constantly to rise yourself, you must intermit.   That man is the best preacher and organizer of a church who knows how to make the most men do the most things.

Q. What is the best kind of pastoral visitation ?

MR. BEECHER. — All kinds.   If I were going to visit the sick, I should go with sympathy and gentleness, with cheerfulness, but not with mirth.   If I were going to visit a family in the ordinary society of life, I should go to the house and call for the children ; that is my choice, always ; and I notice that where I have the children, I have the old folks too.   But then, never go in any formal, set way ; go naturally, go as a man, go because you like the people.

Q. What do you say as to praying in families ?

MR. BEECHER. — I should never thrust prayer upon a family.   I would always go in such a state that, if it were desirable, I should be, at once, ready and willing to pray with them.   That leads me to another point. When I came to Brooklyn, all the young folks were disposed to avoid me ; that is, outside of the church and the meetings.   They thought that I would *talk minister* to them.   But I said to them all in my congregation, " My young friends, I want you to understand that I will never open my lips to you on the subject of religion till you ask me.   If you think I am going to follow you up, you mistake me ; I shall no more do it than I

would insist, if I were a physician, upon throwing my
pills around in a promiscuous party, and asking the
guests if they did not feel bad, and if they would not
like to take some.   There is a fair understanding between us.   You may meet me and travel with me all
day, and I won't bother you ; but whenever you want
me, and will give me the least hint, you will find me
right there, ready to talk, and help, and do everything I
can for you."   That understanding changed our relations
at once.   Thus the most perfect freedom was established
between us, and now, if they want anything, they come
to me without the least hesitation, and I never pursue
them.   I do not lay down this as a rule in reference to
prayer, because there are some men who have an art
of pursuing people which is blessed of God, and which
is natural to them.   There are some persons who will
go into a family, and at once say, "The Lord be with
you!" and everybody feels at once that it is the natural thing to say.   I could no more do it than I could
go in and enunciate a proposition out of Euclid, — and
that is an absolute impossibility.

. Q. In regard to the relation of the Sabbath-school to the
church, a matter which has often been discussed here, should the
Sabbath school be a part of the church, or should it be a separate
organization ?   .

MR. BEECHER. — The question never came up with
us.   We never let it come up.   As far as possible,
I always sought to let the Sunday-school have its
own autonomy.   I have avoided, in all my ministry,
the exercise of authority.   I have refused authority in order that I might have influence, which is a
great deal better.   There is nothing that I want in my

parish which, if they find it out, is not done instantly; but I avoid letting them know it if I possibly can. If they are to elect a superintendent, unless it is a critical case, I refuse to do anything about it. I say, "You are competent; do it yourselves." I have refused to have any secret councils with my own members. I have refused to lay any pipe whatsoever in respect to church affairs. I say to them, "I feel that I stand four-square here among you. I am a member in the church; I am not a dictator. Because I am a pastor, I am not a master. You shall not make me budge an inch from my place, nor will I attempt to make you budge an inch from your place." So perfectly amicable relations have always subsisted, and we have never, during a pastorate of nearly twenty-six years, during the stormiest periods that any nation ever went through, amidst questions that have agitated the community so that it was red-hot, — there has never been any difficulty in my church that I have had to call my deacons together to settle, or a difficulty of any description whatever.

Q. What is the best visitation ?

MR. BEECHER. — The best of all visitation is that which is casual and on purpose, — that which is apparently off-handed in the freedom of casual visitation, but which in your own secret mind forms a part of the system by which you go through your whole parish. But, young gentlemen, a man has a right first to the visitation of the family where his own soul is fed. You have a right to your own society, and a minister ought to be jealous of that. If the whole parish are jealous because you visit in two or three

families for your own sake, stand your ground. You
have as much right to your friendships as they have to
theirs. It is not necessary for you to give up your
manhood in order to please them, if they are wrong.

Then there should be visitation amongst those that
need it the most. Begin at the bottom and go up, and,
if anybody is to be neglected, let it be the rich and
those that are intelligent. In other words, the more
highly organized families are able to get along without you, except so far as friendship is concerned. I
know dozens of families in my parish, — yes, I may
say a great many more, — in which the average intelligence and the average spirituality are far greater than
the average intelligence and spirituality of the whole
church, — families that are churches above churches,
as it were. Now, it is very pleasant for you to go
there by elective affinities. Yet they are the ones to
neglect, if anybody is to be neglected. Take care of
the widow, the orphan, the unfriended. If a man
is under a cloud, go to him. If a man fails in business,
and the tongues of all men are against him, do you be
right by his side and say to him, "Now, let me hold
you up; I don't want to ask any questions or to have
you say anything, but here I am; by and by, when
you want me to say or to do, here I am." Go down into
the deep waters with people, and be all the time looking out for the people toward whom you are to act the
part of the chivalric man. Take the weak side, and
keep on the weak side all the time.

Q. Should the apparent proximate object of visitation be simply to cultivate good feeling between you and those families, or to
exert a direct religious influence?

MR. BEECHER. — Both, sir. If, in the community where you live, you are among a flood of magazines and newspapers, and the intelligence of the community is as great or perhaps greater than yours, it would be like carrying coals to Newcastle to go into a family and try to instruct its members. But you might go into another family, where they did not know the news, and then it would be a mistake if you did not impart information to them. But adapt yourself without routine, without an absolute, stiff rule, to the exigency. When a man goes out for botany, and sees a hollyhock, and puts his hand up and picks it, and sees another flower down there, and stoops down and picks it, he does not have a rule to pick flowers in any particular way.

Q. What do you do when you go into a family, and the mother is desirous to show off the excellences of her daughter on the "pianner," as she calls it, and is full of pride in her little ones, — what do you do? Are n't you tried sometimes?

MR. BEECHER. — Well, sir, my Master carried his people's sins and their burdens, and I try to carry my people's too. I do not know that the pianos are so trying to me as the pictures are. But, above all other things, it is the babies, the prodigies, that I have in my parish! I do not know that you ever had them, but there are born unto us children that are immense, wonderful! These, however, are little infirmities in people. I sometimes think, while we look upon them, and mark them, and amuse ourselves over them, that we have never had a chance to look into the note-book of the angels, to see what they thought of us. My impression is that, if we could get the notion of superior beings

8 *   L

as to the thousand things that they see in us grown folks, we should find that we are more childish in their sight than children are in ours. At any rate, there are a thousand considerations that should cause us to be very patient and to put the best face on those things ; only *don't tell lies.* Dr. Humphrey was told by a lady, " Doctor, you know that mothers think very much of their babies, but I have one that I think is a paragon." " I don't doubt it, ma'am," said he. " I have eight just such at home."

Q. Did you mean to have us understand, in some of your remarks a little while ago, that children from nine to twelve years of age were not often true Christians, worshiping God in spirit and in truth ?

MR. BEECHER. — Oh ! far from that. I believe that children worship God at four and five years of age. I believe there never will be a conversion of this world until the cradles are the sanctuaries. We have got to bring children up in the " nurture and admonition of the Lord"; this transplanting of old trees is better than nothing, but that is all that can be said of it.

VII.

BIBLE – CLASSES — MISSION SCHOOLS — LAY WORK.

CONTINUING the general subject of the social forces of the church, I shall to-day speak especially of Bible-Classes, of Mission Schools, of the Lay Element in the church, and of Young Men's Associations, — all of them very nearly connected, though their names would seem to put them at some distance apart.

There never was a time, I think, in which there was so much direct and indirect movement, from so many sources, against the sacred books which we call the Bible, as there is to-day. There was never so much effectually said against them, which every honest man ought to hear. And yet I think there never was a time when the Bible in its main objects and ends was so inexpugnable, so superior to criticism, and so manifestly admirable, as to-day. That is to say, while you may find fault with the time element, the mere external vehicle by which truth has been conveyed; while you may find some disagreements of dates, or some erroneous historical statements, or the like, — yet, when you consider the end which the Scriptures have in view, namely, the formation of perfect manhood in Christ Jesus, science has not touched the Scriptures, except to illustrate and to fortify them. For example, there is not a single element in them that goes to constitute social or civil morality, that has been set aside either by any experience or by any scientific deduction. The Book of Proverbs, although its aim is comparatively not high, yet, considered as a resultant of observation and experience in the ethical relations of society, is just as applicable to-day as in the hour when it was issued. If there has been any effect produced by the immense revolutions and changes which have gone on in the world, it has been to brighten the sentences, and make them clearer.

If you go higher than mere ethics, you cannot find a single thing that Scripture has pronounced evil, that has since been shown to be good, or that by any modification could be made good. You cannot find a single virtue that is admired and highly extolled in Scripture, that has been shown in the development of man and in the process of scientific investigation to be other than a virtue. You cannot find that the scriptural ideal of Christian character has been in any part impaired. It never stood so high as to-day. Never was there a need more apparent (and, I think, soon to be universally felt), of the contact of the soul of man with God's, for the sake of developing its higher and restraining its lower powers. So that if the Word of God be considered simply as a guide-book to manhood, and through manhood to immortality and blessedness, it stands unchanged and unshaken to-day.

Now, the teaching of that book — while it has, per-haps, been taught too narrowly and literally, and there is room for improvement in our methods of study — was never more important in the training of the church, in the cultivation and direction of its resources, than it is to-day.

IMPORTANCE OF BIBLE-CLASSES.

The matter of Bible-classes is a very difficult one to manage. But the outcome is so admirable that every pastor should find some way to manage them, and to make them a working part in the life of the church which he supervises. We are not to allow the vast flood of literature, the immense increase and populari-zation of what may be called solid learning, especially the exceedingly interesting and growing developments of natural science, to draw away, as they are now tending to do, the minds of the young. Our houses have libraries as they had not formerly, and our young people have a good deal more to read. When as a child I was, for any reason, shut up at home half a day on Sunday, I was not allowed to read "Robinson Cru-soe." I had "Little Henry and his Bearer," and "Pil-grim's Progress," and some of Hannah More's works, as well as a few moral treatises, which, if one began to read, he would retreat from them into the Bible, quick! .These were about the whole of my literature, and the Bible was, after all, the most interesting book in the house.

But now the Sunday-school library has opened upon the children a flood, or rather a swarm, that can some-times be compared to little else than the locusts, the lice, and the frogs of Egypt. There is, I think, an immense amount of wishy-washy stuff, wrought together with a certain sort of fictitious and unwholesome interest, and eagerly taken in by children. The most difficult book in the world to write, is a book for a child; yet it is upon this that everybody thinks he can begin his literary career. And so we are in danger of being carried away by what may be called the "swill of the house of God."

STUDYING THE BIBLE AS A WHOLE.

For all these reasons, the intrinsic value of the Bible, the wide discussion going on about it, the multiplicity of literary works and of religious works, called so by courtesy, — for all these reasons, it is very important that in every church there should be great attention paid to the study of the Scriptures for their own sake. Bible-classes are next to the pulpit, and are sometimes even far more educating than the pulpit itself. A Bible-class, if properly trained, may at last reach almost every question that ever enters the minister's own study. I think it very desirable that the whole structure and genius of the Bible should be studied, aside from its essential contents. The prevalent infidelity and doubt, the sneers that are thrown at sacred things, the talk that men hear of discords in the Bible, undermine the confidence of a great many persons unnecessarily. I know of but one remedy, and that is a clear, bold study of the thing itself. If there were a man in my parish who was an acute infidel, I would secure his presence in the class, if I had nobody else. I would show the young people of my parish either that the difficulties were only apparent, and were solvable, or else that they so inhere in the infinite nature of the subjects discussed as to belong to all views of those subjects, whether religious or not. At any rate, I would produce the impression either that the infidel objections were not true, or that the trouble lay in my own ignorance and incapacity to·answer. But to leave the impression in the community that the minister has got his church around him, and is cuddled there, and that it is his professional interest to stand up for his book, and that his book is susceptible of being riddled if you could only get fair play at it, — if you allow this, you produce latent scepticism throughout your congregation. Therefore, have courage, and allow fair discussion. Let in light, let in air. If there is any book that will bear it, it is the Bible. I think, therefore, that the discussion of the structure of the Scriptures, the nature of inspiration, — its metes and bounds and varieties, and the inferences deducible from it, — all these questions, which are to-day so much in the very air, you must meet. If you do not go to meet them, they will come and take you captive.

VARIOUS METHODS OF BIBLE STUDY.

Consider also the Scriptures from beginning to end, taking them as a matter of history and as a matter of literature, following the text *seriatim*. (I am speaking of different methods in Bible-classes, of which sometimes one, sometimes the other, is to be taken.) Or, instead of taking the Evangelists in course, and then some of the letters of Paul or John, men might take, in the course of the Bible-classes, such topics as the great questions of conscience; the questions of faith, courtesy, hope, love, temper, selfishness, disinterestedness, and a thousand subjects of that kind. That is, events that are occurring in the community, the thousand ethical difficulties or incidents that come up in daily life in the community, might be considered in their relation to the Scriptures, you yourself being all the time the guide and director; so that, in one way or another, you will have pretty much the whole course of life brought out in the most familiar way in the Bible-class. You will be able, in this way, to touch elements that no man can reach in a sermon.

ADVANTAGE OF PERSONAL TEACHING.

When I was in Birmingham, I went in to see how they manufactured *papier-maché*, and I saw the vast machinery and the various methods by which it was blocked out and made. I watched the various processes from room to room, until I came to the last, where is given the finishing touch, the final polish. They told me that they had tried everything in the world for polishing, and at last had been convinced that there was nothing like the human hand. There was no leather or other substance that they could get hold of, that had such power to polish to the very finest smoothness, as this living leather in its vital state, — the human hand. It is very much so with people. You can teach them from the pulpit in certain large ways, but there are some things that you cannot do except by putting your very hand on them and working them down, polishing them off by hand. In the Bible-class, where all sorts of questions and thoughts and feelings come out, and where various tastes lead to all sorts of matters, you can put your hand out and bring the truth into all crevices, nooks, and corners of human thought and feeling and imagination, as you cannot do in a sermon.

Of course, it will require on your part no small range of knowledge. He that knows the Bible well knows pretty much all the world, not in the more modern developments and disclosures, but in ancient history, ethnography, geography; in a thousand questions of manners and customs, of ethics, of equities, of general law and legislation. All these come into the illustration of Scripture; and a minister that carries on a Bible-class,—a live one,—and has in it people who have heads, and are not afraid to speak, will find that he has to use his study abundantly. I should not wonder if you found that, for years, in the beginning of your ministry, the Bible-class taxed you with more study than your sermons. But it is worth the cost. Your people will be rooted and grounded in the truth, when that truth has been derived from the direct study of the Word of God. Truth will have to them a vitality and an authority which it cannot have when it comes from *you*, even under the most favorable circumstances.

In the institution and conduct of the Bible-class, one of the difficulties to be overcome, after the listlessness and general indifference have passed away, will be a controversial spirit, which will often rise up, especially when you have persons who have been catechetically instructed. Almost invariably, the questions put at first are out-of-the-way questions of mere curiosity, and of no value; or else there will be questions of

abstract moral government. Men will want to go at
once right into Decrees, Foreordination, Election, Repro-
bation, or something of that sort, and you will have to
guard your Bible-class from the tendency to purely intellectual debating. For, while doctrinal discussion ought
to be in order, and it is worth while to make provision for the discussion of such questions by themselves, when you can lay out the subject, and invite
questions, and be prepared to go into the whole matter, yet, when a class has been instituted for all sorts
of people, it is very unwise to let it take on a controversial habit. Now, there is a difficulty here. I
have a man who is active, self-sacrificing, excellent, and
who works among the poor all the time; but his ideas
are very curious, and he is incisive in his thought, and
at every teachers' meeting he wants to put questions
on passages of Scripture and carry the meeting off into
philosophical discussion. Now, the object of the head
of the school is to prepare his teachers to edify their
scholars, and he does not wish to invite doctrinal dis-
quisition, or to become an antagonist; and yet, to stop
that man's mouth looks very much as if he were afraid
to defend his own ground, or as if he did not want free
discussion. It will require a good deal of wisdom and
tact and management to go right. One way to meet
the case is to come to a fair understanding with the
person, by personal conversation with him. There are
a great many men that will help you, if you confide
in them; but if you do not, they will hinder you. If
there were half a dozen of this kind, I should call them
together in my study, and say to them: "Now, gentlemen, you are acute, I see; your minds are active, and

you have a great deal of curiosity on this or that subject. I want to do so and so with my Bible-class.
This is my plan, and I want your help. I will agree,
as far as in me lies, to meet your desires. I will have
other meetings, which shall be especially for discussion,
and you shall have free range; but in these others I
want you to help, and not hinder me." Thus I throw
myself on their confidence and honor. Most men that
would come to a Bible-class at all would respond to
such an appeal as that, and would help you. But
don't set up your authority. Don't use your spiritual
bludgeon. Don't say to a man, "Sit down, sir!" Don't
ridicule a man, or shut up his mouth by authority,
because you are a minister. It is the worst possible
policy. No policy will surely keep you out of difficulties, young gentlemen. I don't care how much you
know beforehand of management, you have all of you
got to carry burdens; you have got to learn a good deal
by failures, stumbling, and falling into pit-holes. I only
give you a few hints and suggestions as to these things,
leaving you to use your good sense in extricating yourselves from the difficulties which you will find in carrying on a successful Bible-class.

Now, allow me to say, I have found in my ministry
much benefit from the Bible-class, — more benefit, in
many respects, than from anything else. In my own
early ministry, instead of having a Bible-class, — for I
had not good material to work into one, — I lectured
on the Bible. I took up the Scriptures *seriatim*. The
whole of the New Testament I went through by lectures. I think I have now, somewhere on my shelves
at home, the lectures I prepared thirty years ago, in

which I went over pretty much the whole of the New Testament, chapter by chapter, verse by verse. I asked for questions, sometimes provoked questions, but mainly I expounded the Scriptures myself. Circumstances were such, in my early ministry, as to make this course desirable. During my settlement in Brooklyn, I have had so much preaching to do, and have had so many helpers raised up around me, that I have been able to put this work upon others; and the Bible-classes, which have been a constituent part of our school system, have been more blessed than almost any other part of the labor in our church. We have three Sunday-schools, — the Home School, the Bethel, and the Plymouth Mission. In the Home School, we have about eight or nine hundred children, and from a hundred and fifty to two hundred young men over fifteen years of age. In the Bethel we have about one thousand scholars, and in the Bible-class about two hundred married men; also a class of married women, of about one hundred or one hundred and fifty. In the Plymouth Mission, there are four or five hundred scholars, and nearly one hundred in the Bible-classes. The admissions to the church-membership have ranged from a hundred to two hundred and fifty or three hundred; and probably from one third to one half of them have been by conversions from the world; and I may say four fifths of them have come through the Sunday-schools and the Bible-classes. So that the body of the members who have been brought in have been trained, and brought to a personal avowal of a religious faith and an entrance upon a religious life, by the influence of the Bible-class.

This Bible-class of married men is a phenomenon.

The gentleman who teaches it was a soldier, who lost his arm in the service.   He is singularly well fitted for this work.   He had a large number of poor, plain, but excellent men; but they were not all such.   He has gathered up from the street the degraded, the literally lost.   At first his class was small, — nine or ten ; but he worked with them faithfully, and set them to gathering up their abandoned companions.   Among those brought in were drunkards, pimps, the most degraded and despicable.   There were men that by their careless habits had wasted their earnings and disbanded their families. Some of them were living in filth and vice, and some in crime.   And yet, last January, about a hundred of these men came up in a body and called upon me, and a better looking set of men I never beheld.   They were clothed and in their right mind.   We received at one time some forty into the church, out of this body of men; and one of the most affecting things I know of is that this class, two or three times a year, gives an entertainment to all the parents of the children in the Bethel Mission. They give it themselves.   We furnish the room and lights, but they order a supper, with cake, confections, ice-cream, tea, and coffee.   They have music, and also some little amusement — tableaux, or something of the kind — got up for them.   They invite all the fathers and mothers of the children in the Bethel Mission. Each of the members of the Bible-class wears his little rosette to show he is a manager, and each one is expected to be on the floor to entertain the guests and to see that every one is happy, comfortable, talked to, and fed.   To see these hundred and fifty men, — one of whom said, in relating his experience, " I know all about rum. I have made it, I have sold it, and I have drunk it to the very uttermost," — to see such men in the house of God, entertainers, calling in the parents of the poor wandering children, is enough to make tears come from anybody's eyes.

I don't believe you ever could have reached those men except by taking the Word of God in your hand, calling them together in a place where they felt at home, and then going step by step with them through the truth, teaching them Sunday after Sunday; and, while you are doing this, calling out their sympathies, making them work for each other, — for that is what this class is still doing, — one here and one there, raising contributions by which they are able to sustain men and get them on their feet till they can get work again. There have been literally hundreds of families regathered.

I have one teacher in my Home School, — I should be within bounds if I should say that in ten years he has been the instrument of converting one hundred and fifty young men, and chiefly by the application of the truth as it is in Jesus, in the Bible-class; and I have found that, while our Sunday-schools are greatly blessed, there has been no other agency employed in our church that is comparable to our Bible-classes for adults, young men and old.

CAUSE OF THE PROSPERITY OF PLYMOUTH CHURCH.

The history of Plymouth Church, as viewed, would seem to be a history of excitement and curiosity. The reason of the prosperity of that church has been simply the abundant, continuous, faithful, humble working of the members of the church, year after year. There is an immense amount of life among the members. They are seeking to follow Christ in a humble, working spirit, and that has made the history of the church.

MISSION SCHOOLS.

A few words on the subject of mission schools. These are highly desirable in large cities, where so many of the neighborhoods are neglected, and are not able to support a church. Such neighborhoods can be better reached under the Methodist system than under our own, unless we employ some such auxiliaries as mission schools. I regard mission schools as the tenders of the fleet. Our churches are men-of-war; our mission schools are little steam-yachts that these men-of-war send out into the shallower waters, or where they cannot go. Every city church ought to have one or two chickens of this kind under its wing.

WHERE TO ESTABLISH MISSIONS.

There are, in the establishment of these mission schools, two or three principles that I think should be borne in mind as the foundations of all success. First, a mission school ought not, in my judgment, to be placed in a slum. If you are going into neighborhoods where there is degradation and vice, and all manner of nastiness and rottenness, it is not best to preach the gospel there permanently. Go in to them, and visit them; but if you are to establish an institution, draw people out of the midst of that miry pit on to the edge of virtue and neatness and order. It will be easier to draw people out of disorder up to the borders of order, than to teach them in the midst of their disorder.

There is something in going out of their ill-ventilated houses, their unlighted, dirty streets, up to a place which is quiet, which has some element of beauty about it. It becomes attractive to them, and they will like to do it, provided they think the place is still within easy reach, and is their own.

THE SCHOOL NOT TO BECOME A CHURCH.

Next, I affirm that a mission school, as a general thing, should remain a mission school. I refuse utterly to allow any of our schools to be nascent churches. Not that it may not be a good way to send out a school, and thus prepare the way for a church. There are many cases in which that is a proper thing to do. But ordinarily, in outlying neglected neighborhoods, mission schools are better for the people than churches ; for this reason, that they really are churches in the primitive sense of the term, and that the mode of instruction obtaining there is better adapted to the wants of that class of people than is the instruction which they would be likely to get in a church of the ordinary pattern. Our churches tend to extinguish sociality. Their congregations are respectable. They rise high in many elements ; but the low, the poor, the ignorant, the vicious, are not susceptible yet of these higher things. Where they are brought into our churches, they are lonesome, they are little interested, and are very soon left behind. But if you send intelligent men and women down into their midst to put them into classes, and then to do the work face to face, looking to the individual man, calling him by name, going over to where you can lay your hand on him, you are rubbing in the truth in a manner that just suits his unsusceptible nature.   You are giving to each man as he needs, not comprehensively as a whole congregation needs.

BENEFIT TO TEACHERS.

There is another reason.   I regard these mission schools as the nurseries for training the teachers themselves.   All the good we have done to the poor and ignorant in Brooklyn is not comparable with that which has been done to my own people in the process.   It would be enough, if only this one thing had fallen out, that the young men and women in my parish had been for years and years giving some of their best time, their best thoughts, their freshest hours, their sweetest enthusiasm, their most disinterested charities.   They have gone down into the field and made the work of taking care of these men their own work.   There are, and have been, many children of wealth and culture engaged in this mission work, who give up to it not only hours in each single day, meeting in council, — meeting in little evening parties that have been arranged for this purpose, — but pretty nearly the whole of their Sunday, except the hour of our morning service ; and who carry this on for five or ten years, — fascinated with it, I might say.   Now, this building up of these persons makes them worth a hundred times as much to society and to the church as they would be, had they merely been recipients, going with open mouth, always eating, and never using the strength which came from digested food.   These missions at home keep alive the disinterestedness of men to such a degree that I have come near to think that the church which has no mission feeling in it, no impetus to go outside of itself, no thought of anything except how to take care of itself, is scarcely a Christian church. I do not think that vital piety is long to be sustained in any body of men gathered together for church services, where there is no mission spirit, — that is, a spirit of disinterested labor for those who cannot repay you.

CHURCH SELFISHNESS.

Our mission schools have also accomplished another thing for which I am very grateful. I am ashamed to see great churches, whose wealth is counted by millions, build themselves stately houses, give to them everything that can make them comfortable in the pew, attractive in the choir, eloquent and desirable in the pulpit, and when they have done, pay their minister and all the expenses liberally, and then sit themselves down and fold around themselves the robe of complacency, saying, "There, if the Lord don't think we have done well, he is unreasonable." What have they done but for themselves ? They have embellished the chariot which is carrying them to heaven, as they think, — though sometimes that is a mistake. They have simply made provision for their own religious enjoyment.

Churches gather together families, and take care of them. They are institutions for families. They forget all outside of their own walls ; they forget the community in which they are, which is under their care. If some few of their members are stirred up to open a mission school in a destitute neighborhood, what usually happens ? With very little interest on the part of the majority of the church, a few disinterested persons go down among the poor, and hire a hall. They have to pay almost all of the rent out of their own pockets. They have a dilapidated hall, neither carpeted nor decorated, gaunt and drear; and they gather together there a few on Sundays, teaching them the best way they can. And this is the offering of that church to the poor! That starveling band of teachers, in a little miserable, wretched, out-of-the-way place, — that is what they give! They themselves sumptuously fed, living in a gospel palace, having nothing neglected which their hearts or tastes could wish; yet, when they come to the poor, they take the scraps and moldy rinds to give to them.

Now, I hold that every church which wants to do good should give, not what it has left over, or what it stingily thinks it can spare, to the poor. That which you give to the poor ought to represent that which God has done for you; it ought to represent the freshness, beauty, art, and sweetness which prevail in the household of the givers.

When, therefore, we wanted to build our Bethel, when application was made to us, as a church, to take the school off the hands of those who had been carrying it, I gathered the people together, and said to them, " It is to be determined to-night by vote whether you shall take this school and care for it; but if you do, I want you to understand what you must do. I will not consent to the taking of this school as a poor, lame poverty school. You must build for them better quarters than you have for yourselves, and must treat that school so that they shall have, in the very offerings you bring to them, some sense of the richness which Chris-

tianity has brought to you." They assented to it.Now, our own church is not to be compared for beauty
and embellishment with the Bethel. That building,
with the ground, cost us some eighty thousand dollars.
The free reading-room is filled with pleasant pictures. .
In the appropriate rooms, we have all the elements of
housekeeping that are necessary. The teachers once a
month have their tea there together. Every quarter
the schools have a festival there. It is a complete little
household, in all its appointments. Every part of it is
fine in taste, ample and excellent in the quality and
quantity of the things provided. We spare nothing for
them. We have given them as good an organ as Mr.
Hook can build. We spend five thousand dollars a
year for the expense of running that school. It is entirely a free-will offering. Whatever they contribute
goes to mission work. In so far as the school is concerned, we have made it no second-class car, while we
are riding to heaven in the first-class. We have given
them the first, and take our chances in the second.

Now, where you organize disinterestedly in this way,
and give the gospel, not in its lean, meager development,
in its poverty and wretchedness; where you give the
gospel in its inflorescence, in that state in which it has
had time to root and grow and blossom; where you
embody the gospel in all its brightness and beauty, as
the source of all that is joyous in your own house, — take
that down to them; send with it your best children,
your ripest and sweetest, your most disinterested. Let
these make themselves at home with the poor, and be
to them, week by week, their counsellors and advisers.

Come in with me, on Friday afternoon, which is the

afternoon for prayer among the women, and for the telling of their wants.   It is enough to melt a heart of stone.   That little saintly woman who presides there, whose name I will not mention, is to them, as it were, what the Virgin Mary is to the more devout and intelligent Catholics.   Her ears are open to all their troubles. If one has a sick child or a sick husband, if one has had a death in a family, if a husband has been abusive, if there is discouragement, if the boys have turned out badly, — whatever their troubles, it is their privilege to come there, Friday afternoon, and make known all their wants.   This woman sympathizes with them, counsels them, looks after them, comforts them.   And this work is going on all the time, from year's end to year's end. There is no vacation in that school.   Our Home School has a vacation, because our scholars are all children of prosperous parents ; but poverty knows no vacation. The grief and sorrow that come in the lower walks of life know no intermission.   We always keep open this house of refuge, to which all the poor and the needy come. I tell you, it keeps the hearts of my people very soft and sweet.   There is a revival feeling in the church all the time, coming very largely from the effects of our mission work.

I have said that the best thing in our church was the Bible-class.   Well, the best thing in our church is the Mission class !   Whichever one you think of last is the best.

LAY PREACHING.

This leads me to speak of the lay element in churches. I have already somewhat anticipated that subject.   I

am satisfied, gentlemen, that you are never going to
have professional ministers enough to convert the world,
— never. You have got to have the whole church
preach, or you will never cover the ground. The population increases a great deal faster than ministers do,
especially in the outlying territories. Just think of the
idea of attempting to closely follow up that rush of emi-
gration, and the opening of those vast intermediary and
far-away States and Territories, with schools and
churches and professional ministers. You never can
do it. In this intelligent age of the world, I do not
understand why a layman has not just as much right
to be a public teacher as a minister has. He knows
as much; he averages as well. He does not undertake
to conduct an organization in all its details, and to be a
leader; but, in his sphere, he is prepared to preach the
gospel. There are many men in the law, in medicine,
in mercantile business, many teachers in schools, many
men retired from active business life, who are competent to take this, that, or the other neighborhood, and
maintain service from Sabbath to Sabbath. Able lecturers they are upon education; able lecturers they
may be upon temperance; and they may just as well
preach also sermons that have in them the root of the
gospel. There was a time when it was feared that they
might err from ignorance. But we have learned to trust
men. At least, the democratic idea has been introduced
into the church; and we have learned to have great
trust and confidence in men. It is said that laymen by
their rash speaking endanger the truth. As though
there never was any rash speaking among ministers,
and never any endangering of the truth among them!

It is said that they will run wide of common-sense. As if all ministers were always in the line of common-sense! "Oh but," it is said, "ministers are rectified; the class spirit brings them up, and they are watched over." Just as though public sentiment would not bring the others up, and as though they could not be rectified! The very work that a man is engaged in has the element of rectification in it. Let men not be persecuted, let them not be questioned, let them not be nettled and irritated; for getting mad, if not the father, is the grandfather, of all the heresy in the world! Men think differently from you, and then you hit them, and then they say, "Now I will stand to it." And they fight for their opinion; so that the anger that is excited by opposition is the cause of the permanency of many and many an aberration that has taken place in the church. If you had let men alone, if you had left them at liberty, they would have exhaled much that was obnoxious; it would have cured itself. Men need the work; the field needs them. They are not only to be trusted, but I think that, being trusted, they will average as well as the great multitude of ministers in the kind of work to which they turn their hand.

WORK IN ONE'S OWN FIELD.

That is not all. I think we must have more work from laymen in their own business and in their own professions. A banking-house is the banker's parish; the landlord has his parish in his hotel; the judge has his parish in the bar, and among the people that are before the bar and behind it. Wherever men are, there is their sphere of work. I knew a man who was en-

gaged in business in Wall Street. Certain transactions
on the part of certain young men of character and
family came before him. He drew them aside and
talked to them. He talked to them as a Christian
man and as a father should. The effect on them was
overwhelming. It was the cause, apparently, of an
entirely different style of manhood in them from that
upon which they had been entering. If I had said
those things to them, they would have said, "Oh, of
course; he says so because that is his business; we expect that from a minister; but he don't understand
much about business." But here was an old business
man, universally looked up to in the street; and when
he talked godliness to those young men, it meant something. If I were to see a young buck spend his nights
in dissipation, drinking, and all manner of license, and
should go and talk to him, he would say, "I thank you;
you mean well, no doubt, Mr. Beecher." And he
would say, after I had gone away, "The minister has
been to talk to me, and he was a good old fellow";
and he might be very grateful. But suppose a man of
the world who had gone through much, a man of society, not altogether clear himself, — suppose he should
take that young man, and say, "Now, Thomas, let me
just tell you something; it won't do, it won't do!"
Let *him* talk, and it will make a hundred times greater
impression, especially if he is known to have had some
experience in these evil courses, but has come out of
them and cleansed himself, and stands high in truth
and honor. When I went yesterday from the lecture,
a man met me and asked me, "You know Mr. So-and-
so?" "Yes," — he was the landlord of a hotel. Said

this person, "That man led me to Christ." "How was that?" "Well, said he, "he took me and talked to me." I inquired of the landlord afterwards, and he said it was so. He saw that the other was living very wickedly, and he talked to him, and told him he was going to the bad. The man looked up in his face in utter amazement, and said, "You, a landlord, talk to me so?" "Yes," said the landlord, "I do talk to you so." It made an impression upon his mind that no minister ever could have made.

Now, I hold that there are some things which can be said by each man in his own field, and by nobody else than the man in that place, and that our lay force ought to be developed in the church and out of the church, so as to supplement and carry out the preaching of the pulpit. That pastorate which does not make the most of all the laymen and laywomen in the church and in the congregation is imperfect by just so much. Many of you, perhaps most of you, will disagree with me in the matter of woman's preaching, but you have got to come to it; and I only throw it out incidentally now, not to argue it, but merely to say that coming events cast their shadows before; and when the time comes, and you see that it is the proper thing to do, you will remember I told you you would have to come to it.

YOUNG MEN'S CHRISTIAN ASSOCIATIONS.

One word as to Young Men's Christian Associations. I think, in large cities, there is a sphere for them. In country places, I don't see what they are but men's churches. I think that the young men and young

9 *

women of the church should form young people's associations in the church. To form them with separate
organizations, with elaborate buildings and large machinery, may be wise in large cities, but in country
towns no reason for it exists. As a universal system,
therefore, extending all over the land, I doubt if there
is a necessity for it; I doubt the wisdom and expedi-
ency of it. But, as a special organization in our large
cities, I think it is eminently wise. But what ought
these associations to do? What is their business? If
it be preaching to the young men, if it be conducting
prayer-meetings, — why, the church does that, and it
had better be done in the churches. If it be merely
getting together classes and giving them free instruction in Italian, Spanish, French, mathematics, mechanics, — why, we have multitudes of institutions that
are doing that. Why need there be a Young Men's
Christian Association to duplicate that work. If, however, there is a work set on foot for mutual guardian-
ship and protection, and mutual combined effort to
procure occupation for those who are out of it, — an
association for taking care of the sick, or for watching
the children that come from the country into the city;
if, more than that, the Young Men's Christian Associations provide in the cities lawful amusements in suitable places, so that, if a man goes to unlawful, injurious
amusements, he does it because he wants to go there,
and not because he needs to go there; if they give to
young men modes of honorable and manly athletic exercise; if they visit the jails; if they look after the
various asylums; if they become auxiliaries of the offi-
cers of the law; if they trace out lotteries and obscene

and abominable publications, — if they attempt to do
these neglected things, which church organizations are
not well fitted to do, there may be a large sphere of
usefulness for them.   Otherwise, I scarcely know why
men should go to the expense, pains, and labor of forming an organization for prayer-meetings, or any other of
those things which could be just as well developed in
their church connections.

QUESTIONS AND ANSWERS.

Q. Do you think the positive religious cast of the Young Men's
Christian Associations hinders them ?

MR. BEECHER. — I do not know that it hinders them,
because the strictly religious element is entirely a matter of option, and the other things in the organization
can be taken without the prayer-meeting. They do not
do as they used to sometimes on shipboard, when sailors
were not allowed grog unless they came to prayer-
meetings.   The different features are disconnected.

Q. Would you have as teachers for your Sabbath-school persons
who are not members of the church ?

MR. BEECHER. — Yes, sir; I would. I hold that no
man or woman who goes into a Sunday-school to teach,
can teach long without becoming a Christian. I would
do it as a means of grace to the teacher. So far as the
scholar is concerned, the teaching will, for the most
part, be correct in idea and general feeling, because in
our Christian society and our age of the world, young
men and young women are educated in such a way
as to carry with them a vast amount of Christian feeling and Christian ethics. I do not believe that a man
before he is converted is a heathen. I think there

is a law in the household, in the principles and customs
of society, a reflex light of Christianity, shining in upon
us from every side of human society ; and there is not
a young man or young woman among us who does not
possess a vast amount of the real Christian element.
The fountain needs to be opened through which the
supply shall come perennially from God. Nevertheless,
a person not fully a Christian may have been trained
so that he is competent to convey Christian influence
and ideas to a class. The attempt to move another
mind toward God is one of the most solemn things that
any man ever undertakes in this world, one of the fruitful things, and the most quickly blest. I was never in
my life brought so near to God by prayer, or by reading, or by anything else, as I have been by the disclosure of the wants of a soul that came to me for succor
and relief. It has exalted me immeasurably higher
than any other instrumentality in the world. I do not
believe that a young man or a young woman, conscientious and susceptible, can sit before a class of eager,
palpitating children for many weeks, and not feel the
arrow in his soul.

Q. Do you believe in graded teaching in Sabbath-schools, such
as we have in day schools ?

MR. BEECHER. — Yes, sir; whenever you are in circumstances where you can apply that principle.

Q. Would you have teachers in Sabbath-schools who believed
in Universalism ?

MR. BEECHER. — Not to teach it. That is, I should
say a man is not honest who would go into an Orthodox
church and teach Universalism in the Sabbath-school,

when he knew that that was not the faith of the church, and not the faith of the school. If I believed in Universalism ever so much, and went into an Orthodox school, I would teach everything but that; I would not teach that. If I were invited to preach for a Methodist, do you suppose I would go into his pulpit and preach Calvinism, even if I preached it at home? There is a principle of equity and courtesy always to be observed.

Q. Would you have the pastor or the superintendent conduct the teachers' meeting?

MR. BEECHER. — The pastor, if he can, unless there is a better man, which is not unfrequently the case. I hold that you have a right to the gifts of everybody in your church. There is not a man in my church that I have not a right to. If he is oak, I have a right to him when I want oak; and if he is pine, I have a right to him where pine is the best thing.

Q. In Bible-classes, do you recommend question-books, or merely taking a text?

MR. BEECHER. — Either way, whichever happens to be the best. Sometimes, a question-book. I remember Cogswell's Question-Book on Divinity, and that I enjoyed the use of it before I went into the ministry; and I have known great good to be done by it; sometimes by doing as old Dr. Humphrey did with Parry, — tearing it to pieces; and sometimes by following it and teaching according to it.

Q. Would it not be better to leave the question-book and take the text?

MR. BEECHER. — What should prevent your doing

sometimes the one thing and sometimes the other? Routine is to be avoided. Infinite variety, continual change, that is the course of nature, and that is the course of human nature in society. Generally it is not the course in churches, and that is the bane of churches. We run too much into regular routine. In most churches, I would not have a Bible-class all the year round. I would continue it as long as it ran fresh and deep; but if I saw it begin to fail, I would say, "Brethren, we will adjourn this class for four months. We will go over the harvest season, — or over so long a time. We don't want to run this thing into the ground. We don't want to gorge ourselves." I would not have a person come to prayer-meeting or Bible-class because he thought he must. I would try to take off the sense of bondage and make things free and pleasant, make men come to church because it is sweet to come to church. In order to keep things fresh and lively, a hundred expedients must be taken. Never let a prayer-meeting die, and then lay it out in tears. Kill it.

Q. Would n't that be murder?

MR. BEECHER. — Well, sir, I have an opinion that discriminating and judicious murders are beneficial.

Q. Would you have those lay preachers formally examined and set apart?

MR. BEECHER. — I would examine them in this way: I would see, after they had gone to work, what they did. And if they did good work, I should say, Go on. If they did not, I would examine to see whether they probably could do good work; and if I found they could by a little instruction and help, I would give it to them.

I would induce the sense of voluntariness and freedom just as far as I possibly could, restraining it only at the point where I thought it needed restraint.

Q. Do you have foreigners in your school ?

MR. BEECHER. — Yes, sir ; a great many of them. We reach the boys largely. We have two reading-rooms that are free, one for boys and one for men. One free reading-room for men — which is lighted and warmed, and made as cheerful as possible, and which accommodates an average of eighty or a hundred every night — was first established. Then the boys wanted to come, and we had no accommodations for them; so we had the whole basement cleaned out, floored, lighted, ventilated, and decorated, and then we provided for the boys books, papers, and magazines, illustrated publications particularly. The boys that came in there were so low that we actually put them in first through the bath-room. We made them wash their faces and comb their hair. Some of them were so low that when they saw each other with hair combed and faces washed, they laughed as though it were the best joke of the season. We had to have policemen to keep the building in order, so wild were they. And yet after they once understood that there was law and power, we took the policemen all away as soon as possible, and threw the responsibility of good order upon the boys themselves. They responded to it, and, through all the later period, we have had just as good order among the boys as among the men. Now these were, to a boy, foreigners ; there was not an American boy in the whole lot. And that is not all ; there was hardly a Protestant boy in the whole lot.

Q. Did you give them amusements?

MR. BEECHER. — We did. We gave them checker-boards, and taught them how to play with them. We could n't very well teach ball, or billiards, or tenpins, down in that little building, but we taught them checkers, which they could play.

Q. How would you treat Sunday-school scholars that are persistently disorderly?

MR. BEECHER. — Well, that is a pretty tough question. In a Sunday-school class that is persistently disorderly, it might come to such a pass that you would be obliged to exclude single boys among them; but I think that patient continuance in loving sympathy and kindness would subdue almost any class. At least, if it did n't do any good to the boys, it would to the teacher.

Q. You spoke of the conversion of a great many of the young men. What was the habit of the teachers in respect to the visitation of those at their homes, besides their instruction in school?

MR. BEECHER. — I cannot say as to that. I only know that, wherever there was sickness and trouble, the teacher or teachers knew of it, and visited there. In other words, there was a perfect system of pastoral care in our Bethel Mission School. The parish is so large that I am bishop now, you know, and my curates, or under-ministers, perform the functions of the ministry. So, if I cannot be had, the superintendent of the Home School is competent to go to the funeral of any of the people in that school, and minister to edification. The superintendent of the Bethel Mission, too, is competent, and there are others who are active and able. The people receive it, because these are the persons who are teaching them, who are all the time doing them good. And when there is sickness or death in the house, these are the very persons whom they like to see. I have twenty men who, I believe, if you were to send them anywhere on the two continents, would not stay a month without establishing what was equivalent to a church center, and they would administer ordinances and go forward with the whole work of the gospel ; because I teach everybody that preaching, ordinances, everything, is subordinate to manhood, and that he who is a man in Christ Jesus owns all things. Sunday does not own him, the church does not own him ; he owns Sunday, he owns the church, he owns the Bible, he owns the ordinances ; and any man who has faith in Christ and love to God, and who sees there is an opportunity of doing good by it, has a right to distribute emblems, bread and wine, to anybody who needs them. It is the Christ in him that gives him authority over everything else. There is a great deal of power obtained by bringing up a set of men who believe this, and practice it too.

VIII.

THE PHILOSOPHY OF REVIVALS.

TWO EXTREMES OF OPINION.

PURPOSE this afternoon to begin the consideration of the general subject of revivals. There are, besides the intermediate view, two extreme opinions which are entertained on this important topic. On the one side, there are those who regard the existence of revivals as perhaps, in our day, the most eminent instance of immediate Divine presence that is vouchsafed to the world. They are regarded with a reverence that borders even upon superstition. Often one would think, by what men utter, that not only were revivals out of the course of nature, but that ordinary laws were so suspended in them that our experience in other relations threw but very little light upon the questions connected with them. At the opposite extreme are those who regard revivals of religion as the most remarkable exhibitions of morbid emotion which can now be found; believing that, if they do not spring from Satanic influence, they yet represent the wildest and most spasmodic forms of unregulated human feeling and fantasy.

THE HISTORIC VIEW.

I purpose to-day to enter upon some general considerations, showing on what grounds I believe in revivals of religion, and answering many of the objections which exist in the minds of those who do not believe in them or labor for them. Looking back over history, we find that all nations have been subject to great swells of impassioned feeling; that these impetuous outbreaks have not been casual and meaningless, but have been intimately connected with some of the most important steps that the world has made; that they stand in close relations to civil policy; that they are intimately connected with commercial impulse and prosperity; that they have their place in the realm of art; that they belong to literature; that they spread, in short, over so much of human history as to take in, from first to last, every part of the human mind and its experiences.

THE REVIVAL ELEMENT IN JUDAISM.

As we all think that the Hebrew history has in it something more sacred than any other; as Matthew Arnold holds that the Hebrews were employed by Divine Providence to develop more perfectly than any other nation the great, deep, moral sentiments, — it is very interesting to look back and see how largely the substantial element of religious revivals entered into their economy. I do not need to dwell on prodigious outbursts like that which took place when Elijah gathered together all the prophets of Baal, and introduced new measures with a vengeance, and slew them all.

That, of course, was not a revival of pure and unde-
filed religion, in any such sense as we understand by
the phrase in modern times; but certainly it was a
wild effort of the people to throw off the domination
of idolatry. They were inspired to a more generous
thought of God and of their own religion, and to a
momentary detestation of the oppressive idolatry that
was fixed upon them by the royal family.

I need not point to those great popular uprisings that
took place in the rebuilding of the temple, in the rescu-
ing of the nation from foreign bondage. I point especially to this, that the revival economy, in its essential
element, was incorporated into the Mosaic system. For
I hold that the three great annual visits of the whole
Jewish male population to Jerusalem were substantially nothing more than "protracted meetings" held by
the whole population of Judæa. The entire people was
assembled at the three great feasts, and we have record
of the transporting effects which often took place when
they all mingled together, and the whole national heart
throbbed in unison to the same thought and the same
feeling. It was a saying among the old Jewish writers,
that he who had never been present at one of the days,
— a certain day in the Feast of the Tabernacles, I
think it was, — and seen the rejoicing on that day,
could not know what joy was. For the Jews, I had
almost said, deified enjoyment. In the Hebrew literature there are expressions of joy, from the lowest up to
the very highest rapture, such as I find nowhere in
modern literature; and they are intimately connected
with the development of religious life. Now, these
great festivals of the Jews were really organized

national institutions for the promotion of revivals. This will be more apparent when we come to look particularly into the nature and operation of the revival spirit.

REVIVALS IN CHRIST'S MINISTRY.

At a later period, if you will look closely into the life of the Saviour, I think you will find that during pretty nearly all of his Galilean life, — which was, I suspect, more than two thirds of the whole of his ministerial life, — the people around him were in what can be regarded only as a state of religious revival. That is to say, there was such an excitement of the whole population wherever he went, that all other things fell into the background, and the mass of the people gave way to one feeling and one impulse, following him. And wherever he went, it was so. When he went up to Jerusalem, it was scarcely less marked than in Galilee. After his conflicts in the Temple, he was driven out for a time and took refuge in Perea, or across the Jordan. And, although we have almost no topographical details of his residence there, it would seem that, in the multitude of parables that there fell out from him, this period transcended any other in his whole life. It was there and then that some of the most stupendous of his miracles, as well as the greatest number of them, seem to have taken place. The same things, it would seem, took place at the other side of the Jordan. So it is fair, I presume, to say that the whole of the Saviour's ministerial life, at least the part of it that stands on record, was passed in what we may call substantially a revival work.

REVIVALS IN MODERN TIME.

Now we know that, in subsequent periods, the church was subject to these great Divine freshets, if I may so call them. The rains upon the mountains filled the immediate channels fuller than they could hold, and they overflowed their banks and spread fertility on both sides, clear down to the time of the Reformation, which was itself a grand revival of religion. And, from that time down to this, revivals have been more and more frequent. In our day, revivals of religion are known, I had almost said, in every denomination. There is that leading primitive sect, the Roman Catholic Church : they not only have revivals, but with their usual good sense, having seen how well they work in Protestant churches, they have adopted the principle, and now they have what are called Missions, sending out revival preachers — for they are nothing but that — and holding protracted meetings two and three days, or seven days, if need be, and bringing their flocks, especially the more ignorant portions of them, into precisely those conditions into which we strive to bring men in revival labors.

In the Presbyterian churches, in the Congregational churches, in the Methodist churches, in the Baptist churches, in all the churches of the great sects in the land, excepting perhaps the Episcopal Church, revivals of religion are prevalent. The universality of this phenomenon would lead one to ask, " Is there not something in the human mind itself that leads to such results ? Ought we not to look for a philosophical undercurrent in this matter ? " I think that if you look a little at the action of the human mind, you will see that there is the explanation of it.

THE PSYCHOLOGICAL EXPLANATION.

There are, if I may so say, three states or conditions of excitability in the faculties of men. There is the state of acquiescence, or the latent condition of a faculty: that is, the faculty exists, but there is no automatic action, no habitual response from it. For instance, there are many persons that have a feeble susceptibility to beauty of color; so that if you bring a compound, intense, and solar red to bear upon them, you can strike through the torpor of their taste and make them feel that there is something beautiful in color; but this capacity is low in them, it is sluggish. There are a great many persons who have faculties and affections of various kinds, which are in just that frigid, inactive state, and which require the intensest stimulation to develop them. The reason why uncultivated people like brilliant colors is no other than this: the principle of taste or the sense of beauty in them is so torpid that it requires intensity to bring from it the same response which is, in cultivated people, aroused by a very much milder tone of color. This is a fair analogy for all the faculties of the mind. There is a second state, in which the faculties of men are ordinarily excitable and in even play. Then comes the highest, the automatic form, in which the mind acts spontaneously and of itself. There are hundreds of men who think, when you *pierce* them with incitement to thought. But there are men whose cerebral activity is such that, whether they wish it or not, they are continually creative. The creative states, the automatic habits, of faculty are the highest.

Now, experience shows that it is not possible to develop these higher forms in the minds of ordinary men, if you take them singly. In other words, you cannot develop the higher feelings to the highest degree, by aiming simply at those faculties. You must stir up the mind in its totality. The passions, the appetites, all the force-giving elements in the mind, — the whole commonwealth of the soul, — has got to hear the trumpet blow, and everything that is in the man, from top to bottom, and from side to side, must wake up, and everything become auxiliary to every other thing in the soul. And here you have the suggestion of a general principle, namely, the necessity to individual faculties of help from collaterals or inferiors. If you take this principle and test its application in a community, you will find that precisely the same law holds good outside of the individual mind, in respect to the great elements of human interest, that exists within the mind as a psychological fact. You will find that the great mass of the community are in such conditions that they cannot rise unless they are socially helped, — they cannot rise alone. There are very few persons in the community, even among those whom we call intelligent men, who are competent to do for themselves any satisfactory amount of thinking. But let them converse ; let them walk from morning to evening with those who are interested in the same things (especially if there be as many as three or four), and you shall find that they will avail themselves of this social influence to become far richer and more active thinkers than they could be by themselves. The same principle works in the elements of moral emotion. Society of feeling helps feeling. There are many of our moral feelings that would almost never act but for auxiliaries. I will take a familiar instance in the case of conscience, a faculty which all have or are supposed to have, and which yet, after all, is far from being a leading faculty. If there are one or two men in a thousand who have the sense of conscience pure and unmingled, then there are more men of genius in conscience than there are in poetry or in art. Nine men in ten, yes, ninety-nine men in one hundred, have their conscience in such a state that it never acts except through some auxiliary feeling. Here is one man who never has any conscience in ordinary things; but when his taste is offended, in other words, when the sentiment of taste as an auxiliary stirs up the moral sense, then he is keenly sensitive to right and wrong. In some communities, and in some churches, you will find that the moral sense is nothing in the world but conscience formed through taste or imagination. That which is beautiful is very likely to be holy to them, and that which is repulsive to taste is thought to be wicked; wickedness covered with all beauty is not so very wicked after all to such men. Their conscience acts through this auxiliary, and takes its colors and hues from it. Again, there are some men who are conscientious, when I present conscience to them in the light of benevolence and sympathy. To a man of benevolence, everything that is cruel is wicked; and anything that has kindness in it can hardly be wrong. There are other men who are affected by the sense of shame and by self-esteem. For instance,

many a man will steal and rob and commit murder,
and never have a pang till you catch him, put him
in prison, and bring to bear upon him the gaze of the
whole community. Then, under the sense of shame
and wounded approbativeness, the man begins to look
back upon his deeds, and to feel that they were mon-
strous. It is only the shame that comes in to represent
conscience that kindles the flame in him. There are men
who, under cover of law, will steal and lie, — in a cred-
itable manner, — and never feel any compunction for
it, never feel that they violate any canon of morality.
You must put the faculty of self-esteem in these men
in such a position that it becomes auxiliary to conscience, and then they begin to have a sense of right
and wrong in the matter of truth and of fair dealing.
Their conscience interprets through these auxiliaries.

Now, that which takes place within the man, I say,
takes place without him. There are in the community
vast multitudes of men who, if they are to be roused
and made to have any vivid emotion, must be reached
by rousing up those about them, so that they shall have
these for assistants. If you should put one man before
a minister, and let the minister preach to him as Jona-
than Edwards would have preached, he could not raise
that man to any high level of feeling, or even begin to
do it, as he could if there were added to him five hundred other men sitting there together, all receiving the
same impulse, and all, through sympathy, radiating the
same impulse to each other.

ACCEPTING NATURE'S LAWS.

When you come to look upon the community as it is, to judge of things as they are, and not as they ought to be, you will reason about men as we reason in the garden about plants. I don't go into my grounds and say, "Look here; these hollyhocks ought not to grow taller than daisies; they do, to be sure, but then they ought not to." I never question Nature in that way. On the other hand, I always humbly importune Nature, saying, "Tell me thy will, and then, by obeying, I will command thee." I take everything according to its nature, — the tuberous root, the fibrous root, the ligneous, the herbaceous, the high, the low, the blossoming, — each and every thing according to its nature. Now, in going out into the community, there is nothing that will be more likely to mislead you than that despotic "ought." A man stands in the pulpit and preaches sermons that are away over the head of everybody, and when you expostulate with him he will say, "Oh, they *ought* to come up to such thoughts ; they *ought* to like such themes." You have got to work among men as they are. To the weak, you must be weak ; to the strong, strong. Among the Jews you must be a Jew, and among the Gentiles you must be as a Gentile. If you can do it half as skillfully as Paul did, — and he could not do it so skillfully but that he was caught a good many times, — you will have more success in your ministry than if you adopt the iron method, and undertake to bring everybody under it. Now, looking upon the subject in this light, knowing these inward tendencies in men, I aver that the contro-

versy between fixed institutions and occasional impulses
is one that will very soon be settled.

REGULAR INSTITUTIONS INADEQUATE.

It is said by those who do not believe in revivals,
"It is far better that you should preach the gospel
regularly, methodically; follow it up by proper visitation and by all manner of appliances; and then you
can control the influences and the results. A community that is educated in this way is a great deal better than if it were subject to these starts and impulses
and wild phantasms that come in revivals of religion."
Now, in the first place, I say that there is not a community on this continent that numbers its population
by many thousands, in which the church institutions
are sufficient to reach the want of the whole population. The church has not wings broad enough to
spread over the whole population and brood it. Even
if there were containing power enough in the church
edifices, the people do not flow into them. Though the
matter has been debated and discussed, and though
every means has been taken, the fact remains that the
mass of the population — and, if you take the continent, I think I may say two thirds of the population
of the continent of America — to-day seldom enter
churches. Two thirds of the salvable men do not come
within the influence of these regular institutions. What
are you going to do for them? Is everything to take
the gauge of these fixed, stationary institutions, which
have in them almost no elasticity, whose very peculiarity is steadfastness, continuity in the same ways?

I do not undervalue the stated institutions of the

church, — which I take to be the household, or the
church itself, with all its schools, and all the schools that
are brought immediately under the direct evangelical
influence of Christian men. All these are permanent
engines doing a great work, which is not to be maligned
nor undervalued in the slightest degree, but which is
supplemented by another influence, — one which they
are seldom able to exert, but which is indispensable
for the whole community.

CHURCHES THEMSELVES NEED REVIVING.

Again, I think that stated institutions need revivals
just as much as people do outside of them. The tendency of all institutions is to formalism. Regularity
begets formalism. The burden and the grief of every
man that ever undertook to administer in a college, in a
theological seminary, or in a church, — whether with or
without liturgy, with or without regular service, — is
the constant tendency to wear ruts and to make dead
machines of things. One of the crying necessities of
the church and of its institutions is, to make provision in some way for the rational, the inspirational.
There is a conflict between organization and the irregular but genuine impulses of men. Spontaneity and
regularity, or organization, are at war. I say they
ought to be friends. I say that while you have your
forts and your solid armies, you need also your cavalry,
your pickets and skirmishers and light troops of every
kind, scouring the whole region around; and that revivals of religion are nowhere else so beneficial and so
necessary as where there are strong, intrenched, and
highly organized religious bodies. They need just this

counteracting influence. It is purgation to them. It clears off the old humors. It gives to them new life and new strength.

NEEDS OF THOSE WITHOUT THE CHURCH.

I have said that revivals are necessary to the churches themselves. In respect to the great mass of the community that lies outside of the churches they are indispensable; otherwise such people will live and die almost under the eaves of churches, without having experienced any salutary religious influences. I do not now speak of the dregs of society. There you will find a class, the treatment of which is a very difficult problem; but that is another and a different case. Go above these; go among the ordinary, the working, the half-intelligent, the commonly ignorant people. Go into the households. Here and there you will find a shrewd woman; here and there you will find a thoughtful man; but take common folks as they are, and my own impression, from acquaintance with them, is, that there are very few households, outside of Christian churches, that generate moral thoughts, or religious thoughts, or religious impulses. The higher feelings are extremely weak in them. If there is any way by which they can be reached and aroused, it must be by some means through which you can lift the whole community,— something in the nature of these revivals of which we have been speaking.

FANATICISM: HOW PREVENTED.

It is said by those who are not in favor of revivals, that they tend to a wild fanaticism. That is precisely as if a man should dissuade us from breaking colts and using them on the farm, and on the road, by saying that horses run away. So they do, if they are not well broken or well driven; but I have never regarded that as a satisfactory reason why horses should not be used. A wild, popular impulse may run away with the community. Let me say here, — though I shall have occasion to repeat it more analytically by and by, — revivals of religion are violent and untamable just in the proportion in which they are rare. They become amenable to good management just in the proportion in which they are frequent. Where communities have been absolutely neglected, when the fountains of moral feeling are for the first time in many years broken up, then you may expect catastrophe; then you may expect a flood on the community. The fault lies not in the recurrence of life; it is the long death in which the community has been left that occasions the irregularities. The rebound will be just in proportion to the long decline and apathy. So far is it from necessary that revivals of religion should run to fanaticism, they are the sweetest, the mildest, the most regulable, as they are, in every respect, the most congenial to the best human nature, of all the states of religious feeling that prevail in a community, when they are recognized, prayed for, and dealt with fairly.

LIFE BETTER THAN DEATH.

But it is said that the work that is done by revivals of religion is not to be compared in quality with the work that is done by churches in their ordinary methods. I do not believe it. I do not think that a

man who has been brought into the kingdom of God
through the instrumentality of the church is likely
to be any better than one who has been brought in
through the instrumentality of a great and powerful
outpouring of the Divine Spirit. There may be some
respects in which he would be even less excellent. One
thing is certain, that revivals of religion do bring people
up, do inspire their moral nature, do root them out of
old soil, do give them an elevation that they had not
before. If, as a result of this, there should be here and
there miscarriages, here and there instances of failure,
is it not so in everything? Does every single head of
wheat fill out in the harvest-field? Does all fruit ripen
that "sets" in the spring? And is all that which
swells till the kisses of summer bring blushes to its
cheek, — is all that fit for the bin and for the winter?
Is there not much wastage everywhere? Do all people
that are brought up in regular church connection turn
out well? Are there not failures among the regulars as
well as among the militia? It is said that these revivals of religion pour a stream of raw, uncultured
men upon the community. No, they do not; those
men were in the community before. "Ah! but they
are religious now." Then you would rather have them
dead in trespasses and sins, and regular, than to have
them trying to be better men and scrambling on all
fours! When the choice is life or death, let it be life.
When Lazarus arose from the grave and came forth,
bound hand and foot, what if, before the word was
given, "Loose him, and take off his head-piece and his
shroud," he had stumbled a little, and the disciples
had said, "Well, this raising men from the dead is

not what we thought it was, after all; see how he
stumbles!" When men have been dead without
knowing it; when men have been long dead, till they
stink in their vices and their evil habits, — pride, selfishness, worldliness, — *anything* that puts in them the
germ of life is better than that long propriety of damna-
tion! But then, respectability rules in such things.

RELIGIOUS EXCITEMENT NOT DANGEROUS.

It is said that, during revivals of religion, men come
under great excitement, and do things which they would
not do when under the influence of calm reason. That
is true. You will notice that nobody is afraid of excitement in politics, though it run so high that it looks
as if, at the touch of a spark, there would be a
universal conflagration. Nobody is afraid of over-
excitement in Wall Street. Nobody is afraid of too
high excitement in the ordinary run of social festivities. It is only when men begin to feel that they are
sinners before God, and that they need to be born
again, and begin to have such a sense of heaven that
they cannot bear to lose it; it is only when gross matter begins to die out of sight, and ethereal visions come
before the soul, that we hear men croaking, "Moderation! moderation! Let your moderation be known to all
men." Moderation in combativeness? "Let that fly!"
Moderation in acquisitiveness? "No, no; catch and
get, catch and get." Moderation in vanity, moderation
in pride, moderation in the ten thousand baser compli-
ances of life? No, nobody is distressed about moderation there. But when there is immoderation in sorrow for sin, when there is excitement, lest men shall

10 *
o

lose their souls, then some begin to be alarmed; they are so afraid that everybody will suddenly become angelic and tumble off the precipice into heaven! Why, that is not the danger; that is not the direction in which you need to set up marks. What if, on a road with an abyss on one side and a cliff on the other, we should put up all the barriers on the cliff side and leave the precipice open; would it be wise? Are we in danger of too much and too continuous excitement in spiritual directions? Do not the sounds of life drown the thunders of eternity in men's ears? Are there not ten thousand boiling caldrons of passion and feeling underneath them? Is not every great interest of society pulling upon them? — the household, the store, the shop, the office, all processes of business and of civil society? Are not men wrecked with the thousand worldly things that are tending to undermine faith, to blind spiritual vision? And is it not a great grace and mercy when, even if it comes with imperfection, — and what man is without it? — there is an excitement that lifts men up out of the slough, lifts them out of all their entanglements?

In early days, in Indianapolis, when the city was first built, an old settler told me the trees were so thick in the streets that he forgot how the sky looked, and, in order to see it, he had to walk a mile down to the White River. There he could look up and see all the sky. He used to go down and look for a long time, it was so refreshing to his eyes. In communities where business is like a thick forest collected overhead, so that one cannot see the stars by night nor the skies by day, when these storms of life come on, — these blessed irruptions of revival influence, — men are carried, as it were, down to the stream where they can see the whole heavens above them. And what if, under such circumstances, there is some little excitement? Cannot you bear with it, for the ends it looks toward? Anything for life! There is no heresy on earth like lethargy. There is nothing so deadly, so dangerous, here and hereafter, as to go on from month to month in a calm propriety, in an external seeming, and yet to have all the fountains of feeling that bring men home to God shut up and frozen!

But then it is said that, when men come under these impetuous influences, these high-toned feelings, it results in deceptions and in spurious conversions. Certainly it does. I do not know any economy that does not bring out those results. Men that attempt to come into the kingdom of God head-first are just as liable to go wrong as those that go heart-first: I think they are more liable to go wrong. The regular church is to revivals what greenhouses are to the summer. Greenhouses do very well; they make heat; they have their own stove and stoker; all they want is brought into their little space; and when, by and by, the robins and bluebirds come, and the elms begin to bud, and the maples show their tassels, and people say that summer is abroad in the land, the old gardener walks out, and says, " Look here, I don't like this summer. There are no toads in my house, but there will be toads abroad now soon. Snakes don't get in here, this is safe; but there will be snakes in the woods if summer comes. It won't do for us to have this thing all over the land." Summer, if it *does* bring mosquitoes, is more desirable than are greenhouses for vegetation, for fruit, or for anything else.

HIGH FEELING AND CLEAR SEEING.

Then, as to the spuriousness of conversions. In revivals where there has been an ordinary — not an extraordinary, but simply an ordinary — degree of care; where there has been a thorough wedding of feeling and intellection, — and they are never to be divorced, — where the work has been seriously entered upon and judiciously conducted, my impression is that there are fewer mistakes made than under any other circumstances. For this reason : there is never a time when the mind conceives so clearly as when it is acting under high stimulus. Its thoughts are clearer, its intentions are better, its decisions are keener; and if it takes ground, it is far more apt to take ground by decision, that is, real decision, than when it is acting in a low, lethargic state. If you want to weld together two pieces of iron, and you hammer them when they are cold, *you* will be hot before you can get them together so that they will stick. But take them when they are hot and put them together, and they will be welded by a few blows so that they will not break asunder. Get men at a welding heat, and then the way of life and duty becomes simple and plain. First and last, the operations of the mind are more thorough, surer, healthier, and better, in a condition of healthful excitement than in a low state of feeling. I stand for *life*. Life is health and activity.

RELIGIOUS INSANITY.

It is said, "Are not many persons made crazy by the excitement under which they are dealt with in these

revivals of religion?" Yes, some. There are some
that would be made crazy by any excitement. But I
have been watching in New York and Brooklyn, during all the time that I have been there, now nearly
twenty-six years, and I have never had to deal with
a person in my congregation that was made insane
by religion; and yet I suppose I have conversed with a
thousand persons that were under very deep religious
impressions. But I have seen man after man, — I could
point to nearly twenty within my own personal neighborhood and knowledge, — that have been taken from
their stores, and brokers' shops, and other places of that
kind, to the retreats for the insane, because of the excitements of business. Twenty men may wear themselves out in business and die, either from softening of
the brain or hardening of the heart, and nobody says a
word about that! But if, in attempting to live a better
life, there are one or two among a thousand, so organized that they cannot bear any excitement, and certainly not such an excitement as religion naturally creates,
these are marked and held up as scarecrows.

REVIVALS RAISE THE TONE OF CHURCH PIETY.

But it is said that, by revivals of religion, the church
is likely to be filled up with unmanageable masses of
men; that revivals, as it were, bolt food into the church,
which, if it were taken slowly and by mouthfuls, mas-
ticated and digested, would become real strength, but
now lies like a burden in the church. Well, my reply
to that is this: It is conceivable that, in some circumstances, such a result might follow, and especially
in communities that are at a low ebb of moral or intel-

lectual culture. It is quite possible that that might be the case where the administration in the church itself is lax and careless. But where the church is intelligent, and filled with genuine religious feeling, and where there is anything like a proper activity in taking care of the products of the revivals, the membership of the church is raised, not lowered, in moral tone. When an iceberg breaks off from the frozen rivers of the north and comes sailing gradually towards the south, it cools all the waters as it goes, clear down into the temperate latitudes. Its influence is felt even upon the atmosphere. But when southern waters go pouring up the Gulf Stream to the north, they carry heat that is felt in all the atmosphere and in all the seas through the vast circuit, till it beats upon the shores of England, of Norway, and of Sweden. It carries with it something of the tropic summer all the way. When we have revivals of religion and receive multitudes into the church, they are not icebergs; they are Gulf Streams from the warm south; they bring into the church, not chill, not death, but life and warmth and joy. These are facts which I do know, which are on record; facts about which the experience of thousands of men of different denominations and varying temperaments agrees.

Revivals of religion are pre-eminently desirable, because they arouse individuals; because they carry up those that were Christians already to a higher pitch of experience; because they renovate the churches themselves; and because they do a work for scattered populations in outlying communities which would never otherwise have been done. There are multitudes of

men that could never get away from the current of
their business, that could never face the public sentiment, the social current of the community, unless the
community itself became warmed, leavened, aglow with
moral influences. Then they would go with the stream ;
and there are thousands of men who in that way come
into the kingdom of God, but who never would have
come into it up stream.

For reasons, then, of spiritual thrift in the individual,
of strengthening the church of humanity towards the
poor, the weak, the outcast, I think we have occasion to
bless God for these outpourings of the Spirit, that come
as the wind comes, we know not always whence, and
that go as the wind goes, we know not always whither ;
but which, like the wind in the mariner's sail, may be
so studied and so used that there shall be over it a
substantial control.

QUESTIONS AND ANSWERS.

Q. What is your observation as to the tendency of religious
revivals to the promotion of religious knowledge and the intellectual character of the community ?

Mr. Beecher. — It is precisely what you choose to
make it. A revival of religion leaves the minds of the
community open as the furrows are. If you choose to
sow the seed of knowledge, it will grow and thrive
wonderfully. If you neglect that, and throw into the
furrows mere executive activity, that will be the crop.
Of all things in this world, I believe there is nothing
that is more under the law of cause and effect than revivals of religion. And, although they are divine in
the most important sense, yet they belong to that side

of Divinity which lies nearest us, and are entirely subject to our control by the appropriate use of instrumentality.

Q. According to your observation, under what we recognize as
the revival influence, does n't a man want to know something; does
he not hunger after some religious knowledge? Or does the revival influence leave him entirely indifferent as to the truth?

MR. BEECHER. — If it ever leaves men indifferent, it
is somewhere where I have never been. I have always
found that not only those that were brought in became
hungry for increased knowledge, but it was peculiarly so
with the old stock. It was like a stirring up of the soil
around the roots of a tree; you had growth all around.

Q. Is n't there a tendency to reaction and increased coldness?

MR. BEECHER. — If you draw a line across a man's
head, half-way between the top and the base, every one
of the faculties below it, when violently excited, tends
to reaction. If you take the faculties above, which we
call moral or divine, if they have anything like fair
usage, there is no reaction to them. If you rouse men
up by the basilar faculties and fill them with horror and
all sorts of lurid phantasma, look out for a reaction, —
you ought to have one. But if revivals of religion
come in with hope, with love, with courage, with faith,
— in other words, if they are brought in by gospel influences in distinction from legal influences, — they are
not subject to reaction. So far from it, I think a man
can work twenty years at the very top of all his strength,
if he is working by love and courage and hope. Those
things never tire out. That is what Christ meant by
saying that there shall be rivers of living water in men.
They are waters which, if a man have, he does not

thirst; it is bread which, if a man have, he does not hunger. He lives on it more than forty days, — he lives forty years.

Q. According to your statement, the half-educated ought to have revivals; but what shall we do with the educated?

MR. BEECHER. — In the fullest sense of the term "education," no man is educated that is not a Christian. A man is not educated who merely has his *knowing* faculties whetted, sharpened. A man is educated only when all parts of his nature are brought up to high condition. In our time I do not think any man is educated who has not gone through the strata of Christianity, if I might so say. But a great many men that are intellectually wise are just as much and as really the subjects of revival influences as anybody. I have seen men in every way my masters in all intellectual knowledge, who were made like little children. In my parishes in the West, I have seen men who came out from New England, where they had been for more than forty years in churches, — and I think a man that has been in a good old-fashioned New England church for forty years, without being converted, is like a side of sole-leather that has been in a tan-vat for ten years; he is so tough that if there is anything that can affect him it must be divine, — and yet I have seen these men melting down like little children, and made truly and thoroughly amiable Christian men.

Some one asked with reference to revivals in colleges, and whether revivals were to be looked for in connection with college instruction.

MR. BEECHER. — I do not know why they should not be. If you once get away from the idea of their awful-

ness; if you once get clear of the notion that they are
directly and solely acts of the Divine sovereignty; if
you assume that they are just as much the subject of
human volition and arrangement as moral instruction
of other kinds, — then I do not know why revivals of
religion might not be had in every class in academies
and colleges, and that without disarrangement of affairs.
A revival of religion is nothing in the world but a
religious feeling in its intense and social form, so that it
becomes contagious, electric. It is not an abnormal or
unnatural condition; it is not one hard to produce.

Q. You know, sir, what revivals have done for your *alma mater*,
for Williams, and for Yale, in former years. It is said that, in colleges and universities, revivals are to be looked for less frequently
than in the primitive state. Is that so, in your observation, and, if
so, how do you account for it?

Mr. Beecher. — I will say, fairly, that I have not
given to the subject any particular investigation. I
am not aware of the facts. I only know this, that I
think there are speculative tendencies unsettling the
minds of men that preach, as well as of men that are
preached to, in our day. That transitional state through
which we are passing has rather broken the power of
faith. Men don't exactly know whether they believe
in certain things or not. When you have that state of
mind in the community, you will not have revivals. A
man has got to believe. . If he doubts, he is damned.
I should rather attribute the decadence or the infre-
quency of revivals, as a general result, to the transitional
state of mind through which, it seems to me, the whole
community is going. It seems to me the whole community is moving in the direction of a revolution.

There are a great many people frightened, a great many anxious, and a great many are taking refuge in the old forms, in order to get away from what seems to be coming. And that unsettled state is not favorable for the production of positive results.

Q. Don't you think those lurid influences are relied upon too extensively?

MR. BEECHER. — Yes, sir, they are largely relied upon by revivalists. Most revivalists that I have known are men with immense bellies and immense chests and big under-heads. They are men that carry a great deal of personal magnetism with them, a sensuous magnetism, too, and they have a great power of addressing the under-mind; and they will set feelings undulating like waves, and will carry men on them. I do not believe you could preach with effect to the boatmen and the gamblers of Arkansas and to all the riffraff of the community, those who really live down in the cellar of their heads, unless you brought the motive of fear to bear upon them. If you could in any way bring the higher feeling in their natures to act in and of itself upon the lower ones, there would be regeneration in that direction. But, ordinarily, men that work among those classes are men largely of the earth, blessed with vigorous circulation and great power of throwing out sympathetic influence upon men; and because they preach largely to the under-class, men who are moved by conscience and by nothing else, they preach these acerb and terrific doctrines, and preach them with all the imagery that has come down to us from the mediæval times, with hoofs and horns, and all manner of exaggerated statements. I have heard a revivalist in my pulpit make statements to my congregation that, if I believed them to be true, would make me abandon the Christian ministry,— I was going to say, abandon decent society and forswear my race! The thing was so hideous! He stood there, — and afterwards, when I was with him, it appeared that he had no compunction, — and he began with this declaration, that the mind was capable of infinite development and increase of capacity. Well, that is pure supposition, to start with. But, assuming that, he went on to say that it would go on increasing forever in power of thought, and power of susceptibility, and power of enjoyment, and power of suffering. That being granted, he went on to say, that if men go to hell they will increase for ever and ever; and when he came to the application, it was this. "I have no doubt," said he, and his great white eye glistened as he rolled it around the audience, "that there are men sitting before me who will by and by be in hell, and will have grown and grown and grown in the power of suffering until they will have reached a point at which they will suffer more in a single minute than all the suffering of all the damned from the beginning of creation to the present hour!" There was his logical inference; and then he multiplied it and went on, saying that there would be multitudes and multitudes of them there, while angels were singing glory to God, and while God was looking over into the pit and seeing that terrific scene, enjoying himself; he wanted me to believe that, and then worship God! Now, where you deal with men in communities in that way, it is you who are to blame; for the reactions are something very terrific in revivals.

Q. Is n't that the style which reaches children, also?

MR. BEECHER. — It reaches them, — hideously, too. I remember, in my childhood, when a minister came to my father's house, I was like a thermometer. You cannot open the stove door that the thermometer does not feel it instantly ; and so it goes up and down, as sensitive as it can be. My spiritual nature was just as sensitive to religious impulses. I was always plunged into the depth of despair about my sins, always in a state of awful anxiety to be converted and to have the evidence of it in myself. This man, whoever he was, — his name has gone from me, — took my brother Charles and me, and began to tell us stories about the Devil and hell, until I had got into that state that I now wonder I did not go into convulsions. It was hideous. If he had put me on a hot gridiron and left me there ten minutes, I could have got over that, but this soul-broiling, this torturing a little child's sensitive nature in that way, without presenting any thought of mercy or love or goodness or Christ Jesus, — why! the man was a heathen, only he had a Christian coat on him!

Q. Do you believe in preaching to flee the wrath to come?

MR. BEECHER. — Certainly I do.

Q. Did you mean to state that, in preaching to those lower classes, you have to use appeals to their lower nature?

MR. BEECHER. — I state this : that any man who will begin, in any community, preaching to those who are morally dead and uncultured, will generally find that he has to use far more acerb and violent presentations than he will afterwards. And, if he preaches successfully, and preaches there for five years or ten years, he

will find, as his preaching carries people up to higher
levels in their own nature, that the same motives will
not any longer produce the same effect; that he has got
to go higher in his motives, and, preaching on that
higher level, he will yet go to a still higher one. He is
carried, all the way along, to higher and higher classes
of motive. My own preaching in the East is not at all
what it was in the West. It is addressed to a totally
different class and totally different conditions of society.

Q. Should the pastor allow evangelists to take charge of a
revival and assume control?

MR. BEECHER. — That is a very large question. I
should never allow any evangelist to take charge of
any meetings in my church. But if he is stronger than
you are, what are you going to do about it? You go
out now and look at the white-oak trees, and you will
see that they have held on to their leaves all the winter
long, just as many churches hold on to old, dry ministers. And you will see that the moment the sap begins
to start in those trees and grow, every one of those old
leaves will go. So with many and many a man who
has pastoral charge of a church; the moment the church
begins to swell, off he will go. It is a very dangerous
thing to have a revival of religion, unless a man is
wide-awake, useful, and active in his church. And it is
a very dangerous thing for a man to build a church
edifice unless he is a very able, powerful man. A new
church has often unsettled a minister. The impulse
that gives vitality, ambition, and movement to the
church, — a man must keep ahead of it; if he does not,
he will have to go.

Q. Do you think that preaching on doctrinal points is deadening in a religious community?

MR. BEECHER. — Yes, if a man deals too much in it, it is deadening; it is mephitic gas. If you want to speculate, speculate moderately, but don't get into an eddy, a whirlpool, and go round and round, and shut yourself up to that thing. If a man wants to study, let him keep that up, but keep close to *folks*, and feel the reality of human life, the need of men. I am just as subject to scepticism as any man could possibly be, all the time; and I have kept my head above water in a real, living faith in God and humanity, by working on the living, palpitating heart of men. Take a living soul into your bosom, and it will give you life.

Q. Do you think it possible for a man to be converted under the influence of fear, unless that fear goes so far as to secure a knowledge of the love of God?

MR. BEECHER. — I make just the same distinction between a man's being a religious man and a Christian man, as I do between a shrub in leaf and a shrub in blossom. I do not think that more than half the people that come into our churches are anything more than religious; they are converted to religion, but not to Christianity. They are converted to the sense of duty, to the will that means to do right, but they are not converted to that faith that works by love.

To excite fear is to produce life and motion. It is the initial step to arouse a man to that state by which you can carry him forward to higher states. But I do not think that fear, in and of itself, ever wrought love or ever will work love.

IX.

REVIVALS SUBJECT TO LAW.

ALBERT BARNES, in speaking on the subject of revivals of religion, says, "The phenomenon itself we regard as the work of the Holy Ghost, alike beyond human power to produce it and to control it." And then he quotes the passage, "The wind bloweth where it listeth, and thou hearest the sound thereof, but canst not tell whence it cometh and whither it goeth: so is every one that is born of the Spirit"; an illustration which was very pertinent before the establishment of the Meteorological Bureau; but, unfortunately for a literal application of it now, we know where the wind comes from and very nearly where it is going to. Still, the figure is just as good, and the truth is more than all figure, and that remains constant. Now, it would be fair to say that this language admits of two constructions. One of these would equally apply to all phenomena of the human mind, — thought, feeling, volition. The other construction would put all the history which is developed under the supposed personal agency of the Divine Spirit of God outside of the pale of scientific observation, of reasoning, of deduction. It is in fact, I suppose, in that place that Mr. Barnes would have put revivals of religion. I suppose he would have said that all nature, meaning thereby the physical universe, is governed by laws, and that by the study of these we may understand and control them; but that God's work in the human soul is secret, mysterious, without law known to men, unstudiable; that it depends upon the sovereignty of God; that God works as he will, meaning by "as he will," that he works without any sense of law or any definite or permanent channel; and that, therefore, spiritual phenomena stand outside of mental philosophy, if by mental philosophy we understand the exposition of the great natural laws which regulate human thought and human feeling. This, I know, was the feeling that prevailed in my childhood. I know that such men as Dr. Heman Humphrey and Professor Edward Hitchcock, for moral completeness and for sturdy and rugged understanding, — the latter for scientific attainment also, in his own day, — were not to be despised. Yet I recollect going down to Dr. Humphrey's under a state of prodigious mental excitement in my own behalf, and asking for some instruction, that I might ease myself of my burden and be brought to a saving knowledge of Christ; and he said to me, "My young friend, you are manifestly under the strivings of God's Spirit, and I dare not touch the ark with profane hand. The Spirit of God, when he strives with a man, is his own best interpreter." And so he left me to the work of the Spirit. Whereas, if I had had but a very little clear instruction, it would have saved me years of anxiety, and, at times, of positive anguish, for want of knowledge. The impression in Dr. Humphrey's mind was, that the work of the Spirit was of a kind so sacred, so apart from all law and exposition, that it was not safe for a man to undertake to interpret it. I recollect, in a meeting held during the same revival, going myself, — although I was then a member of the church, — to be conversed with by Professor Hitchcock. He came down on the side of the house on which I sat, until he nearly reached my seat ; then, turning from me, he walked back to the desk and said, substantially, "I see that this room is filled with the Spirit of God. I am awed and subdued. I dare not attempt to mingle human wisdom with the workings of the Spirit of God." Now, the reverence, the humility, and the childlikeness of the man were admirable ; yet I cannot but think the whole judgment and feeling in respect to the work of the Spirit were wrong, and not only inconsistent with the truth, but utterly inconsistent with the administration, in other departments, of both Professor Hitchcock and Dr. Humphrey themselves. They were perpetually laying the foundations of procedure in matters that belonged, according to their own definitions and showing, to the province of spiritual enlightenment. They did prepare with great skill ; they did lay out paths where men might walk, expecting certain results to follow. They did, in a latent way, — in a way, perhaps, not so clearly announced as we enunciate it, — they did imply, in their other spheres of labor, that cause and effect ruled in spiritual things, as in intellectual and material things, and that the foundation of knowledge was the study of the methods of the Divine economy, so that men might co-operate with God. And that study, by implication, requires that we should believe the methods by which God acts to be stated, to be constant. Not but that there is a Divine Spirit working according to its own free will. So, also, do I work according to my free will, and here, on you, turning this way, or that way, or the other; but I always, when freest, act along the line of certain definite mental peculiarities in myself, according to the law of the structure of my mind, and always produce impressions on you, according to the working of the laws in your mind. And yet I am free. I am free to reason, to appeal, to persuade, to pour one or another motive, by sympathy, upon the congregation. Freedom does not imply that one does not move along traveled roads; does not imply caprice, fitfulness, and perpetual unlikeness of method to method. The freedom of the Divine Spirit, the freedom of God's will, does not require that he shall never do twice alike, so that we cannot follow his footsteps, or know *how* he works, as well as *what*.

I remember that in the earlier revivals — the revivals of my childhood — nothing was so impressive as Mr. Nettleton's constant, emphatic, and, I may say, awful recognition of the Divine Spirit. He so represented the Spirit of God as to make everybody quake in his shoes. I think he had the art of inspiring fear, without denunciation, in a very much higher way than usually belongs to preaching of the same general class. But then his representation of the Divine Spirit was, that God was a jealous God, a sensitive Being. And he would whisper this utterance, " *Take care* that you do not *grieve* the Spirit of God ! " Why, I felt like a

man walking in the midst of torpedoes, — I did not
know where they were; but I might step on one, and
away I should go! It was a vague terror. I was full
of fear; afraid to go to the right or to the left, forward
or backward, up or down. I felt that the whole air was
full of a sensitive, jealous spirit that was ready to smite
down, I knew not when, or how, or where. I only
felt, in a general way, that I was a sinner, and that
God was ready to strike me, and that if I could not get
under the lightning-rod, where the flash would be carried off, I should be gone. It produced an intense
moral nervousness; but, in a sensitive nature such as
mine was, it overacted. An obtuse nature it would
hardly bring up to the point; but in others it would
overwork, and produce that kind of *curdling* of the
blood out of which comes no good, but much mischief.

THE DIVINE SPIRIT NOT CAPRICIOUS.

Now, in regard, not simply to revivals of religion,
which I believe to be the work of the Divine Spirit,
but to the whole department of spiritual experiences,
I say they are in analogy with mental experiences;
not that they are on the same level, but that the administration of God over the human soul is in analogy
with his administration over the lower or physical elements in man, the intermediate emotions of the social
and the intellectual processes. Spiritual developments
are, all of them, under law, administered by law, as
much as any other part of nature, and to be studied,
therefore, as we study every other department of human
life. And in regard to the moral elements, all the
graces of the Spirit and all the fruits of the Spirit be-

long to education. They are to be developed by education, just as much as every other part of the mind. The belief in the immediate presence and efficacy of the Divine Spirit is not inconsistent with the belief that its immediateness and efficacy are exercised through definite laws, with a constancy that makes those laws comprehensible. It is in the possibility of this definite knowledge that the foundation is laid for a wise procedure on the part of the minister and the members of the congregation.

Once, this would have been a very audacious avowal, — I do not know but it is yet. That is to say, it may be considered audacious to preach that men, when they need humility, meekness, rapture, ecstasy, should be put upon seeking these things precisely on the same general methods as when they want the knowledge of criticism, the knowledge of history, or intellectual development in any direction. Suppose, when a father brought his boy to the Sheffield school, in order that he might be trained in engineering, the child should say, "I find it exceedingly difficult to get algebra and geometry into my head"; and his father should reply, "My son, you do not spend enough time in your closet; you ought to pray more : that would open your mind to geometry!" I should not blame a father for saying to his son, "Pray for God's help in studying geometry." But, suppose the father meant to imply that that was the way to learn algebra; that algebra would come as the fruit of prayer; and that if you only humbled yourself and prayed enough, and were in an open and receiving mood, by and by would come in algebra! Yet that is about the way in which many people pray for spiritual states. They think that if they withhold themselves from known sins, if they put themselves in a waiting position, if they open their minds freely, and then pray for meekness and humility, they will receive those conditions. Some seem to think that such things are kept already prepared, and that when one is in the right state, or has the right temperament, or the right constitution, and has prayed enough, some humility is taken and given to him; that it comes down to him in some way unsearchable and unknowable.

I should be very unwilling to be understood as setting aside, a whit, the faith of the church in the existence of the Divine Spirit, in its universality, in its speciality and personality, — I mean in the sense of acting upon individual persons. I believe it all, heartily. I believe it a good deal more than I should if I were shut up to the old theory. I regard laws as so many limbs in which, in this opaque and material world, and in that other unexplored world within us, I may trace the form of God. I think we never come so near to God as when we are in the immediate recognition of the relations of cause and effect, in regard to the operations of the outward world, or of the inward world. And by believing that all moral results are conformable to the established constitution of things, we do not obliterate faith in the Divine Spirit, but only mark out the ways through which experience and observation teach us the Divine Spirit acts. Its action is universal. It is not, I think, this secret, subtle substance by which men themselves are vital, by which they come above the line and level of physical and material organizations into that state which has never

yet been explored, whose metes and bounds no sur-
veyor can ever measure by chain or rule, whose quality
no alembic and no analysis can ever discover, — that
yet unknown thing called mind. I believe that when
we come into that state in which this begins to efflor-
esce, we enter the region where the Divine Spirit,
universal, stimulating as the sun is throughout the
hemispheres, exerts its power ; that the soul is waked
into life by the Divine Light, and that our higher raptures, rulable according to law, according to definite
exposition of law, are yet vitalized and sublimated by
the direct impact of the Divine mind. If there is such
a thing conceivable as one mind being brooded by another, one mind resting upon another, such I believe to
be, at least in figure, the method in which the human
mind is awakened and stimulated by the Divine mind.
What I plead for is, that the gifts of the Divine Spirit
are not exceptional, or capricious, without rule, without definite purpose ; but that they are to be just as
definitely expected as the results which the farmer
seeks when he sows his seed. Although God is the
God of nature, and although all the processes of nature
are under Divine sovereignty and power, yet, in that
realm there is a definiteness of expectation which is
justified by experience. All men think that when you
educate a person physically, you are to do so, not without
a belief that God helps all things and is everywhere, and
everywhere operative, but yet with a definite purpose
to make them stand, walk, throw their bodies into pos-
tures of grace, and so discipline themselves to strength.
We teach the hand all manner of manipulation and
skill, and feel that there is no irreverence in saying

we do this by natural law.   So we teach children a
thousand intermediate disciplines of affection, of love,
of taste, of obligingness, of self-denial, — a thousand
things that they must or must not do, in order to perfect
themselves.   In other words, we perfect the lower part
of men's natures by education.   That we do this with
the intellect, every one knows.   Reading and writing
may "come by nature," but we always supplement
them by teaching, and act in the schools as though the
intellect had certain laws, as though there were appropriate methods of cultivating it.

REVIVALS UNDER THE LAW OF CAUSE AND EFFECT.

But now, when we come to religion, men fly the track.
They seem to think, "Here is vagueness; here is a
realm too sacred to suppose that law operates in it,"
and it is just there that I say, in respect emphatically
to revivals of religion, that they are conformable to law,
and that that conformableness to law is in the foundation of education and knowledge, in the production
of emotion, or in the production and conduct of all
spiritual processes.   You will see, therefore, that the
ridicule which men heap upon the efforts made for the
promotion of revivals is altogether without just foundation.   They say, "Mr. Jackson has gone down to
Mill Hollow to get up a revival, I understand"; and
everybody laughs, and feels that that man is put down.
But suppose I were to say, "Mr. Jackson has gone down
to Mill Hollow to hold a temperance-meeting, and to
try to get up a public sentiment on that subject."
"Very good; they need it down there, and I hope he
will succeed."   Suppose I were to say, "Down in Mill

Hollow, I understand, there are a hundred children who have not been to school, on an average, one month in three years; and Parson Jackson has gone down to stir the people up on the subject of education, and try to get up a public spirit on the subject." Nobody would laugh at that. But if I say, "Parson Jackson has gone down to Mill Hollow to try to get up a *religious* feeling, a revival," then everybody laughs and scoffs. This could not be but for that background of impression, that a revival of religion is a thing so absolutely above human knowledge, and depends upon such capricious conditions in the Divine Spirit, that human effort in that direction is absolutely ridiculous.

If I should say, " Parson Jackson has gone over to the White Mountains to try to get up a tornado," they would laugh; or, if I should say, " Parson Jackson has taken a lever and gone east to try to pry the sun up in the morning," they would laugh : because these things are known to be outside of human power. But to say that a man is going to stir up the community in behalf of railroads, causes no one to laugh. To get up a reformation in the matter of gambling or drinking, is looked upon as normal and right; but to stir men up in behalf of the whole extent of their moral character and life, — is not that normal also? Is there anything ridiculous in that?

WHAT IS NATURE ?

It is such statements, however, that many feel to be an upheaval of the foundations, and a departure from the faith of the fathers. For example, some will ask you, "Does not such a view as this confound

11 *

nature and grace? Is it not bringing all gracious
operations down to the level of nature?" What is
nature, then? Is it a flat plane of matter? — something that lies at the very bottom of God's creation, and
is on the whole very unworthily there? Many people
talk as if nature were the lowest and the last of things.
And therefore they speak about reducing a thing to
the level of nature. What is nature? Everything that
God ever organized into being and maintained, is
nature. The rock, the soil, the herb, the insect, the
animal, man, in body and in soul; all the way from
the lowest inorganic rock up to the most inspired
genius in humanity, all that long line upward, is through
the realm of nature. Nature does not wait, either,
on this side of death; for when we shall break through,
— not by far traveling, but by dropping opacity and
the cumbering flesh, — and stand in the spiritual light
with spirits that are now perhaps nearer to us than a
hand's-breadth, — when we shall come into the other
life, still it will be nature, as I believe. For nature is
all heaven, and all earth, and all the universe of God.
Wherever, along the lines of space, the word of God has
thrilled and something has happened, there is nature;
and nothing is or can be that does not circle into that.
To reduce things to the level of nature, is to reduce
them to the level of God, which ought not to be a very
great degradation.

PHYSICAL NATURE NOT IGNOBLE.

But there are two things to be thought of, even in
respect to that use of the term which men have been
accustomed to make. I have not such an ignoble

sense of nature, — meaning by that simply the economy of the physical world round about me, — as to believe that a spiritual intuition or emotion is degraded by being spoken of in the same connection. There are a great many men, acting under the old theological heresy of the intrinsic sinfulness of matter, who curse material nature, as though God had had nothing to do in the making and sustaining of it. I do not consider that unthinking matter is to be ranked or classed with sentient matter, but *this* I think: The heavens declare the glory of God, and the earth shows his handiwork. Oh, there is not a place in the old Litchfield house where I was born that is not dear to my eye! I go back there sometimes; and the last time I went I chose not to go in the glare of day, they had so changed the place. But I stood at twilight, when just enough darkness had come down to hide the changes, and yet there was light enough to throw up above the horizon and against the sky the substance and form of the old house. It was full, to my thought, of my father and my mother, of my sisters and brothers. My heart blessed the old house for all that it had had in it; for all the care that it had had, for all its sweet associations. It was stained through with soul color. It was full, as it were, with the blood of life.

The mother who, by reason of increasing wealth, is selling off the old furniture as she moves out of her cottage into her mansion, sells everything cheerfully till she comes to the cradle. " No, my dear, no; you never shall sell that." What is it? It is an old, rude, heavy, clumsy thing, which rolls, when you rock it, like a farmer's wagon going over bridges, and makes all sorts of noises. But there is no money that can buy that. There her seven children have lain; there she has had songs and prayers; there have been tears and heart experiences unutterable, — and they have sanctified the cradle. The globe on which the foot of Christ has trod cannot be ignoble to me. The heavens and the earth are full of God to me. There is not a bird that sings, there is not a flower that blossoms, there is not a lichen that colors the rock, there is not a thing that happens in the world, that I do not say to myself, "That is God's thought and matter." The world is embossed and embroidered and filled full; it records the tastes, the habitudes, the thoughts, the feelings, of my God. Matter by association becomes sacred to me. If you hear men talk about degrading things to nature and to matter, say to them: The right way is to level up, not to level down. Carry the idea of nature and of matter up so high that it will not be a degrading association.

When men say, therefore, that to declare the work of God in revivals of religion is entirely compatible with the system of moral laws, and the results which are the works of the Divine Spirit actually producible by taking advantage of these laws, — when men say that this is to reduce grace to the level of natural law, I think they talk either on a false system, or without knowing what they are saying. For it is no degradation, any more than it is a degradation for me to say that men learn refinement, intellectual culture, taste, beauty, or any other thing, by the application of suitable laws. It is undertaking to find out what God did, and thought, and meant, and to follow that.

Then it is said, "Does it not dishonor God? Does it not take from him his prerogatives? Is it not a vain assumption on the part of man, that he can do what it is the province of the Divine Spirit to do? Can man convert himself? Is not conversion the work of God directly?" Admit that it is — which I do not admit — the sole work of the Divine Spirit; this would not interfere with the ground of moral education, and would not touch the ground on which I place revivals of religion. Although some specific parts of any general system may be more immediately personal and absolutely divine in their causation, it does not affect the fact that the system itself may be a mixture of divine and human volition. But it seems to me that every element that goes to the constitution of a revival, and every element, too, that goes to right teaching, and right training, and the production of all kinds of Christian feeling in a church, — every one of these will one day be solvable; they will come within the circuit of human knowledge; and we shall profit just as much by this knowledge as we have profited by knowledge in the whole economy of society. Do not men live better, are they not wiser and better, for having studied out those phenomena which by the old Hebrews were supposed to be the immediate results of Divine power? God spoke to the Hebrews, when it thundered. We do not any more suppose that thunder is the voice of God. God made grass to grow, as it were, by touching it with his finger. We know that grass grows through the impulse of the Divine Spirit, but it is the Divine Spirit sent through various channels. Are we worse off for the knowledge that the Divine agency is both immediate and remote? So it is said that God, in old times, put it into the hearts of men to do a thousand things with irresistible impulse, using them as machines, starting them as an engineer starts his cylinder, setting it going and pumping right and left. That used to be substantially the idea of the way in which the Spirit acted upon the minds of men.

THE SCIENCE OF RELIGION.

Now, more and more is the study of art and science making man powerful, facilitating his efforts, raising the tone of society, stimulating general civilization. So, I believe, one day, piety itself will be carried to a higher level; it will be purified, it will be systematized, it will be better studied, more easily understood, less fitful, less disposed to moods. The Spirit of God is bringing his church into that higher state in which religion also becomes a part of science. That is to say, the way of God in religion will be made known to us just as God is made known to us in physical and intellectual affairs. In that day, I believe we shall have a higher state of piety, for I do not believe that the church of God has more than come to its blossom, if to that. I do not believe that it is going to die under the rocks. I think that it is going to be purged out by the life of science. I believe that many of the systems now held will change the forms and the economies of civilization; but the great substance of religious life is so true, it is so ineffably and transcendently superior to every other, that, in the last unfolding of the Divine Providence, it will be as conspicuously superior to what it now is as every other part of the human economy is superior to what it was in times gone by.

DEPENDENCE ON GOD NOT GIVEN UP.

But this teaching that all moral and spiritual results are subject to the investigation and control of men, — does it not weaken our sense of dependence upon God ? It may, but it ought not to. What is our sense of dependence upon God ? I depend on God for the continuation of my reason; but while that is preserved fresh and strong, I feel bound to depend on myself. I do not feel at liberty to depend on God, and then sit up all night; to depend on God for the bright exercise of reason, and then use myself up by twenty hours of continuous study, when I have immediately before me a great effort to make in a public assembly. If I have to preach on Sunday, I pray God to help me. Help me do what ? Help me not to be foolish on Saturday; help me not to use myself all up in talking and laughing, not to eat anything improper; help me to be in a perfect state of bodily health; help me to have elasticity of spirit; help me to have such entire control of myself as that my life shall beat in the higher part of my mind, so that all my moral nature shall be luminous, full, impetuous, and wanting to corruscate. So I ask God to help me. Not directly to help me reason, but to help me that I may use reason according to its laws, that I may understand what he gave to me and how to employ it. No man depends on God so much as he who believes that laws are the indexes of the Divine will ; and he truly depends on God who, seeing natural laws, obeys them. There is no other explainable dependence but that. And certainly the rational explanation of revivals does not decrease that dependence, but rather increases it.

" But does it not inspire in men a vain sense of confidence ? " Is a farmer inspired with vain self-confidence, because he can build a wall ? Because a man can plow his ground and get forty bushels of wheat to the acre, does that inspire in him vain self-confidence ? Is not success in following revealed laws the way to encourage men to normal action and feeling ? If I find out how the graces of the Spirit are produced by the constitution of my nature and the constitution of God in my nature, if I find out the truest and the best way by which to develop them, does that inspire, or tend to inspire, me with vain self-confidence ? The augmentation of the sense of power in right channels and right directions is wholesome, it is good.

Without, therefore, arguing any further on this subject, which is preliminary, I say that we may approach the topic of the production of revivals of religion with perfect boldness, without any sense of irreverence, and without feeling that we are in any way transgressing either the revealed word or the truth as manifested through God's providence.

WHAT IS A REVIVAL ?

What is a revival of religion ? Describing it from the outside, it is a deep interest in personal religion, in a church or in a neighborhood. Or, to give a very general definition, it is the existence, in a large number of persons at the same time, of strong moral feeling. It is the excitement of a great many persons together, their excitement having social relations. It is the excitement of many people together on one subject, and that one subject their moral state, their religious condition. It is the excitement of a great many persons together on the subject of religion, each one with reference to his own personal feeling. It is not with reference to the public well-being, but to each man's own personal well-being. These, I believe, comprehend the phenomena of revivals of religion. They will vary according to circumstances. That is to say, sometimes the impression will come silently, like the dew through the night, and all you know in the morning is that it is there. At other times, it comes with a rush, as a summer storm comes after long drought. At other times, this great, pervasive feeling in the church or the community is the result of deliberate planning or action. In other words, it has all the varieties that belong to nature. It adapts itself to the conditions of men, the nature of the community, and the moods in which that community exists. The phenomena are infinitely various.

THE AWAKENING OF CONSCIENCE.

In the first place, revivals sometimes take on the form, simply, of increased attention. I have heard my father say that his first effort at all revivals was to produce attention, thoughtfulness. But as this is merely the swelling of the seed, the first germ in the development of a true revival feeling is an unusual sensibility of conscience, or of moral sense. More usually, a revival begins with a feeling arising from the application of an ideal rule to life. It is accompanied with

a sense of low living. Men have generally this feeling
in a community: "We are not living right; we are
not fit to die. Something needs to be done before we
are prepared to meet our God." Now, all these impressions are a kind of obscure utterance of conscience.
The real thing that is taking place is that the conscience of the community is waking up, and is beginning to apply to thought and feeling new measures, or,
if not new measures in conception, yet new measures
in practice. Old knowledges become vivid, and there
is, throughout the community, an actual personal sense
of unworthiness, guilt, sinfulness, whatever term you
choose to employ; and that is the first marked
symptom. It may be tender, gentle, sweet as a song,
or it may be impetuous and harsh, rending as a storm.
That will depend upon the conditions in which the
community is and has been, the nature of the instruction the people have had, the obliquities through which
they have gone, the degradation or the elevation which
has previously taken place in them.

THE SENSE OF DANGER.

Then, there is the sense of danger, too. Under some
administrations that sense of danger will predominate,
and all that goes on in the church and community will
go on under the stimulus of fear. But if this renewed
excitement of conscience, or this activity of the moral
sense, could be made to act under the consciousness of
the essential hatefulness of wrong, and thus create a
revolt from moral inferiority, a sense of something
nobler than fear, — a sense of obligation to God, of the
shame and dishonor of 'receiving everything from the

hand of the benefactor and returning nothing but selfish and quarrelsome ingratitude, — that would be a far more wholesome feeling. But it runs through the entire scale of motive, from this more noble sense of the unbecomingness, the unworthiness, the ingratitude, and the dishonor of sin, clear down to the lowest tone in the base, — the fear of the consequences of sin, a deeper sense of moral responsibility, an increased apprehensiveness of danger.

THE STRUGGLE.

. Then comes the struggle. The struggle that takes place in revivals of religion, psychologically stated, is the attempt of the reason and of the moral sentiments to take ascendency of the passions and appetites. It may assume a doctrinal form, or it may assume a practical form. That is to say, sometimes the struggle is of a dissipated man to break away from his dissipation; sometimes, of an ordinary, respectable business man to break away from certain improprieties in the conduct of his business; and sometimes, in highly intellectual, theologically indoctrinated natures, it may be the struggle as to whether a man will submit his will to the supremacy of the will of God. But these are only forms. The real thing that takes place is a nascent effort of the superior faculties in man to dominate the inferior and come to sovereignty in the soul. It involves a clear and emphatic view of God, of the future of our existence. I have ridden many and many a night in storms and darkness, especially in the West, where my early life was largely missionary, when it was so dark I could not see the horse's ears before me, and sometimes when storms were coming on or were actually raging. I think there are no phenomena, not even burning prairies, or, still more terrible, burning forests in the night, through which I have ridden when the swelling streams threatened to carry me away, — nothing so impressive to me as those sudden flashes of light that revealed to me, as I rode over some elevation, the whole outlying country, so that I could see hill and valley, distant hut, log-cabin, the outlines of the trees, the whole shape of the clouds in the heavens. The whole was instantaneous, and but for a second, and then darkness shut down again. Now, where men are riding, as it were, in the profound darkness of an unconverted and sinful life, and these moral illuminations come and throw the light instantaneously, so that the eternal world is brought near to their consciousness, — immortality, all that is meant in God and heaven, so far as they can comprehend them, all that is meant in life here, all that is right and wrong, — when all this is brought, as in a moment, in a vision, before a man's mind, it is one of the grandest experiences that ever comes to the human soul. You may laugh at men under conviction, but the evolutions that are taking place in the souls of men, when God's Spirit is working upon them in revivals of religion, have in them more grandeur than the evolutions at Waterloo, or in any battle that was ever fought upon earth.

THE VICTORY.

Then there is a transition from this state of struggle to one of victory, purpose, consecration; one in which, by the Spirit of God working co-ordinately with human reason and with the human will, a man determines his character and his after-life, passes from the lower plane of selfishness and pride into the plane of love to God and love to men, with a purpose permanent, irrefragable, supreme. These, briefly stated, are the points of the phenomena that take place in a revival of religion. Thoughtfulness, leading to an excited moral sense; a new measure of life and duty; a struggle and a victory, in which, when the constituent elements are examined, it will be found that a perfect revolution has taken place in the interior economy. The man that before lived for himself, now lives for God and for his fellow-man. He who lived only for time is now living for eternity as well. These are the things that take place.

HOW TO PRODUCE THESE RESULTS.

Now the question arises, How shall we attempt to produce these? You have said that they are producible, how shall they be produced? I may mention briefly, as the result of my own observation, that there are favoring circumstances in Providence which determine times and seasons in this matter. All seasons are not alike favorable. All methods, we know, are not alike wise, neither are all seasons propitious, for the procuring of these results. For example : it would be unwise to attempt to excite in a community or in a church a very wide-spread, deep, and general moral excitement while the whole community is burning and blazing with political excitement; because you cannot have two such excitements at the same time, and the religious feeling in any community is generally so feeble that it is not

strong enough to resist this greater excitement. There
are single instances in which revivals of religion, well
inaugurated, have survived political excitements; but in
those cases they have been strong before the other excitements began, and they have been shielded and sep-
arated. Two rivers of equal force may come together
and flow on together, but rills entering a river are lost
in it. These major excitements overmaster the minor
ones; and the moral excitement in this world is usually
the minor one, because of the feebleness of this element
in men. You must lie upon your oars and wait for
day, watching times and seasons. Then there is a great
deal of difference in the time of the year, whether
people can get out to meetings or can spare the time.
Among hundreds of revivals I have known only one
that occurred in the midst of harvest; because men
cannot spare the time from the harvest-field. You want
time and leisure, and therefore you want those intervals
of the year when men's occupations favor. Business
has much to do with times and seasons. For instance,
sometimes men are hot with speculation, and the whole
air is full of it. That is not a favorable time for any
processes leading toward this production of common
moral feeling. But, on the other hand, the reaction
comes. Once in about ten years you may make up your
minds that things will go down; and immediately following the universal bankruptcy, or the feeling that
men are bankrupt, is a good time to strike in. I do not
think that times of general sickness are opportune, — a
little remarkable, that. But where wide-spread sick-
nesses afflict the community, they generally harden the
heart. It is almost never a good time for revivals after

the prevalence of sickness, but business overthrows make the best of all preparations. There is nothing that seems to cut the roots of man's dependence on this world like that. There is no other state in which men seem so to want something to hold them up, no other state of mind in which men are so drooping, despondent, and longing, in which they feel so much the vanity of this life, and the need of something better than anything in this life, as they do when the hand of God's providence has crushed their idols, — their money. Those are precious times, — times never to be lost sight of.

Then there may be specially favorable circumstances in communities. And, although general sickness may not be favorable to revivals, sometimes the death of a single person will be blessed to the whole community. In a case within my knowledge, the drowning of two young ladies was the means of producing such universal tenderness and seriousness, that it culminated in a general revival of religion. So a young man, the pride of the village, brought home from college to be buried, of whom his townsmen had hoped the best and the noblest things, and in whose death they were stricken, will produce a state of mind which, if wisely followed up, will lead to the raising up of a score of other young men that will more than fill his place. All these things are to be watched in the community, and your efforts at revivals are to be at particular seasons of the year. As you sow in spring and reap in autumn, as you adapt all the economies of industry to varying seasons, so you are to adapt your moral culture of men to those peculiarities of God's providence, which, with a little care and observation, every one may discern.

QUESTIONS AND ANSWERS.

Q. Do you say that revivals are sure to follow when means are employed in the appropriate way, at appropriate seasons ?

MR. BEECHER. — Just as sure as results are to follow in husbandry. It is not every man that plows well and sows well who gets his harvest; but still, that is the average course of things, and the probability is such as to encourage everybody. It is not every ship that is well built that is lucky, and makes good voyages. There is n't anything that is absolutely certain. I feel, though, in regard to revivals of religion in my own church, that if the circumstances of the community favor, if those means are taken by which men are brought together and kept together long enough to produce a distinct moral impression upon them, and follow it up continuously, the result is just as certain as any other result in the operations of cause and effect in life. I believe, you know, that religion is right living, according to the nature that God has given us; and that when you begin to open up to men their nature and show them what is the great law of rectitude, and then press that right home upon them, ordinarily those who have been raised in Christian families will go right forward. I honor God in the faith that the mind will act according to those laws which God has given to it.

Q. Yesterday, in speaking of different denominations as having seasons of revival, our Episcopal brethren were mentioned as, in some sort, an exception. Where would you place their season of Lent, with reference to its bearing upon revivals ?

MR. BEECHER. — I thought afterwards, on returning

home, that revivals, in the usual sense of that term, were believed in by Bishop McIlvaine, and by his successor in Brooklyn, Dr. Cutler. I have known individual instances of that kind, but my impression is that, in general, our brethren in the Episcopal Church prefer to rely, not upon spontaneous and irregular influences, but upon steady and constant action of training institutions. The Lenten services may possibly be considered as an approach towards a revival state.

REV. DR. BACON. — Isn't it an arrangement to have a revival of religion every year, at a certain season ?

MR. BEECHER. — Yes, that is the design. It is to have the spring of the year come in with a very strong impression upon the minds of men of the great historical facts of Christianity, with their appropriate results upon the heart.

Q. You speak of some seasons as being more favorable than others to the production of revivals. After all, don't you think that one of the great duties of ministers and of churches is to watch the indications, the leadings of God's providence in the spiritual world, as by analogy we do in the physical world ?

MR. BEECHER. — Yes, sir, unquestionably. Only, I have known a great many ministers who spent the most of their lives in waiting for God. I suppose there is scarcely any church in which two consecutive years pass without possibilities of developing more or less the revival spirit. I repeat what I said yesterday, and what I shall have occasion to speak of more fully, that revivals have themselves a progressive history in any church. The first revival, in many of its features, will never be repeated. The next one will be an advance upon that, unless the interval has been so long that the first has been forgotten. But, take a period of twenty years, and let there be in that twenty years eight revivals of religion, and the revivals themselves will show that there has been a process of development. The last one will be purer, sweeter, more efficacious, less physical, with less of the awful, if I may so say, than the first one. In any two or three years, it seems to me that a man whose heart is warm, whose zeal is strong, will find openings and opportunities for either partial or very general revivals. In almost any large parish, with outlying neighborhoods, a revival may take place in one neighborhood, but not in the whole parish, — sometimes in one portion, and sometimes in another. And these little affairs are to be taken care of, no matter if there are only five or six gathered in; they are precious fruits. Never refuse to glean.

Q. My question would relate to the philosophy of revivals: Where is the real initiative? Is it in the human agent, or is it in the Divine?

MR. BEECHER. — Everything that I have is divine when I am acting in the line of law. I believe myself to be under the inspiration of God at all times, and that that is covered by the injunction, "Whether ye eat or drink, or whatever ye do, do all for the glory of God." If I sit down to-day to write to those whom I love, the very act of writing is something sweet and pleasant to me. Not that I like to write, for I do not, very much; but, after all, it is the perfume that comes over from the other side that makes it sweet. Now, if one has the sense of God, and lives with God, and feels that God is his father; if he has the sense of sonship, and carries within himself the thought, " All things are mine, because I am Christ's," — then there is no part of his life that will not refer to God. Under those circumstances, I say, that when I see there is a little opening, and I am moved to go right into it, it is the Divine Spirit that moves me. This body is divine. God took a spark of himself, and put it in me, and called it Beecher. There may be an irreverent way to take that, yet there is another, — the affectionate and the real way.

Q. As I understand it, you look upon a revival of religion as what might be called a phenomenon, and not, perhaps, the regular, normal condition of a church. Would you consider that a church ought to be, or can possibly be, in a continued revival state ?

MR. BEECHER. — Yes, and no. That is to say, no, if you take your type of a revival from that condition into which churches go when they have not for a long time had one, and which is like the first throwing up of the soil, with the disintegration of rocks, full of violent effects, and therefore full of reactions and rebounds, with much allowance to be made all the way through. In that highly wrought state, a church could not possibly exist all the time. But suppose that to be the first in order, and that the same church, after about two years, has another revival; it will come in less violently, with less retort, with less intense convictions. And your unthinking, unwise, good old men will pray that God would give them another such shaking as they had two years ago. Well, he won't give them another such shaking, because that was a shaking with twenty-five years of deadness before it; this has had but two years of comparatively little falling off to precede it.

It will be much richer, sounder, safer, deeper, more comprehensive, but less phenomenal. Then, after two or three years, will come in another divine work of grace. That will come as tranquilly as the morning breaks out of the night. And some will believe that the work is not deep, because there are so few physical manifestations in it; that is, nobody breaks down, crying, "God be merciful to me a sinner!" with a shout of "Amen!" all over the house. That is what is called a very powerful work of grace. I think the silences of nature are greater than its thunders. I think that what is going on to-day in the meadows, where millions of pumps are drawing up the water through the trees and through the air, is far more tremendous than any enginery which men build and set in noisy motion. So, oftentimes the silences of religion are far the more powerful. And when you adopt that belief in the management of revivals, till men are accustomed to religious things, there is no violent contrast to the foregoing state, and they will have grown and grown until the whole congregation have come up to the higher level of thinking. Revivals of religion in that state are continuous, but not in the lower, convulsive form in which they usually begin in untrained populations, or in churches which are not accustomed to them.

When you ask me, therefore, if revivals of religion can continue all the time, I say that these climacteric revivals cannot. I do not think there is a month in the year in which there are not conversions in my congregation, and I do not think there is a year in which there are not hundreds of converts brought in. We do not look for very great overflowings now. One reason, I

think, is, there are a thousand men and women there
who are living very near to the sweetness of the divine
life, living sympathetically active lives all the time, for-
getting themselves, working for others, cheerfully, hope-
fully, socially, and gladly; and people, coming in, are
at once affected by that spirit, and they begin to blossom, as a bush transplanted from the north to a far
southern latitude begins to blossom.

Q. Would it not be consistent with your view to hold that
prayer is more essential to the production of effects in a revival,
than it is to the production of effects in farming?

MR. BEECHER. — Certainly.. That is to say, prayer is
more nearly related to the results you want to produce.
Guano is better for farming than prayer, but prayer is
the guano of spiritual life. Pray always. I hold that
prayer is to a man what perfume is to a flower, — it
cannot open its mouth without perfume coming out of
it. And the praying always, the thought, the feeling,
the taste, the sense of pleasure, the social gladness,
all the while effervesces, so that it takes the upward
tendency. It reports itself continually through the
higher feelings towards God, and that I suppose to
be prayer, — communion, God with us. I suppose you
sought to prevent the impression getting abroad that
I regarded a revival as a kind of mechanical matter,
like farming, or a stroke of business.

Q. No. But you say the supernatural is exerted in both, and
is exerted according to law. I simply wanted to have you bring
out this, — which I supposed was implied in your view, — that
among the antecedents in the production of this class of effects is
prayer; and in a sense different from what it is in the production
of effects in husbandry, for instance.

MR. BEECHER. — Ah, I do not know that I should say that.

Q. Well, farming goes on in heathen countries, it may be, if they are equally acquainted with husbandry, as well as in Christian countries, without prayer.

MR. BEECHER. — Well, that shows that without prayer you can farm, but it does not show that you can farm without the divine effluence. It only shows that God does not always measure his influence by prayer.

Q. Can revivals be produced without prayer?

MR. BEECHER. — I have seen many men produce revivals of religion that I did not think were very praying . men. I thought their work *limped*, and was very imperfect. Although I do not disesteem — I exceedingly value — the use of prayer, yet it does not seem to me that it bears the same relation to this result which you seem to think it does. It has *a* relation, and a very important one.

Q. It seems to me it is perfectly consistent with your general view of the government of law in the case, to suppose that prayer is one of the appointed antecedents in regard to spiritual blessings.

MR. BEECHER. — It is one of them.

Q. And a very important one?

MR. BEECHER. — Well, I put this case to you: Suppose that I go home and find my little girl, five years old, in whom my heart is bound up, dead: that I am so constituted that I would not stop preaching because of my child's death, but would feel a heroic sense of duty to preach on that very account: that I should go into my pulpit, and it were known to all my people that my little girl Mary was gone, and I should stand there and preach just as well as I could, the tears running down my cheeks, my utterance choked, and that the word should come back to me on prayer-meeting night, when the lecture-room was crowded, that there was a powerful impression there. Would you say that that work had been brought on by the superior instrumentality of prayer? Was n't it that Divine providence, acting on the sympathies, the imagination, the heart and its best feelings? On the other hand, I have known, in churches where it was as dry as Sahara, many a godly man labor through weeks and months without any external encouragement; but, after all, there was gathering there a moral momentum, to break out by and by in tides. Now, I say that prayer is an aid, a powerful antecedent; yet I would not say that it is the indispensable and inevitable one.

Q. Suppose that, when all those young people were got together in the lecture-room, there were no prayer, would there be much of a revival of religion?

MR. BEECHER. — But the revival has begun, and of course you could not help praying under the circumstances.

Q. Suppose it has not begun. Take Habakkuk, for example, where he says, "In the midst of the years make known; in wrath, remember mercy." And then the Psalmist, "Wilt thou not revive us again, that our people may rejoice in thee?" There are two instances of prayer, and Mr. Barnes founded his series of sermons on revivals upon one of these very texts. And on the day of Pentecost men prayed for the outpouring of the Spirit. What do you make of these instances?

MR. BEECHER. — I don't want to make anything of

them. They *are* made. You put the question as if I had propounded the theory that revivals of religion are possible without prayer, and that there was no important relation of prayer. I say, No ; I say that that is one of the channels through which causation seems to flow. It is but one. You brought up Habakkuk's revival, — or one that he prayed for and did n't get.

X.

THE CONDUCT OF REVIVALS.

CLOSED last week, in discussing the question of revivals of religion, with the consideration of times and seasons, such as might favor, or such as might hinder, the development of a religious enthusiasm in a community. We must bring to mind again, in going forward with this subject, the prime idea, the root of revival; it is the development in a church, or in a community, of a deep religious enthusiasm under social aspects and with reference to some immediate results. That, then, which shall tend to arrest the attention of men, to interest them in religious matters, to produce a normal excitement which may be called enthusiasm, and to turn this enthusiasm to certain immediate and personal ends, — that is the thing to be sought by every one who strives to develop among his people a revival of religion. Revivals are in no sense to be regarded as antagonistic to regular institutional work. They do something which cannot be done by ordinary instrumentalities. They do many things far more easily than they can be done in any other way. There are men who can be lifted out of the conditions in which they are living when there is a swell in the whole community, that could not be lifted without this collateral social aid. I am not speaking of what is within the power of the Divine Spirit. I am only speaking of what we know to be facts in the ordinary development of Christian work. Without a doubt, by the exercise of Divine power, anything might be done; but, without a doubt, the Divine power does not act in communities, except by methods, channels, laws, instruments; and we are to watch and study these, in order that we may put ourselves in the line of the working of Providence.

EFFECT OF REVIVALS WITHIN THE CHURCH.

The results, then, at which we aim, in revivals of religion, are twofold. First, the immediate conversion of men from selfishness and worldliness to a Christian and godly life; and, secondly, the exaltation of Christian character in the church to a higher plane, to a nobler form of development. Even if there were to be no ingathering from the world, a refreshing — as it is called in old-fashioned language — a refreshing of grace in a church is pre-eminently desirable, pre-eminently a blessing from God, though it may stop with the members of the church. For, as our power is not numerical, but moral, it is not so much the number as the quality of the members in a church that determines its power. A church of twenty men who are eminent in grace and goodness is a larger church, if you measure size by power, than a church of two thousand that are living a very low and worldly life. So that when men in the church have been living in routine Christianity, without any very active development of personal faith and of the sweetness of the Christian graces, it may often be the case that a revival of religion will do its Divine work within the church, and, though there are not many to be counted as added to the list, the church itself will be immensely strengthened, and its power augmented. The desire of gathering in a large number from without is not indeed unnatural or reprehensible; nor is the work unimportant. But it is still more important that, in gathering in these men, those that gather should themselves be built up, developed, and made more powerful.

BORN AGAIN.

As to the former purpose, we seek in a revival of religion the ingathering of men to a new life. I read in the Word, — I had almost said, with regret, — "Ye must be born again"; because my heart looks at it in such a way that I feel that, instead of being a duty, it is the greatest privilege; it is a wonder of grace almost contravening the order of nature. "Ye *may* be born again," as if it were a permission, would seem to me almost a better rendering. It is true that it is imperative, — "Ye *must* be"; but, after all, "Ye may" is still more sweet, and not less imperative. If a man, after living forty-five or fifty years, had committed such errors and mistakes as to be compelled to retire bankrupt into private life, all his business experience only showing him that he had gone wrong, and could then have the privilege of beginning again, with all his added experience, just as fresh and hopeful as if he had never made a mistake, what a privilege that would seem to him! But this he cannot do. He has no credit; and, in the ordinary tenure of life, there is no time, after the fiftieth year, for a man to change the impressions of the community about him. The circumstances are all against him, and he must go on, and probably end his life in poverty. See how it is with Christian character. The community is unspeakably more lax than God is, and permits all manner of prevarications, all manner of deceits, all manner of cruelties. While men are moderately respectable, it winks at them and covers them and indulges them, until they go below a certain line, and then there is nothing that has such lion's-teeth as the community. When a man is broken down by sinning and wants to come back again; when he has stolen; when he has betrayed fiduciary trusts; when he has been sent once to the penitentiary for a public crime, and every man stands against him, if not with fierceness, yet with cold distrust, and with unwilling-ness to help him,—if then a man could come back from the prison and have it said to him, "Now, then, by proper conduct you may stand just as you stood before in the community," what a bounty of blessing it would be to him! But here is the word of God's grace, saying to men that have lived for ten, twenty, thirty years in the way of transgression, "Now you may begin again just like a little child, and take a new start. God is lenient, gracious, merciful, slow to anger, abundant in goodness, forgiving iniquity, transgression, and sin." It is this one thing that we bear in mind,—the possibility of renewing the moral character of men. The great point of doubt has been whether it is possible to renew moral character suddenly, whether it can be done by afflatus. No, it cannot. That is, character is a thing that grows slowly, but the beginnings of it can be established; the foundations can be relaid of elements which go to establish new habits, and a character can be begun on a new basis. This may be very sudden. A gambler may cease in a moment to gamble, and never touch again the instruments of deceit. A drunkard may, in a single moment, come to a decision by which he shall never again touch the fatal cup. The effects of his past misconduct will not pass away at once; but the man has made a stand that will affect his whole character for time and for eternity. A man may be pursuing a dissolute life, and in a single hour he may set the rudder so that his whole track after that will be upon another line. The beginnings may be sudden. It is the knowledge of the fact that there is a power by which men, not in single instances alone, but in ranks and in multitudes, may be brought in, that inspires us to work in revivals of religion. Men may be changed. We do not get up, therefore, a religious enthusiasm in a social form simply to enjoy ourselves and to exalt the feeling of the church, but because in the heat thus generated you can develop in wicked men a newness of life which it would seem very difficult to develop under any other circumstances. This is the language of experience and observation, and not merely of theory.

WHERE TO BEGIN REVIVAL WORK.

The first question that would naturally come up in treating of how to begin is: In working for a revival

of religion, shall the man who has the conduct of affairs begin with the church, or shall he begin with the
community? And this question becomes somewhat
more important, because there have been a great many
revivalists, as they are called, who have had the gift or
power given them by the Master of the church of developing this enthusiasm of religion in a social form in
communities. Mr. Avery was accustomed — and, if
alive, I suppose he would still follow that course — to
refuse to say a single word to sinners until he had
dealt with the church. He usually called them together, set their sins in order before their eyes, and
demanded of them certain expiatory experiences; and
when he had got the church broken in, then he turned
to the other sinners, and opened the doors of hope and
grace for them. I don't say that this is not proper sometimes; but it was, I think, his uniform practice, on the
theory that it is in vain to expect anything to be done
with men out of the church, while the stumbling-block
of the church lies right in their way. Others have pursued a directly opposite course, and have begun first to
deal with the congregation at large. Others — as Dr.
Finney, for instance — have attempted to develop a
large system of doctrinal views, and to bring the community very generally under a common theological
influence, before they began to make any important
strokes for results; intellectualizing, indoctrinating the
community for a long time. I am not here to criticise
that; but this I say, there is no prescriptive way, and
there is no one way. You must determine by circumstances. If you were to ask General Moltke what was
the proper mode of taking a fort, from the north or the

south, from the east or the west, he would laugh at you. He would say that the way to take a fort is to find where it is weakest, and to attack there. There are circumstances in which your force should be concentrated on the church; there are circumstances in which it should not. In my own ministry, I have considered the church and the people outside of it as all sinners together, and I have worked for the whole crowd. It is true that a united church, brought into a high spiritual state, will have a very powerful moral influence upon the world outside; but it is just as true that a single conversion outside will be a trumpet-call to wake up a whole church. The action from the outside to the inside is just as easy, often, as from the inside to the outside. Carry on both systems. Help the church by society. Help society by the church. Work one against the other. Don't fall into routine, or into set schools of revivalism. It is spiritual engineering, and you are to judge by the circumstances and the facts in the case what is the wisest and best thing to do.

PREPARATION IN THE PREACHER.

As to the means that are to be employed to develop a revival in the church, first and foremost I mention preaching; and, in order to this, much depends on your own state of mind. I think that, almost always, a man has in his own heart the prophecy of these things. I have waked up in spring mornings, and the air has smelt differently from what it did before. I have gone out of doors, not thinking that it was spring, but it was brought home to me by the changed aspect of things around. So I have found, in my own ministry, that

when my heart was right for this work of God, I somehow had it brought to me in a way which inspired courage and zeal and purpose; an intensity of feeling that
assured me I was going to succeed,—not I, but the grace
of God that was in me.   I had a courage, a sort of certi-
tude in me.   "The time has come! the time has come!"
and I went down into the work with the feeling, "I will
not be denied! I will have this blessing!   Slay me, but
give me this!" And where a man has even the smallest
beginnings of this feeling, he is pretty sure to impart it.

Now, how shall a man come at it, if he has n't it?
I might say to a pastor, "Art thou a master in Israel,
and knowest not these things?"   You have not had a
charge, and so I don't blame you.   In what way shall
a man who has the cure of souls and is waiting for
souls; who believes in God and immortality, in the
Lord Jesus Christ, in the dying and necessitous condition of men, — in what way shall he come into active
sympathy with them?   Suppose a surgeon should say
to me, going down to a great military hospital, "I am
going down to a great work, and I don't know but
my zeal and courage will flag; how would you advise
me to prepare to take an interest in this thing and
sympathize with these poor wounded soldiers?"   If
he needed telling, he would not be fit to be a surgeon.
The circumstances themselves will be all the incitement he needs.   When a man looks over his congregation, and thinks of them, feels for them, prays for
them, carries them in his heart, when they are really
dear to him, — in part because they are dear to Christ,
who is dearer to him than life itself, — it seems to me he
needs very little instruction on this matter.   Only this:

if you have cares that are freighting and harassing you, lay them aside. If you have worldly business, or anything of that kind, that is absorbing your time and preventing the kindling in you of an enthusiastic devotion to your work, put that aside, no matter what it may cost you. If you find your own spiritual feelings have been scattered, take those means which you recommend to your people, — your Bible, your closet. Humble yourself before God. But I beseech you to avoid that kind of crawling, that prostration, that takes the very manhood out of a man. I don't think God wants to have a man crawl before him like a worm. I don't think he is any more pleased to see that than you would be to see your children act so. I have a little dog at the farm that, when I come home, is so exceedingly glad that he lies down and squirms and rolls over on his back, so that I want to kick him. If I had a child that acted so toward me, · I should not esteem him the more. That same dog, although he is so affectionate, will kill chickens, and he never can hide the working of his conscience, — for he has a moral nature in him, — and I know just as soon as I see Frolic, whether he has been killing chickens. If I point my finger downward he is so submissive, and flattens himself like a pancake, and crawls up to me for forgiveness! Now, a dog don't know any better, but a man ought to. And I have seen men who seemed to think that if they *emptied* themselves before God and made themselves mean, and said all manner of self-abasing things, it would fit them for the work. No! Manliness! No doubt every man has enough to confess, but God wants men to come to him as though they were his sons. I am a son of God, discrowned, dishonored by imperfection, by manifold transgression, but my Father's blood is in me. I am a son of God! I will confess my sin, but I will stand before him as his son still. I am willing to be chastised, but I am not willing to crawl in the dust, as if I were not an immortal creature. It is not necessary to weaken yourself so. But pour out your heart with strong desires before God. Love men! Love God! Work!

Now, as soon as a man comes into that state, if he is going to be successful, his preaching will be intensely earnest, it will be exceedingly clear, it will be personal. So much for the state of mind preparatory to preaching.

SPECIAL KIND OF PREACHING REQUIRED.

At other times you are giving general instruction, but now you converge the knowledge that men are supposed to have. You are bringing it to a definite purpose. When a man is stating law in the lecture-room, he pursues one course; but when he stands before a jury, to win a case, all that he ever knew is concentrated for a definite purpose. He thinks of their verdict. We preach a great many sermons, and properly, which are to promote meditation, which are to bring forth their fruit gradually in the family and in the community at large. That is well enough; but when revivals have set in, our preaching is for immediate results in the hearts and souls and consciences of our fellow-men. So that, while every sermon is an instruction, it is also a plea. Every sermon is to have in it a grasp, an intensity of hold upon men, that shall, from day to day and from week to week, have its influence. You shall feel

in yourself that every time you preach a sermon you
have drawn some man, you have gained some man.
That is the ideal; that is the aim.

In preaching, in revivals of religion, the great things
you wish to secure are the reason, the moral sense, and
the imagination of men. Men work more by imagination than we suppose; not in the form in which it is
associated with poetry, but with that action of it which
brings invisible things to sight, which enlarges the
scope of existence, — in short, which brings the eternal
future very near to men. Sermons must bring out
those truths of God's word that are sure to have effect.
They must bring out those truths which satisfy the judgment, the common-sense of men; which also frequently
arraign and satisfy the conscience; and which do these
things in the light of the higher relations which men
sustain to the future and to the government of God. I
say this, because many people suppose that, in revivals
of religion, the only thing to do is to address the feelings, to sing men along, to exhort them along, to carry
them along they scarcely know how. There is a place
for singing and for the social exercises in the subordinate meetings; but a minister ought never to preach so
well, so strongly, so clearly, and so compactly, never
with such appeal to a man's deepest nature and through
his imagination to his whole being, as in the initial state
of revivals of religion.

FREQUENCY OF SERVICES.

As to the amount of preaching that is to be done, or
the number of meetings that are to be held, I would
say that depends on circumstances. In good old New

England times, to a reflective people, accustomed to argue, cautious, conservative, you might preach powerfully on Sunday, have one extra meeting during the week, and perhaps one or two more prayer-meetings in neighborhoods. That would serve to bring people forward. They would get along on that. But take later communities that are full of vital influence, nimble, enterprising, active, with fugitive plans and thoughts, changing every day, rushing, — why, that would produce scarcely any impression upon them; and the proper treatment is by frequent meetings and continuous meetings, by iteration that shall overcome all the distractions outside of them. The aim is to bring men into a state in which they are susceptible of moral development, of the higher forms of Christian feeling; and, therefore, how frequently you are to preach depends very much upon the parish you are in. Sometimes once or twice a week, sometimes every day in the week, with prayer-meetings besides. I think, in a time of revival, a minister can generally preach once a day and once or twice on Sunday much easier than, at other times, he can preach once or twice in the week. Nothing so strengthens a man, or makes him so fertile, or enables him to carry work so well, as to be in a revival of religion. There is some difference among men. Some have so slender a constitution, their vital force is so insufficient, that they cannot bear the strain on nature. Yet, on the average, men can carry more work than they think they can, if they don't squander themselves. I don't hold up my own case as an example. I have an uncommonly strong constitution, and have great resiliency and recuperativeness; but I have preached every day for long periods, and twice on Sunday besides, holding an inquiry-meeting and a prayer-meeting and doing a great deal of visiting intermediately, and that too, as far as I could see, without any weariness or reaction afterward. It was not merely because I was strong. It was because I worked on the saccharine juices, and not on the acid.

COURAGE GIVES STRENGTH.

If you work on the principle of "awful responsibility," if you have all the time the feeling of anxiety and care, if you go about bowed down with worry, you will be exhausted very quickly. You cannot bear much. But go about from day to day, in the midst of the outpourings of God's spirit, with this feeling : "The Lord Jesus Christ is my elder brother. He thinks of me and of my people a thousand times more than I do. This is his work. He will surely accomplish it, and he says to me, 'Trust in me, love me, hope, and be courageous.'" If I go on the principle of love and trust, I can do ten times the work that I could do on the principle of anxiety and conscious responsibility. There is nothing that wears a man out so soon as worry, and there is no worry like that which comes from the attrition of anxiety in ministerial life. Ministers are so afraid they shall not do things just right ; so afraid they have not dealt with this man just as they should do ; so afraid that sermon was not quite right. Of course it was not. You may as well take that for granted in the beginning. You will never do anything just right, never say anything just right. God knew it when he made us, and he made us notwithstanding; he knows it, and employs us with that understanding.

No man is perfect here. All our best work is full of chaff. If we could see the truth as God sees it, and then as we preach it, the last would seem to us despicable. The old figure of our righteousness being filthy rags is true, in this higher interpretation of moral feeling. Therefore, let it be true at once and for all. Dismiss it forever; and do not, all the time, act as if you thought you could be perfect, and it was only from want of vigilance or anxiety that you had not been perfect. Let a man simply have this testimony in himself: "I am ready to do anything; I am willing to put all the strength I have into my work. Here I am, what there is of me; I throw it all into the work." Thus let him have some use for his God; trust him; believe in him. What is the use of having redemption through Jesus Christ, reconciliation and love, and all promise and hope, and then going bowed down as if you were a galley slave? Be yourself, before your congregation, what you want them to be; and, while you preach the love of Christ for human souls, show them that *you* have it, by your confidence and cheer. For there is no time when a man ought to sing and whistle and laugh and feel so happy as in the coming of a revival of religion. In Litchfield, when I saw a thunder-storm coming up, I used to run into the house and ask my mother to let me put on my old clothes and go out in the rain; for nothing was so grand to me as being out in the tempest, and seeing the elms swayed and the long drought broken by the coming on of the storm. I exulted; and though the birds were

all gone, I was there to sing. When, after a drought in
the congregation, things are beginning to move again,
that is the time for exultation. You need not be afraid
you will grieve God's spirit away. If God's spirit
could be grieved away, it would have been done long ago,
when you were preaching old tinkered-up sermons,
repeating for the five-hundredth time the message you
did n't care for, first or last. But when men begin to be
alive, when there begin to be some real affinities with
God and Christ, then is not the time to be anxious and
low-browed. It is the time for gladness. In this
spirit, a man can preach every day. He can't help himself. The days will not be long enough, not enough of
them in the week, for him to preach, provided he has
this impetus, this " rejoicing in God." You know Paul
said, — he had a double-barreled gun to fire, — " Rejoice
in the Lord ! " and when he fired off the other barrel,
he said, " Again I say, Rejoice ! " This buoyancy, this
cheerfulness, this hopefulness, this holy confidence, this
radiant gladness in the minister, will have a direct bearing on the production of the effects he seeks by preaching. Under ordinary circumstances, make that your
main reliance. Preach the gospel, — the power, the
nature, the love, the justice of God, the condition of
men, their sinfulness, their profound danger ; open the
future to them ; let them see into what they are going ;
analyze their character ; measure them by their own
standards, and show them how low their condition is ;
lift the standard higher, and show them how much lower
they are, until you come up to the ideal and measure
them through and through. Deal with them with all
the earnestness and vigor that God has given you.

DO NOT WORK BY AUTHORITY.

Then, while you are preaching in this way, remember that while you are master, while you dominate them, while you have authority over them, while you are zealous for the truth and glory of God, on the other hand, — strange and anomalous condition, — you have got to lie down before them, you have got to let them walk over you, and be their servant. When you go fishing, you have no authority to lay upon the brooks. You have got to find out how fish are to be caught, and you have to catch them in that way. If you are fishing for trout, you go to work one way, for perch another, and for bullheads another, and you bob for eels. You may throw the net for some, and some you never can catch in a net. Some you never can catch with a set line; and, if you want to get them, you must begin afar off. I have seen a man, when he came into the meadow where the trout-brook ran, lie down some four or five rods before he got to the brook; for, said he, "The very jar of the ground, light as I step, will be felt by them"; and he crawled up to the edge of the brook, and then, lifting himself up, he threw his line; and when he had got his trout, he did not care if he had crawled an acre over. Now, a man that fishes for men has got to fish for them in all sorts of ways. You cannot put your royal robes on and walk down the street and have men come out and cry, "Convert me! convert me!" You have got to treat proud men in the way that proud men have to be treated. Some men come to you that you did n't expect. Some will hold back, from whom you expected the greatest help. You will have all sorts of surprises, and your business is constant and various. Suit yourselves to emergencies; your business is to win men. Win them one by one, one by one. I don't think there is any joy so great in this world as the joy of working in a revival, when a man is in good health, and when there is a genuine work of grace going on, and those whom he respects and loves are breaking out, one by one, into new life and uttering their joy. I don't think there is anything this side of heaven that is comparable to that; and I have said, in these moments, that all the kingdoms of the earth would be nothing to me compared with the royalty I carried in my heart, when I saw men bowing down in this way and coming to God. It is reward enough. A man never seems to himself to have so little personality, never seems to care so little about himself, to have so much thought of God, such insight into theology, such perception of moral truths, as when he stands in the presence of men roused by the spirit of God, and is obliged to meet their case, and to administer to their wants. It is astonishing what revelation, refreshment, reinvigoration, indoctrination, inspiration, is given to men who are engaged in the same work in which God is engaged, — bringing sons and daughters home to glory.

VARIETY OF METHODS.

I am speaking of the variety of instrumentalities that can be employed. I have given an emphasis to preaching, though not more, I think, than it deserves. There is a variety of other instrumentalities that bear more or less directly upon the social side; and I may mention, first, the multiplication of meetings and prayer-meetings. It is sometimes well that a meeting should be thrown entirely out of its shackles of custom. So prone are we to run in ruts that, once in a while, it does us good to break up accustomed forms and methods, and make the meetings stand out as something singular and peculiar. Thus, before my time, in early days in Brooklyn, meetings were held in the lecture-room of the church that stood on the ground where Plymouth Church is now, at five o'clock in the morning, and they were thronged. Well, it would not have been wise, the next year, to put the meetings at such an hour. But, for that one time, the very singularity of it kindled men, and, during the whole of that season, the room was not large enough to hold the people. Something out of the ordinary way serves to arouse the attention of the community and draw their interest.

PROTRACTED MEETINGS.

Protracted meetings are eminently useful in the conduct of revivals of religion. We all know that protracted meetings are necessary for the development of the social in other things. Political campaigns are one continuous series of protracted meetings. If you wish to get up an enthusiasm in anything, it must be by constant repetition, iteration. Suppose a man should undertake to make a sword, and should come to-day and give it one blow and go home, and to-morrow should come back and give it another blow and go home, and so on; how long would it take a man, at that rate, to be an artificer? No; he must repeat his blows, one after the other, while the iron is hot. It is

not enough that a man should go to meeting once on
Sunday, in order to do certain things.

Thousands of men are not able to carry the Sunday
far down into the week. They need to have their impressions renewed. They are fitful, feeble; they don't
generate thought easily for themselves. There are
thousands of persons not able to generate much feeling
for themselves; but if you bring them into a mass-
meeting when there is a great deal of feeling about, they
catch it by sympathy; it helps their weakness: and
this is the theory of protracted meetings, that while
the strong may not need them, they are of benefit to the weak. Their poverty of thought and of
feeling, their want of continuity of will, are met in
that way; and protracted meetings are thus great
blessings.

How long ought they to be protracted? Just as long
as you want them. Four-day meetings? Yes, four days,
or eight days, or twelve days, or sixteen days, or twenty-
four days, or forty-eight days. You own all the time
there is, and you can keep them up as long as they
are profitable. Suppose my boy should come to me and
ask, "Father, how long ought I to shake the chestnut-
tree?" "As long as the chestnuts fall; as long as there
is a chestnut left," I say to him; "shake till you can get
no more nuts. As long as they fall, club it." I remember, in one case, carrying on a protracted meeting in my
own parish for over eight, nine, ten weeks; and when,
on Sunday morning, I made up my mind to close the
series of meetings, I had looked over the congregation
and could count but ten that were not hopeful Christians,
and they were persons for whom I did n't believe it

would be of any use to keep the meetings going; so they were closed. But there is no rule about it. So long as protracted meetings are useful and good, employ them and keep them up. As soon as they cease to be beneficial, quit them; use liberty and good sense.

There are also many things in vogue which are good in some communities and not in others, and are, in fact, matters of taste and discretion. In some communities, it is the custom to invite persons to rise for prayer in meetings. I have seen the very best results from that, yet I never could do it in my own congregation. I have tried it a few times, but always in a faltering way. It did not come naturally to me, and it did not harmonize with my style of administration from year to year. Yet I have seen men who, in times of revival, had the happiest results ensue from employing that method of bringing people to a decision. The theory is, that there are hundreds and thousands of persons floating about a community who have a certain amount of moral sensibility, but it does not take on any form of will. If, however, you can in any way concentrate that, and get these persons to commit themselves by an avowal, then their pride and vanity, and all their other feelings, will tend to press them forward in the right way; and so, by public commitment, they are put in a better position. There is no harm in it, when it works favorably, and there is no obligation attaching to its use.

The same is true of "anxious seats." A great deal has been said against them. It is a very common practice in Methodist churches, and with them it works extremely well. There is no reasonable objection to them. But if there is anything in yourself, anything in the character of your people, that should make this inexpedient, you are not bound to try it.

INQUIRY-MEETINGS.

Inquiry-meetings are of universal use, but more in New England than anywhere else. They bring the mind of the minister to bear directly on a single individual mind. They are more thorough; they explore a man, they find out his habits, they learn his disposition, they apportion the truth exactly to his want. Preaching to a whole congregation is very much like giving, in time of pestilence, hygienic instructions which every man must apply for himself; but an inquiry-meeting is like the visit of the physician. He takes each man by the pulse, and determines the medicine especially needed. I have always, in my own charge, dealt very largely in inquiry-meetings, frequently calling them after every prayer-meeting; not disconnecting them, not making them formal, but saying, "If any persons wish to converse with me after meeting, I will remain." And after the Friday-night meeting, I do the same, making it as little awful as possible; making it social and genial and inviting; winning people to it.

CAMP-MEETINGS.

Camp-meetings are scarcely within your probable range. I believe in them. I think they are excellent in new countries, and under certain circumstances they may be employed in old communities. Still, they are not ordinarily within the habits of our sort of people. I have spent some very blessed days in camp-meetings; and no man with poetic feeling, an eye for the sublime, who has seen a genuine camp-meeting, can ever revile it. The night, beautiful in its radiance overhead, the trees lit up with lamps, the songs of Zion sung by three thousand people, the strange mingling of light and dark; and after the great meeting is over, and the people have retired to their several tents, and had family prayers, I have lain in my little bunk and heard, in the night, six, eight, or ten little meetings going on all around me. One dies out, another dies out, and another; there are only three; another follows, and there are only two left; and finally, as the last bell strikes, I hear but one. After that, low murmurings, and then silence comes down over the great camp, and all is still. I think the life is almost a fairy life. It is enchanting. And yet, while it is eminently proper for a sparse population in a new country, and may be used occasionally in old communities, it can scarcely come within the range of your probable settlements.

EVANGELISTS.

Only a word now on the subject of evangelists. In general, in the induction of a revival of religion, it is better that the pastor should do his own work. It is a great deal better for you to be the father and the brother of your people, and, taking the spirits that are in sympathy with your own, to do your own visiting, get up your own meetings, conduct them, and have the domestic element, as it were, in your own parish. If you need further force than this, the next best thing is to call in your brother pastors. There should be a fellowship in churches in this way, and you should have help from those that are congenial. But there is no reason why, under certain circumstances, you should not have the help of men who have shown themselves to be gifted by the Master with a special. talent for developing religious feeling in the community. But, in the admission of evangelists, or revivalists, all may not alike be useful to you. There are many men whom I trust, and whose names will stand far above mine in heaven, that I would not have in my congregation under any circumstances. There is a genius that belongs to every church development which has its own individuality and peculiarity. "But if you introduce a revivalist whose whole style of thought is different from your own, and in antagonism with it, you will introduce a discordant element." Even so; but then I would object to none because they are evangelists.

In the selection of help of this kind, I should say one needs to be very judicious in calling in to his help those that are professional evangelists or revivalists. I incessantly develop in my people hope, courage, faith. I work by that myself. I have taught them to work by it. My congregation is genial and cheerful, and there is an atmosphere there of fellowship and of kindliness. Now you bring in a man that preaches harshly, and begins to bear down upon the conscience with that stern sense of awful responsibility, — there would be rebellion in the congregation; you could not hold them to it. And therefore, although that man might, in another relation, be an excellent man, do much good, and be owned and blessed by the Master, yet he is not adapted to that

place.   There are a thousand wheels that are just as
good wheels as any in a certain watch, but the difference of the ten thousandth part of an inch would make
any wheel inappropriate for that particular watch. The
wheels must have a certain relation to each other, or
they won't keep time.   And so of the genus Evangelist.   There are a good many species; and while it is
best to do your own work, or to do it with the help of
a brother pastor, still, if you are obliged to, call in an
evangelist, but do not do it at hap-hazard; call one
who will work on the same lines and in harmony
with you.   That will be likely to help you; and he
will probably leave your church stronger than he
found it, and you better rooted in the church than
when he came.

QUESTIONS AND ANSWERS.

Q. Does not such an evangelist as you have described meet
the wants of some people?

MR. BEECHER.—Yes, sir.   But then, suppose he meets
the wants of a few at the expense of a great majority?
You cannot make a net, you know, that will catch trout,
and at the same time be fit to catch sharks; it has to be
so very thin.   I do not think that any one administration can take every sort of person.   I think it is to
the interest of every Episcopal church in the community that there shall be a Congregational church
alongside of it; and it is to the interest of every Congregational church that there shall be, in the immediate
vicinity, a Presbyterian or a Methodist church: that
thus elements may be developed outside which will

affect them beneficially. My dear old father used to think that it was his interest to keep out all churches except his own from Litchfield. The moment he found a Methodist was getting up a fire, he would go and put his foot on it. And I heard him say, in the exuberance of his zeal about it, "Why! when I heard the Methodists were getting in, in such a district, I would go over there and I would preach so much better than they could, that they couldn't carry their meetings along!" Well, that was about the spirit of that time. If I had my choice, I would never have, in any community, less than one good representative of each of the various forms in which churches develop themselves; no church can develop all sides. And so we get from the formular worship of the hierarchical churches some elements in the direction of veneration and taste, that we do not and cannot very well develop in our congregational churches. On the other hand, there are certain enthusiastic social elements that are developed by the Methodists: there is a royal — jollity, shall I say? — a heartiness among them, that it is very hard to get in a Presbyterian church. But there is an intellectualization, and a certain element of righteousness and ethicalness, in Congregational and Presbyterian churches that is pre-eminently fundamental in a community. And if this view of the church as the body of Christ, and all the individual churches parts thereof with various powers and functions, — just as a single church is represented as one man, with members carrying different gifts, — if this view might prevail, sectarianism would be disarmed of its sting.

13 *

Q. Don't you think it is necessary to bring men to a decision in regard to the subject of religion?

MR. BEECHER. — Certainly it is. But decisions, you know, are very different things with different people. Decisions take place in connection with different faculties. A person with very large conscientiousness and self-esteem would come to a decision that would meet together with a snap you could hear all over town! But, take a person who lacks in those elements, and who is genial and gentle, and he will decide as clouds do, — that change their form in a rosy, round-edged, soft, flushy way. You must remember that decision takes on a great many different forms; but, somehow or other, everybody must be brought to the point of decision. There are some men who decide as an engine flies the track, and there are others who go off on switches, but keep to the track. There is every possible variation.

Q. Don't you think that a revival has a tendency to bring men to a quick and rapid decision?

MR. BEECHER. — Yes, sir.

Q. What is the philosophy, or reason, or cause, of that?

MR. BEECHER.— The reason is very plain, — that you are causing everything to converge to that very end. That is the thing you are exerting your whole influence for. You have indoctrinated them; they have learned their duty; they have learned moral government; they have learned a thousand truths. Now you take all the elements that they have been gaining through your pastorate, and by your instructive preaching, and concentrate these upon them. This reminds me of the first sermon I ever preached that I felt did any good at the time. I was in despair, at Lawrenceburg. I could preach to interested hearers. I hoped that I instructed them in some measure, but I never could carry the congregation beyond a certain degree of excitement. In the West, they always had two or three days of preaching before a communion season. By the preaching, in the preparatory days, the interest would grow and deepen, and the people would become intense, and come on the Sabbath day to partake of the communion of the Lord's Supper; but by Monday, it had all gone out again, and there was nothing left. I would think the church was getting on its legs to march, and it would fall flat again. I sent out for Dr. ——, and asked him if he would not come down and help me, but he could not. · I sent up for father, and asked him if he wouldn't come down, and he said, " No, you must find out, yourself." I went over there to Indianapolis, and my heart burned within me. I could not be preaching for nothing. I determined to sit down and study how the Apostles did it; for, though I was not an apostle, I thought possibly I could do something, in some way, according to my size and shape. I took the book of Acts, and studied Peter's sermon on the day of Pentecost. I analyzed it, I looked at it all the way through, I formed a theory of the way in which the effect was produced, and I then constructed a sermon, — not of the same material, because Peter was preaching to a Jewish audience and I was preaching to Hoosiers, — but I constructed a sermon on the same principle, as I understood it. I was preaching in the hall of a little academy that would hold a hundred or a hundred and fifty people. The legislature was in session, and a good many lawyers and public men were there. I went down, on Sunday morning, as anxious as a boy with a new gun would be to try and see how it would shoot. I fired my sermon, and there were about ten men awakened. If there was ever anybody delighted, I was. I had learned how to preach. I said to myself, " I have got the knack of aiming now ; I know what to do." Well, the trouble was, that, though I had preached that sermon of that sort, I had materials to preach but one or two more, and then I ran out. But I had got the ideal, after all, — the sense of aiming at certain points, and carrying them by the direct application of the truth. That was everything to me. My horizon enlarged and enlarged, so that by and by I came into the possession of my profession, so far as I have ever attained it.

Q. You have said a good deal to make us feel very kindly towards all denominations, and to make us feel that it is very consistent to have a good many of them ; but how do you get along with the fact that in so many of our towns, East and West, especially West, every denomination considers it its duty to be represented, as much as if there were not any other denomination there, and so they all become weak ?

Mr. BEECHER. — Yes, that is a misfortune that ought to be striven against as far as possible. I know we had sixteen denominational churches in a population of four thousand, in Indianapolis.

Q. Did you consider that too much of a good thing?

MR. BEECHER. — I did consider it a great deal too much, but it did not argue that a little was not good. I think that, in making a sandwich, a little mustard improves it; but I would not put in a quart.

XI.

BRINGING MEN TO CHRIST.

 PURPOSE, this afternoon, to confine my remarks principally to the consideration of what may be called the clinical practice in revivals, or the treatment of cases as they arise. As nearly as I can judge, there has gradually come to be, in our time, a very great difference in the way in which persons in whom religious sensibility has been developed are treated, as compared with the custom that prevailed twenty-five, and still more fifty years ago. I have no doubt that if the venerable and noble ministers who lived in those times were to stand by now, retaining their views, and look upon the development of Christian character as it takes place in intelligent churches and under intelligent ministrations, they would think the world was coming to an end; and that men were being converted entirely out of the proper way; and that the church was likely to be filled up with material feeble in spiritual life.

And yet, on the other hand, I think none can deny the fact, that never before at any period were the churches possessed of so many members of so high a type of piety; and never was piety based upon better, clearer knowledge; and never did Christian emotion so co-operate with Christian activity as in our time.

While, then, it would seem that the technical processes with which men are treated have suffered great change, the result of those processes in the hands of the Christian ministry in our day is the production of a higher type of Christian character, not in individuals, but in communities.

I purpose to consider the phenomena of conviction of sin and of conversion, of the obtaining, in the old language, of a "hope"; and of the various experiences that stand connected with these things.

THE OLD AND THE NEW PRACTICE.

I admit freely that there is no such attempt now made, that there are no such lessons in working with respect to the promotion of conviction, its depth and its continuity, as prevailed in earlier days. In working, it will be found that you cannot control things, that they will have their own way; that one class of your hearers will develop moral sensibility in one degree, another class in another degree; and they will assume aspects so different that the contrast between the extreme cases at the two ends of the scale will make it seem as if only one could be right and the other must necessarily be wrong. There has always been an effort to countervail this. That is, there has been a theory that, in conviction and conversion and the entering upon the Christian life, there are certain great marks common to all; and therefore there has been an attempt made to bring men up to certain tests, and to compress, as it were, experiences into certain molds; to prevent elasticity and liberty of being, if one may so say. Or, as I have been accustomed to say, the old-school men refuse to allow God his own sovereignty in the way of convicting and converting men, but insist that the sovereignty should be exercised according to certain prescribed patterns, deduced from experience. It will not be difficult for men of a certain moral organization, that is, men organized so as to be susceptible in religious directions, who have been under continuous religious culture, who are apprehensive of the truth, candid, fair, — it ought not to be difficult to produce in such men, and that, too, by very slight and gentle means, all the conviction of sin that is necessary, all that is of any use. On the other hand, persons of a torpid disposition, slow of thought, not easy to move in their emotions and inward life, will require a pressure 'far greater. So it falls out in preaching, continually, that sermons which are adapted to rouse the lethargic and torpid overact upon those that are sensitive and mercurial; and that allowances and explanations and concessions which are strictly right, as adapted to more sensitive and advanced natures, are taken advantage of by those lower down; so that, in dealing with men, there is no one single way. There is to be incessant adaptation to the individuals, or, in large communities, to the classes, into which individuals fall.

The character of conviction of sin will very largely depend upon the theology which you preach. If you preach the theology of Dr. Emmons, you may expect several results. The first is that you will lose most of your congregation; secondly, those who remain will be very hard and stubborn; and, thirdly, when conviction does come, it will come like the rushing of a mighty wind, like a tornado, like an earthquake, breaking up the foundations of things. The results will be in some such proportion all the way through.

If you preach the higher forms of Calvinism, if you represent God as he is represented in what is called hyper-Calvinism, a congregation will stand it and hear you through; and if you bring men into such a state that they feel guilty for not loving such a God, though it may take a good deal of time, yet when the result does come on, it will be something terrible, and will very nearly break up the foundations of moral consciousness, very nearly take away a man's reason. If, however, a milder type — ordinarily considered the New England type of Calvinism — be presented, so that God is represented as supremely just, not upon impossible conditions, or conditions so extraordinary as scarcely to come within the range of human comprehension or feeling; if you represent the administration of the universe as in the hands of God, who maintains for the welfare of all a system of righteous law, who deals with men in such a way as to address himself to their reason and moral consciousness, — it ought not to be either a long process, or an exaggerating process. That is, feeling ought not to be driven to such wild extremes in the process of satisfying men that they are guilty for disobedience to such a God and to such laws.

In general, the more the element of coercive gentleness — if I may say so — the element of paternity, the

T

element of Divine love, is preached, the milder will be the type of conviction, but the more efficacious, the more rapid in its workings, and the more rich and beneficent in its results.   Let me guard you, however, against supposing that the infusion of a larger element of love in the Divine character, with a less element of justice, will work beneficially.   I would not be understood to teach that the Divine love is that vague and colorless good-nature and kindness which some suppose.   In my thought, love carries in itself the highest truth and the highest justice, and the most absolute requisitions of right and duty; and it carries both justice and truth in the spirit of love.   The atmosphere differs; the elements remain the same.

DIVERSE PERSONAL ELEMENTS.

The variety of cases which occur under pungent and faithful personal, applicatory preaching, is very great. I cannot attempt to mention all, but will take some of the more common and conspicuous.   There will hardly be two persons awakened alike.   You must not expect it.   Take, for example, the awakening of children.   How impossible it is for a child to be affected with any such sensibility, or any such introspect or retrospect, or any such burden of conscience, as belong to an adult, who has gone through life organizing selfishness, cultivating passions!   The child knows none of these things.   You can say to a child, "You are a great sinner before God," and it trembles; here is some vague mystery, it does not know what.   You can work upon its sensibility, and teach it that it must give up its heart to Christ; and it may in a helpless way lift its little hands and try to deliver itself up to the Lord Jesus Christ, and by and by be told that it now may be happy, having passed through all the stages. Who that looks into the heart and reads things as they are does not see what a work has been wrought upon that sensitive nature? But the child that has had no life, whose experience is nearly nothing, how can you expect a manly disposition to be developed in that? It is said that jugglers in India will take an acorn and extemporize a tree before your eyes. That may be done by jugglery, with a seed; but in childhood you cannot develop a virile experience.

Among the mature, conviction will generally vary with the disposition. In one class reason will be predominant, because that is the structure of their mind. Another class will not reason much, but they will be chiefly influenced by emotion, because that is the structure of their nature. Some persons will have a light playing about their conceptions of right and wrong, which shows that they have the element of imagination largely developed, and they get the view which imagination alone enables the reason to give of moral qualities, of right and wrong, of the present and of the future.

DEGREES OF INTENSITY.

All these elements you will find developed under any searching ministry. Their intensity will depend upon the constitution of a man's mind and upon the history of his life. I should suppose, for instance, that a man with a slow and torpid moral sense never could arrive at any vivid convictions. The Divine Spirit

that shines alike upon all the earth does not make
all things upon the earth alike beautiful; nor does
it change the inertness and sleep in all plants at the
same time; nor does it produce a like development in
all. So the Divine influence, working through the truth
that falls upon the human heart, acts according to the
laws of that human heart, and men that are slow of
belief, slow of intelligence, torpid of feeling, will come
up but a little way comparatively. If you wait for them
to develop paroxysmal feeling, if you have an impression that no man can come into the kingdom of God
unless he comes in with a sweep and a whirlwind of
experience, you will find yourself overmatched perpetually, and you will do one of two things; you will either
throw them back in despair upon the world, or else
lead them to simulate an experience, so that they will
unintentionally, but really, come in upon a false basis.
Understand that every man will have an experience
corresponding to his organization and his nature. In
some there will be very little feeling, slowly educed;
in others, very much; and, as respects that, one may be
just as good as the other.

The wickedness — that is, the overt wickedness — of
a man's life will also have much to do with his sense
of conviction. I mean that conscience is largely formed
by the public institutions of society, by what prevails
in the domestic circle, by what are understood to be
the civic virtues; and a man whose conscience is not
merely instructed from the pulpit, but has also been
formed in civil affairs and social relations, will have an
experience the proportions and character of which will
be taken somewhat from this education. So, if a man

has been a drunkard, a licentious man, a thief, a pirate, or a liar, and has come home and been brought under the power of religious teaching, and has something of manly nature yet left in him, — when the truth falls on that man, you might well suppose that he would have a concrete conviction of sin ; a conviction that he is a desperate sinner. But his idea of a desperate sinner would not be that he had broken the law of God, but that he was a liar, that he was a robber, or a pirate, or a lewd man, or a drunkard. It would fasten itself upon some of those physical, external forms of sin ; and while you might attempt, by and by, to enlarge his view, it would not be best to do it before you had brought him forward into a Christian life.

PRACTICAL INFLUENCES TO BE USED.

While, however, I say that you should accept the development as it comes, in respect to the general character and in respect to its depth and strength, let me also say that there is an interference which you can practice, a guidance which you can effectually furnish. You can do it by personal intercourse with your people. You can do it, but not very well, by general preaching. For example, you will find in a very large class of easy-going people, ordinarily well doing, according to the current opinions of society, a state of moral feeling that is susceptible of great excitement. You preach to them the Divine law and the claims of God upon them, show them that they have been great sinners against holiness, and they will all begin to feel that they sinned in Adam and that they have sinned since Adam. They feel that they are very guilty and need change of heart, and they

will put you off with that. Now, if a woman is a ter-
magant, you must make her conceptions of sin include
that element. If a man is cold, hard, proud, it will not
do for him to confess Adam's sin, nor any of the generic
sins. His sense of sin must cover his particular disposition. If you find a man notoriously stingy, mean, and
avaricious, no matter if he shakes in convulsions for his
sins against God, that man must have his convictions
kept down until he comes to the question of avarice.
In short, generic conviction, instead of personal conviction, will not answer ; and it is part of your business
to produce the latter. If you care to have men really
changed, if there is to be something more than ecclesiastical translation, if there is to be a personal reno-
vation, by which a nature is to be sweetened into
benevolence, by which a sodden and sordid nature is
to be exalted into some of the elements of nobility, by
which a coarse and physical nature is to reach up into
spiritual realms, — you must search out men and
make them search themselves, and find out where
there is too much or too little ; and their sense of sin
must be brought personally home to them, so that all
these elements shall be distinctly in their consciousness,
when they make their submission or choice before God.
That brings matters to a practical reality, and into such
a form that you will avoid, or tend to avoid, bringing
men into the church under strong general impressions,
who, after all, have not changed materially in those
individual elements of character that fashion their
life.

THE APOSTOLIC THEORY.

The question is not an unimportant one: How thorough ought convictions of sin to be? And that leads me to say that there seems to have been, in times past, an impression that a conversion was more thorough in proportion to the depth, if I may say so, or quantity of feeling which had been expended in the beginning, and that the conversion was probably a shallow one in which a man had not felt immensely and intensely.

I remember very well the time when four or five weeks was a moderate term for a man to go under conviction of sin. I remember when it was supposed that general attention would occupy a week or ten days, and then would come seriousness, which would occupy several days more; then convictions of sin in their lighter form would come, and at last wrestling convictions, and, finally, the crisis; and if, in my childhood, a man was converted in four weeks, it was almost thought an insufficient time. It was against such notions as those that my father used to contend. He was, in some sense, a reformer in those matters.

On the other hand, when we go clear back to the apostolic age, we find men gathered together in great crowds, receiving the truth, and under a single sermon breaking down and crying out, "What shall we do to be saved?" and before they departed becoming so transformed that the Apostles considered them worthy of church-membership.

Here, then, are the two extremes. In the first preaching of Christianity, it was understood that when a man's character and condition were clearly presented before him, and the question of his adhesion to Christ was pressed upon him, he had it in his power to determine then and there, and if his determination was right, and was carried into practice, the feeling that led to it was enough. In the old New England practice, the impression was that a long-continued, but especially a deep and thorough, conviction of sin was very desirable.

CHANGE OF LIFE THE REAL AIM.

What, after all, is the object of sorrow? What is the use of it? What is the use of pain, when we break a law? To bring us back into obedience to law; simply to rectify that which created the sorrow; and to produce such an impression upon the memory that we shall not be likely to transgress again. Sorrow is not like a dye-vat, in which a man ought to lie over-night in order to bring him a conviction of sin. If a captain wishes to leave port, and the wind is blowing ten miles an hour, he heaves up the anchor, for this is enough to get him far out of port. If he gets out on a breeze of ten miles an hour, it is as good as if he went out on one of twenty. If it requires twenty pounds of steam to work an engine properly, then all above that is waste. Every grain of powder beyond what is necessary to throw a ball where you want it to go is superfluous. And every particle of feeling you expend of this kind, — regretful, sorrowful, remorseful, all that strange medley of emotion, and all that which we do not now analyze, which goes to constitute what is called conviction of sin, — the elements of reason, of imagination, of memory, — all the various sensibilities that play and interplay; of all this, every particle you expend more than just enough to make a man say, " I am wrong, I will do right," is unnecessary. Just so soon as you get enough feeling to bring about the change, you have accomplished your purpose. Everything more is so much surplusage.

DIFFERENCES OF DISPOSITION.

This is an important consideration, because, in the first place, there are many persons who are thought not to be safe Christians, because they are mild, gentle, and not liable to strong feeling of any kind. I recollect an elder in my church in Indianapolis, when I was a Presbyterian, whose whole life, I think, never had an inch of undulation in it. I think he would smile gently when he married his wife. I think he would smile gently when he buried her. He possessed a perfectly even, tranquil nature. Now the idea that this man should be convulsed with any feeling was absurd. And when he came into the church he said, " I don't remember that I have ever had any exercise of feeling"; and persons were rather slow to receive him. Some men thought there should be more exercise of feeling. Still, he was one of the best of men I ever had in the church, although he glided in almost without emotion. Spring came, in his case, without any breaking up and freshets and storms.

On the other hand, there are many persons whose consciences are never satisfied. They hear a man tell how the Lord led him into the kingdom with terrible manifestations of feeling and with anguish and suffering; how, when he went into a monthly meeting where a revival was going on, conviction struck him and he went home; how he could find no rest, how he could not attend to his business, he was so wretched; how he kept it from his wife for a week, and by and by such anguish and agony came that he could not eat or sleep, and it seemed to him that soul and body would be rent asunder; how he prayed and prayed, and at last, as he prayed, he saw a vision as a light in the heavens, and he called out, " O Lord! O Lord!"—and there was a terrible wrestling, and something seemed to flood him with the glow of peace, and he came out of his darkness and began to cry, " Hallelujah! hallelujah!" and was so happy! Now, all that is genuine. It is genuine for him; not for me, not for you. But a man hears this,—a man who has been endeavoring to walk honestly with God and honestly with men; who really has the spiritual life developed in him; whose soul dominates his body; who is disinterested, and is always working upward toward higher and higher degrees of excellence, and never has had this dramatic experience, this pictorial conviction of sin; with whom, indeed, it has always been a matter of doubt whether he was really converted or not,—and he says, "If I had only had *that*, I should feel that I had a ticket, a pass that would be valid."

CONVICTION ONLY A MEANS TO CONVERSION.

A man who sleeps on the ground-floor of a tenement house is roused in the night by the cry of fire. He springs up, gathers his wife and children about him, attempts to rush down the main hall-way, and meets the flames coming up. Beaten there, he runs to the rear stairs,—up comes the bulging smoke. He flies to the next story, and after him comes the flame, roaring and crackling at his heels. From story to story he runs, until he is driven to the roof, while all below him is a sea of flame. He is about to give up, and feels, " I am a dead man, and my household are lost ! " when a voice from the gable hails him. A ladder is thrown up. He hands over his children and his wife, and finally he himself gets down and escapes. Everybody congratulates him. " Wonderful escape ! " — and so it was a wonderful escape. No wonder he remembers it. And so he is narrating it; and a young man says, " I slept on the ground-floor in that building, and when the engines came thundering along, I jumped up and dressed myself, got all my clothes and valuables, and quietly walked out at the lower door and went away. But if that man's experience is called *escaping*, I fear I have not escaped ! "

So it is in respect to changes that are produced in men's minds. The point is this, — that a man shall be born again; that there shall be a new arrangement, if I may say so, a crystallizing of particles, a transformation which consists in the shifting of sovereignty from the bottom of the head to the top. Whereas, before, the animal spirit ruled the man, now, through Jesus Christ and the inspiration of the Holy Ghost, all the upper part of a man's nature is vitalized, comes into dominancy, and controls the lower. And whatever process, whether long or short, with visions or without them, with literalness or imaginativeness, with deep or little feeling, — whatever brings a man into that condition, is enough. For conviction of sin is cause merely. If it produces effect, that is all you want; all the exaggerating conception is needless.

PRESENT CHRIST AS THE STANDARD.

Then, if that be the object of conviction of sin, of course all your preaching will tend to the development, the measuring, of a man's character, so that he shall be able to determine continually that he is sinful. You will, in other words, hold out the standard of life, — not an exaggerated one, or an ideal or imaginative one, but a real standard of life in Christ Jesus, as laid down in the New Testament. Measure a man within and without, his understanding, his sensibilities; hold this measure up before him with such continual appeals to his practical knowledge of himself that he will come to the conviction that he is altogether sinful. When I say "altogether sinful," I do not mean total depravity, a very infelicitous phrase, framed under a philosophy in which we do not believe, the technicalities of which we should abandon. But I believe there is not a single faculty in a man's nature that does not sin. I believe in the correlation of faculties. They are all put into false relations with each other in the practical matters of life; and man is in a state of antagonism towards God, towards the Divine law or order.

HELP MEN TO ACTIVELY CHOOSE.

Now, when you have produced that impression upon your congregation, the question becomes simply one of transition. They are satisfied that they have lived wrong; that there is a better way. The point, in the next place, is how to determine choice. I speak with profound feeling here. My own experience, through many stormy years, is wrapped up in this matter. I feel the profoundest pity for those who are so vaguely stimulated by preaching, but not taught or led to know what to do. As a little child, I was so susceptible of moral impressions that I don't remember a year of my life, after I was seven or eight years old, that I was not under conviction of sin; that I did not go about with a feeling of sadness, — a feeling that I was in danger of exile from heaven, all because I was a sinner, which I did not want to be. There were times when it amounted to positive anguish. There were times of revival in my academic and college course, before I was a member of the church, when, if I could have had the simple truth as it now appears to me, in less than an hour, yes, in a moment, I should have come on to ground of peace and trust, of faith and love, and therefore of hope and courage.

BE SPECIFIC, NOT VAGUE.

It is to the last degree important, therefore, that, in dealing with men, you should know exactly what the point of difficulty is. Do not arouse in your congregation the feeling that they are in danger, and then leave them to hold up their hands vaguely for something, they don't know what.

But this belonged to the old system, to the idea that God acted in his sovereignty upon the hearts of men as he would, when he would, where he would; and that man could do nothing but wait on God. In past times, a man suffered more just in proportion as he was better, — that is, more sensitive in conscience, — and as he yearned for something higher and better; as he added all the susceptibility of a poet to all the intensity of the moralist; and was left groping for light, without any knowledge of what to do or where to go?

Under such circumstances, how did a man get into the kingdom of God? A great many men did n't get in. They became weary and fell back. A great many got in because, in some way or other, under the general stimulus of singing and social meetings, there did come a vision of Christ that their souls embraced. It filled them with joy, and they passed in.

I sometimes think people get into heaven as a blind man gets into a garden. He happens to strike the first picket on the right-hand side of the gate, and he turns to the next one to the right, and the next, and he finally goes around the whole enclosure, butting against every single picket, though he gets in at last, because finally, in the order of time, he reaches the gate. In other cases, a man may come in by the first intention. What histories might be written of the experiences of Christians! Talk about the Inquisition! The Inquisition has no chambers in which there has been such suffering as in the silent chambers of unrecorded spiritual histories, — such excruciating sorrows, such useless sufferings! If you don't know how to lead men into light, don't plunge them into darkness.

THE TWO ELEMENTS OF ACTION.

What, then, is the thing men are called to do when they are awakened and become conscious of their wrong estate? It seems to me there are simply two elements in it. One is the presentation of the Lord Jesus Christ as the manifest idea of God. Jesus Christ, as he walked on earth, is to be presented to man. That is the pattern of himself which God wishes men to have before them when they determine whether or not they will serve him. It is in that point of view that I condemn Calvinism with such severity, if not acerbity. When I take Calvin's view of God and put it by the side of Jesus Christ, who suffered that men might not suffer, who came to shed his blood and die that men might be redeemed, — when I put this by the side of the systematic God that Calvin has erected, I feel an unspeakable horror, a shock in my whole moral being. I say to my people: Whatever may be the logical excellence of that system, — and it is a wonderful system of ratiocination and skillful construction, — whatever may be the general truth of it, one thing is certain, that the cross of Christ bore up no such conception of God as that which is given to us in the Calvinistic representation of God. I take, therefore, the Lord Jesus Christ as the manifestation of God. I take the life of Christ as it was upon earth, and hold it up to my people, and say: Here is the companionable God, who would in heaven do just as he did on earth, only more gloriously and abundantly. As he himself said, " If ye, being evil, know how to give good gifts to your children, how much more shall your Father which is in heaven give good things to them that ask him."

Now see what he was among men. See how he took them to his arms of helpfulness! What humility! What patience! What gentleness, sweetness, instructiveness, long loving! What balm in his sympathy! What healing power in the application of his loving heart to the hearts of those that were around him!

The presentation of Christ's character as the sinner's friend is, beyond all other things, the most sublime and the most glorious. That my soul knows right well. I had wandered through years and years, trying to submit to a theological God, trying to submit to a catalogue of attributes. I had gone through the seminary, and had nearly completed my theological course, inwardly unbelieving. It was my duty to take a Bible-class. I did it unwillingly. I undertook to do what the German commentators did, with whom I was then familiar. They undertook to interpret the New Testament just as they found it, without saying that they believed in it any more than in Homer and Virgil. I took the subject of the relations of Christ to men out of the four Evangelists and presented it to my class in that way; and, as I went on, gathering everything of Christ as a conversationist, Christ as a personal friend,— I remember the brightest day that ever dawned on this earth, since moon and stars shone upon it, was that morning while I was studying the thought of Christ, and it flashed upon me, as the result of all the facts and instances that I had been selecting, that Christ was one who by perfect holiness and purity knew how to be sorry, not for the man who was converted, but for the unconverted man, because he was sinning. He was sorry, as the nurse or the mother is sorry for the child because it is sick. It dawned upon me, "This is God, to be sorry for imperfection; this is God, to be sorry that men are in the bondage of sin and in the thrall of death; and the resource and power of the Divine nature are offered to those that are bad to help them out of their badness."

So there had been my trouble always. I could not make myself good enough for God to take me; and I spent hours, yes, I squandered days and days, in fruitless prayer and agonizing search to find a God who would do something for me, or to find that experience that was to come radiant down through the atmosphere and lodge upon my soul. I could never find it. But when I found that the nature of love is to make lovely things; that the nature of purity is to make uncleanness pure; that the nature of holiness is to inspire holiness among men; and that God's government is to take the poor, the needy, and feeble in his arms to help them, loving them all the time while he is doing it, to help them to himself, — I no longer suffered, for I had found my Father which is in heaven.

Now, present that character of Christ to men, saying, "Do you want this Christ, do you want this God? Is this your choice?" I think you will find them coming quick and thick around such presentations of Jesus Christ, to say, "My Lord and my God!" Everything that is good in man responds to it. Everything that is base in man slinks away, dishonored and disgraced, if it obstructs the heart's allegiance to such a God as that.

THE IDEAL MANHOOD.

Then, secondly, you want to present the character of typical manhood as laid down in the New Testament. Are you prepared to say, to-day, " I will accept and love that blessed Saviour, and that life and that character shall be my search from this day forward to the end of my life"? When a man says, "Yes, that I take, and

14 *   U

that I acknowledge to be hereafter my life," the man is
a Christian.   What is a Christian?   A saint?   Yes, I
hope so, though it is tough for some saints in the calen-
dar.   But so is a man a Christian out of whose mind
has leaped that purpose.   When is a seed a plant?
Just as quick as it has begun to shoot a root down one
way and a stem up the other.   It is not a grown plant,
but it is a plant just as truly as it ever will be.   And
when is a man a Christian?   The moment he accepts
Christ and the purposes of life which Christ ordained,
by precept and example; the moment he says, "That
is the charter of my life.   I hold myself bound by
those laws."   The instant a man puts the honest purposes of the Christian forward, he has begun to be
a Christian.   "What! without any transport?"   Yes,
with or without.   "Without any fruit yet?"   Yes,
with or without.   That is the initial point; — the point
at which a man with his purpose or will goes over to
that view of Jesus Christ, and accepts that ideal of manhood as his own, and then begins to act accordingly,
he has started.

VARIED EXPERIENCES.

Now, in the development of this purpose, you will
find, as in the process of conviction, a wide range of
variation which you ought not to desire to contract.
You ought to rejoice that the God who made ten thousand forms of flowers, and who differentiates throughout
the physical world, also makes every man different from
all others.   This variety constitutes an element of intense interest and profound sympathy.   There will be
many persons who will come gliding into this state of
mind as naturally as a cloud forms.   Of all the

things that take place in nature, there is nothing so ethereal, so ineffable, as the birth of a cloud. If you have spent a summer in a mountain region, you have had an opportunity of seeing them form in long sequence. Overhead there is perfect clarity, deep blue, the air as clear as crystal, and when you first look there is nothing else; but before you have ceased to look, within a glance of the eye, there is a slight opacity, a haze; — you look again and it is a cloud. A breath brings it, swiftly and silent. And there are some souls that move almost as ethereally as that. I have known persons who came into the Christian life with as little friction, as little ado, as little conspicuity, and yet with as much certainty, as a cloud forms in the pure summer mountain air. Bless God for such! Praise him, thank him! Do not disturb them. If they love Christ, if their hearts gush out in praise, if they betake themselves to the ways of Christian life, its dispensations its bounty, its magnanimity, its generosity, its truth, its self-government, its ardent passion of life, its self-denial in love, — if they betake themselves to these moods and life, never put them back by asking "In what way did you come? What was your experience?" If a child brings me to-day a bunch of spring beauties, or hepatica, or that sweetest blossom that grows in the breast of humility under russet leaves, the mayflower, the trailing arbutus, I will ask no questions where they grew. The flower itself is its own evidence of orthodoxy.

There are many that come into the kingdom of God by this attraction. I know that a great many persons would say to such people, "Was there a very great struggle when you began to love God?" I used to have a member on my examining committee who questioned everybody that came into the church with "Do you remember any time when you hated God?" "No," said a sweet young maiden; "I do not remember a time when I did not love him." That would not do; that was a fatal defect, in his judgment. Why, I rejoiced in it! I said to her, "Hold on, my child, hold on; don't let him dash you. You are right, and he is wrong." It is good sometimes to make deacons ashamed before young people. When the image of the Lord Jesus Christ comes before such a soul, its nature goes right over towards him. Who shall dare stand between such a soul and the Master who has found it?

I have presented this picture to many persons, who would clearly understand the conditions of salvation, as they are called, and yet who had a vague impression that something else had got to come. They had had none of those Dantean purgatorial experiences; they did n't know that they might *believe* and call that being Christians; and so they waited. I have often found that, by bringing the amplitude and impetuosity of my own hope to bear upon them, I could give them great help. Why, I have for a man, in such times as that, labor-pain. And when I find a man that has got the right condition and the right feeling, I can *put him in*, if he won't go in otherwise. I can put him in with an afflatus of hope, with an exulting push of my soul on his soul, and say to him, "O gazer! O lingering child! you are right, you are right; that is your Christ. Take him, take him, you are near him, his hand is on you." And with my certainty and the excitement of my soul and its sympathy with his, before he knows it

he is right over on the other side of the rise. Well,
may not men be brought over by hope? I say that
when you bring before men the vision of Christ, not
crucified, but the Christ that lives again and lives forever, compared with whose bright face the sun itself is
darkness, — bring that conception of the living God of
love before a man, and I do not care by what door of
his faculties he may come out to him. He may come
by fear; it is the worst one. He may come by conscience; it is good enough. O, but let him come by
love, by sweet sympathy; it is better than all. It is
better that the child that has gone away should come
home for the most selfish reasons, than that he should
not come at all; yet if he come by filial sorrow and
noble motives it is the best way to come. But *any*
way, so that he comes! In general, however, I think it
may be said that more persons may be won by the love
of Christ, by the presentation of these brighter views
of his character and love, than by any other means.

Of course I do not purpose, in this brief lecture, to go
into the analysis of all the phenomena, — they are
endless, — nor to give you a registration of the classes,
of the infinite number of cases that will occur. It is
a part of your privilege and your enjoyment to learn
these yourself, in your own ministry. I wish only to
leave an impression of the simplicity, the naturalness,
the ease, with which one may make the transition
from the natural life, in which the lower faculties predominate, to the spiritual life, in which the higher or
religious faculties are in the ascendant.

AFTER CONVERSION.

When men have been brought to this state of conscious sinfulness and feel their need of a change of life within and without, when they have had the part which they are to choose clearly presented before them, and made the choice, what will be the result? Well, that will depend a great deal upon circumstances, too. I have heard men say that they went to bed unconscious of loving God, and woke up in the morning in a transport. They think they were converted in their sleep. I don't think so, — though I have seen men in church who, if they ever were converted, would have to undergo the process while asleep. But I have no question whatever that a change often takes place unconsciously in men, when the mental processes have been so graded, the instruction and the approaches have been so gradual, that they could not tell when it came. When you go by the Pacific Railroad to California, you do not know where the maximum grade is. You go up over the Rocky Mountains with such a gentle slope, all the time rising, rising, rising, that when you stop at last, and they tell you that you are on the summit level, you are amazed; you thought that the summit level was such that you would be plunged up and plunged down in getting there; but it was like going through a meadow, the rise was so gradual. I have seen many men with such experiences as that in regard to their Christian growth. And the question should be, simply, Do they live right? have they the right dispositions? are they moving in spiritual directions? If they are, no matter how gradually they passed from death to life. When the spark is first struck, it does not glow; you shield it darkling, you feed it, you have smoke before flame, and then by and by a little light; but if you still feed it, the light shines brighter and brighter unto the perfect day. So a person may be soundly converted and really a Christian, and may have passed over into the promised land of faith and hope, though he has no milestone to tell him when he passes the line, and there are no phenomena to flame it in heaven or to proclaim it on the earth.

Then there are persons who have the most distinct and clear perceptions of change. Mr. Riggs, who was in college when I was, and who afterwards went abroad as a missionary, was one morning sitting in his room conversing on the subject of religion with a friend, who told him what he thought was necessary in order to become a Christian. "Is that it?" asked young Riggs. "Yes, that is it." "Then," said he, "I am going to live that life." And without any conviction of sin he made a purely intellectual decision, and it was followed at once by his affections and his actual honest life. He he became not only a Christian man, but an eminent Christian man.

On the other hand, there are tempestuous natures, natures that break out into intense emotion. I do not think these dramatic conversions are necessary, but still, if a man's mind works in such a way that when he first gains a clear vision of God and embraces him, and is conscious that all resistance has ceased, and that he is willing to abandon all evil ways and enter upon all righteous ways; when he feels within himself, "I have passed from death to life,"—if there is a transporting sense of joy and surprise, I stand by and say he has a right to his individuality and his own experience. All I ask is that he shall not make that experience a despotic standard for his quieter brethren.

There was an old Methodist preacher in Virginia, in earlier times, who gave his experience, in which — as he said — the spirit of God "walloped" him, and he could get no peace. He told how it drove him out of his house, away from his business and into the fields; how he "wallowed in conviction," as he expressed it. He seems to have been a great, strong nature; and he finally bowed down in the field before God, he said — he was a slaveholder and had nine negro men, — and prayed, "Why, Lord, why is it that you deal so with me? Tell me what is in the way, and I will give it up!" "And, brethren," said he, "I saw nine black niggers standing right up before me, and I said, 'Yes, Lord, I will give them up.' And the next moment I was on my feet hollering, 'Hallelujah! Hallelujah!' That was genuine. I think there are a great many men that might be converted in that way. Men who give false weights and measures, who are doing iniquity on the sly, when they come to the Lord Jesus Christ, they come with a consciousness that they are bringing such unworthy things! When you go to see one whom you love and who desires to love you, what care it inspires within you! How you apparel yourself with that which is sweetest and best! How you take from yourself everything that would be disagreeable! How you seek beauty, and wear it in flowers! How you come into the presence of those you love, honoring them by everything that you think would be sweet and pleasant to them! And when one goes before the Lord Jesus

Christ to offer himself up in love, a loving sacrifice, shall he hide deceits? Shall he hide gross appetites and lusts? Nay, verily; when a man has come to the time of decision, let him take the worst things about himself, the " nine black niggers " before him; and then let him place Christ right over them, ascendant, triumphant. Let him put down his sins, — let them go down in the act of consecration. If there is this transport of emotion, that is his way; he has just as much right to it as the English have to speak English, the French to speak French. But the test of his conversion from the love of sin to the desire for holiness is to be found, not in the manner of its happening but in the life that follows it. " By their *fruits* ye shall know them."

I draw my lectures to a close this evening. I never part for a whole year's separation from any one without the consciousness that it may be the last parting. It is not sorrow that this inspires in me, though it is sadness; but it is a sweet sadness, a tempered sadness. Young gentlemen, many of you may cut short your labors on earth before the time comes round again for the resumption of this course of lectures, should they ever be resumed. Some of you may pass to a higher ministry before that time. Many of you will pass out into the field and begin your earthly ministration. I can ask for you in either case nothing so good as this, — a sense of the love of Jesus Christ to you; — not how much you love him, but the sense of the overflowing affluence of the love of Christ for you! And I can bear you this witness, that not all friendship, not praise, not success in life, not the joy which I experience in communion with nature, not the rapturous and exquisite sensations in the presence of things beautiful, nothing in earth, has ever been to me such strength, such constant joy, as the sense that Christ loved me while I was a sinner, and as I am a sinner, and because I am a sinner; that, because I am sick, he is my physician; and because I am weak, he is my captain; and because I am imperfect, he is my "all and in all." And, therefore, as the consummation of every earthly ambition and as the assurance of everything that is richest and best, I can only wish you the consciousness of a living Saviour; a high-priest, merciful, patient, long-suffering; a present help in time of trouble. Christ loves you with overwhelming love; may you know it and rejoice in it! ·

Cambridge: Electrotyped and Printed by Welch, Bigelow, & Co.

September, 1873.

J. B. Ford & Co.'s Publications.

THE CIRCUIT RIDER.

A NOVEL.

BY EDWARD EGGLESTON.

1 vol. 12mo. [*In Preparation.*

Mr. Eggleston is making this his best novel; and is giving it his most careful attention. Its own superior merits as well as his brilliant reputation will command for this, his latest work, an immediate popularity.

A GOOD MATCH.

A NOVEL.

BY AMELIA PERRIER, Author of "Mea Culpa."

1 vol. 12mo. Cloth, $1 50.

A clever and amusing Novel, agreeably written, racy, and lively.

BRAVE HEARTS.

A NOVEL.

BY ROBERTSON GRAY.

1 vol. 12mo. Cloth, $1 50.

A characteristic American novel under the *nom de plume* of a favorite story-writer, heretofore known by the brilliancy, wit, pathos, humor, and readableness of the shorter tales published under his own name.

SILVER AND GOLD.

AN ACCOUNT OF THE MINING AND METALLURGICAL INDUSTRY OF THE UNITED STATES, WITH REFERENCE CHIEFLY TO THE PRECIOUS METALS.

BY ROSSITER W. RAYMOND.

Commissioner of Mining Statistics; President of the American Institute of Mining Engineers; Editor of the Engineering and Mining Journal; Author of "Mines of the West," "American Mines and Mining," "Mines, Mills, and Furnaces," etc., etc.

1 vol. 8vo. Cloth, $3 50.

27 *Park Place, and* 24 & 26 *Murray Street, New York.*

WINNING SOULS.

SKETCHES AND INCIDENTS DURING FORTY YEARS OF PASTORAL WORK.

By REV. S. B. HALLIDAY.

1 vol. 12mo. Cloth, $1.

The author of this volume for some time past has been, and now is, engaged as assistant in the pastoral labors of Plymouth Church, Brooklyn (Rev. H. W. Beecher's), where, in visiting among the sick, the poor, and the afflicted of that large parish, and in attending to many of the social and business details of the church, he is continually encountering new and interesting phases of heart-life struggling to turn from sin and sorrow toward godliness and peace. These simple records of scenes among his earlier labors will possess a peculiar interest to all who love such work for their fellows.

NORWOOD:
Or, Village Life in New England.

A NOVEL.

By HENRY WARD BEECHER.

Uniform Edition of the Author's Works.

1 vol. 12mo.   [*In Press.*

This is Mr. Beecher's only novel, and it affords a most remarkable illustration of his versatility. Full of exquisite descriptions of scenery and delineations of social and domestic life, exceedingly graphic and trustworthy in detail, and abounding in passages of genial humor and kindly wisdom, it is altogether one of the most enjoyable novels ever published. It is fragrant with the genuine raciness of the New England soil.

PLEASANT TALK ABOUT FRUITS,
FLOWERS, AND FARMING.

NEW EDITION, WITH MUCH ADDITIONAL MATTER.

By HENRY WARD BEECHER.

Uniform Edition of the Author's Works.

1 vol. 12mo. Cloth, $1 75.

This volume, when it was first given to the public some years ago, was most favorably received, both in this country and in England. The present edition contains many recent additions to the original book, dealing with both the poetical and the practical side of gardening and farming, the whole making a volume of rare interest and value.

YALE LECTURES ON PREACHING.

FIRST SERIES.

BY HENRY WARD BEECHER.

Uniform Edition of the Author's Works.

1 vol. 12mo. Cloth, $1 25.

Delivered before the classes of theology and the faculty of the Divinity School of Yale College. This series treats of the personal elements which bear an important relation to preaching. The Lectures are rich in suggestion, not only to the minister, but to the lawyer,—to everybody to whom the study of human nature is of interest or value. As an expression of the methods by which this master-preacher works to produce such resulss as have crowned his ministry, their usefulness cannot be over-estimated.

"What a charming, what a 'fruity' volume is this last venture of Henry Ward Beecher! The 'Yale Lectures on Preaching' can be read by everybody, layman or clergyman, with delight. We can point to few recent novels which are more entertaining than this book."—*Boston Globe.*

"Vigorous, eloquent, and practical." —*Philadelphia Age.*

"We know of no dozen treaties on the preacher's work which contain so much of sensible and valuable instruction as is compressed into this little volume."—*N. Y. Independent.*

YALE LECTURES ON PREACHING.

SECOND SERIES.

BY HENRY WARD BEECHER.

Uniform Edition of the Author's Works.

1 vol. 12mo. Cloth, $1 50.

The second course consists of eleven lectures delivered at Yale College during the winter of 1873. In this course Mr. Beecher considers the social and religious machinery of the church as related to preaching.

STAR PAPERS.

NEW EDITION, WITH MANY ADDITIONAL PAPERS.

BY HENRY WARD BEECHER.

Uniform Edition of the Author's Works.

1 vol. 12mo. Cloth, $1 75.

These experiences of Art and Nature are perhaps the most widely known of Mr. Beecher's miscellaneous writings. The original edition, issued many years ago, met with a most gratifying reception, and, although it has been out of print for some years, has been frequently inquired for. It is now reissued with fresh and charming additions.

"We have nothing in the way of descriptive writing, not even the best sketches of Washington Irving, that exceeds in richness of imagery and perspicuity of statement these 'Star Papers.'"—*Methodist Home Journal.*

"A book to be read and re-read, and always with a fresh sense of enjoyment." —*Portland Press.*
"So full of rural life, so sparkling with cheerfulness, so holy in their tenderness, and so brave in nobility of thought."—*Liberal Christian.*

LECTURES TO YOUNG MEN

ON VARIOUS IMPORTANT SUBJECTS.

NEW EDITION, WITH ADDITIONAL LECTURES.

By HENRY WARD BEECHER.

Uniform Edition of the Author's Works.

1 vol. 12mo. Cloth, $1 50.

This was Mr. Beecher's first book, and is known all over the world. The present edition is enriched by the addition of several new lectures, and some reminiscences of the origin of the book by Mr. Beecher. The book should have a place in every family. It can scarcely fail to interest every intelligent reader, nor to benefit every young man who reads it.

"The subjects are all practical, and presented with characteristic impressiveness."—*Albany Evening Journal.*

"Wise and elevating in tone, pervaded by earnestness, and well fitted for its mission to improve and benefit the youth of the land."—*Boston Commonwealth.*

"These lectures are written with all the vigor of style and beauty of language which characterize everything from the pen of this remarkable man. They are a series of fearless dissertations upon every-day subjects, conveyed with a power of eloquence and a practical illustration so unique as to be oftentimes startling to the reader of ordinary discourses of the kind."—*Philadelphia Inquirer.*

MOTHERLY TALKS

WITH YOUNG HOUSEKEEPERS.

By MRS. H. W. BEECHER.

WITH CARBON-PHOTOGRAPHIC PORTRAIT OF THE AUTHOR.

1 vol. 12mo. $2.

Mrs. Beecher's notion of woman's sphere is, that, whatever exceptional women may be able to accomplish by reason of peculiar circumstances and talents, the place of labor and achievement for most women, and for all married women and mothers, is *Home.*

This book, composed of brief and pithy articles on almost every conceivable point of duty, is an admirable monitor for young wives, and a mine of good sense and information for growing maidens.

"An admirable corrective to ignorance in the household."—*N. Y. Tribune.*

"A useful and entertaining work, crammed with friendly and admirable monitions and instruction for young housekeepers."—*Philadelphia Evening Herald.*

"This book is exactly what its title sets forth—a kind and motherly way of helping the young and inexperienced make agreeable, well-regulated, and happy homes."—*Boston Globe.*

"What she has to say she says so well, with such good sense, ripe judgment, and such a mother-warmth of heart, that she cannot fail to help the class for whom she writes, and guide them into good and useful paths."—*Presbyterian.*

NEW LIFE IN NEW LANDS.

NOTES OF TRAVEL ACROSS THE AMERICAN CONTINENT, FROM
CHICAGO TO THE PACIFIC AND BACK.

By GRACE GREENWOOD.

1 vol. 12mo. $2.

This is a gathered series of letters, racy, brilliant, piquant; full of keen observation and pungent statement of facts, picturesque in delineation of scenes on the plains, in the mountains, and along the sea.

"Among the best of the author's productions, and every way delightful." —*Boston Post.*

"The late William H. Seward characterized her account of Mormons and Mormonism as the most graphic and trustworthy he had ever read."—*Methodist Home Journal.*

"Grace always finds lots of things no one else would see; and she has a happy knack of picking up the mountains and cities and big tress, and tossing them across the continent right before the reader's eyes. It's very convenient."—*Buffalo Express.*

MY WIFE AND I:

OR, HARRY HENDERSON'S HISTORY.

A NOVEL.

By HARRIET BEECHER STOWE.

Illustrated. 1 vol. 12mo. Cloth, $1 75.

This charming novel is, in some respects, Mrs. Stowe's most thoughtful and complete book. It is eminently a book for the times, giving the author's individual ideas about the much-vexed *Woman Question*, including marriage, divorce, suffrage, legislation, and all the rights claimed by the clamorous.

"A capital story, in which fashionable follies are shown up, fast young ladies weighed in the balance and found wanting, and the value of true worth exhibited."—*Portland Argus.*

"Always bright, piquant, and entertaining, with an occasional touch of tenderness, strong because subtle, keen in sarcasm, full of womanly logic directed against unwomanly tendencies. —*Boston Journal.*

THE OVERTURE OF ANGELS.

A SERIES OF PICTURES OF THE ANGELIC APPEARANCES ATTENDING
THE NATIVITY OF OUR LORD. A CHAPTER FROM
THE "LIFE OF CHRIST."

By HENRY WARD BEECHER.

Illustrated. 1 vol. 12mo. $2.

A beautiful and characteristically interesting treatment of all the events recorded in the Gospels as occurring about the time of the Nativity. Full of poetic imagery, beauty of sentiment, and vivid pictures of the life of the Orient in that day.

"The style, the sentiment, and faithfulness to the spirit of the Biblical record with which the narrative is treated are characteristic of its author, and will commend it to many readers, to whom its elegance of form will give it an additional attraction."—*Worcester (Mass. Spy.*
"A perfect fragment."—*N. Y. World.*

BEECHER'S SERMONS.

FROM PHONOGRAPHIC REPORTS BY T. J. ELLINWOOD, FOR FIFTEEN
YEARS MR. BEECHER'S SPECIAL REPORTER. UNIFORMLY
BOUND IN DARK BROWN ENGLISH CLOTH. EACH
VOLUME CONTAINS TWENTY-SIX SER-
MONS, AND THE PRAYERS BE-
FORE THE SERMONS.

Eight vols. 8vo. Cloth, $2 50 each.

Each succeeding volume will contain also, six months' sermons (from
450 to 500 pp.), issued in uniform style. The *First Series* has an excellent steel portrait of Mr. Beecher; the *Second Series*, a fine interior
view of Plymouth Church. The other volumes are not illustrated.

"These corrected sermons of perhaps the greatest of living preachers—a man whose heart is as warm and catholic as his abilities are great, and whose sermons combine fidelity and scriptural truth, great power, glorious imagination, fervid rhetoric, and vigorous reasoning, with intense human sympathy and robust common-sense." — *British Quarterly Review.*

"There is not a discourse in all this large collection that does not hold passages of great suggestiveness and power for the most ordinary, unsympathizing reader—illustrations of great beauty and point, eloquent invitations to better life, touching appeals to nobler purposes and more generous action," — *Springfield Republican.*

MATERNITY:

A POPULAR TREATISE FOR WIVES AND MOTHERS.

BY T. S. VERDI, A. M., M. D.

Fifth Edition.

1 vol. 12mo. $2 25.

This book has arisen from a want felt in the author's own practice,
as a monitor to young wives, a guide to young mothers, and an assistant to the family physician. It deals skillfully, sensibly, and deli-
cately with the perplexities of married life, giving information which
women must have, either in conversation with physicians or from
such a source as this. Plain and intelligible, but without offence to
the most fastidious taste, the style of this book must commend it to
careful perusal. It treats of the needs, dangers, and alleviations of
the holy duties of maternity, and gives extended, detailed instructions for the care and medical treatment of infants and children
throughont all the perils of early life.

"The author deserves great credit for his labor, and the book merits an extensive circulation."—*U. S. Medical and Surgical Journal* (*Chicago*).
"We hail the appearance of this work with true pleasure. It is dictated by a pure and liberal spirit, and will be a real boon to many a young mother."—*American Medical Observer* (*Detroit*).

"There are few intelligent mothers who will not be benefitted by reading and keeping by them for frequent counsel a volume so rich in valuable suggestions. With its tables, prescriptions, and indexes at the end, this book ought to do much good."—*Hearth and Home.*

THE CHILDREN'S WEEK:

SEVEN STORIES FOR SEVEN DAYS.

BY R. W. RAYMOND.

ILLUSTRATED BY H. L. STEPHENS AND MISS M. L. HALLOCK.

1 vol. 16mo. Cloth, $1 25.

Seven cheery stories with a flavor of the holidays about them. Mr. Raymond's conceptions are ingenious, and while the glimpses of fairy-land and its wonders will open the eyes of the little folk, the book possesses many attractions for older persons in its simple, artistic style, and the quaint ideas in which it revels.

" The book is bright enough to please any people of culture, and yet so simple that children will welcome it with glee."—*Cleveland Plaindealer.*

Mr. Raymond's tales have won great popularity by their wit, delicate fancy, and, withal, admirable good sense. The illustrations—all new and made for the book—are particularly apt and pleasing, showing forth the comical element of the book and its pure and beautiful sentiment."—*Buffalo (N. Y.) Commercial Advertiser.*

OUR SEVEN CHURCHES:

EIGHT LECTURES.

BY THOMAS K. BEECHER.

1 vol. 16mo. Paper, 50 cents; Cloth, $1.

A most valuable exponent of the doctrines of the leading religious denominations, and a striking exhibition of the author's magnanimity and breadth of loving sympathy.

" The sermons are written in a style at once brilliant, epigrammatic, and readable."—*Utica Herald.*
" This little book has created considerable discussion among the religious journals, and will be read with interest by all."—*Phila. Ledger.*

" There is hardly a page which does not offer a fresh thought, a genial touch of humor, or a suggestion at which the reader's heart leaps up with grateful surprise that a minister belonging to a sect can think and speak so generously and nobly."—*Milwaukee Sentinel.*

HISTORY of the STATE OF NEW YORK.

FROM THE DATE OF THE DISCOVERY AND SETTLEMENTS ON MANHATTAN ISLAND TO THE PRESENT TIME. A TEXT-BOOK FOR HIGH SCHOOLS, ACADEMIES, AND COLLEGES.

BY S. S. RANDALL,

Superintendent of Public Education in New York City.

1 vol. 12mo. *Illustrated.* Cloth, $1 75.

Officially adopted by the Boards of Education in the cities of New York, Brooklyn, and Jersey City, for use in the Public Schools; and in Private Schools throughout the State.

PRINCIPLES OF DOMESTIC SCIENCE

AS APPLIED TO THE DUTIES AND PLEASURES OF HOME.

By CATHARINE E. BEECHER and HARRIET BEECHER STOWE

1 vol. 12mo. *Profusely Illustrated.* Cloth, $2.

Prepared with a view to assist in training young women for the distinctive duties which inevitably come upon them in household life, this volume has been made with especial reference to the duties, cares, and pleasures of *the family*, as being the place where, whatever the political developments of the future, woman, from her nature of body and of spirit, will find her most engrossing occupation. It is full of interest for all intelligent girls and young women.

The work has been heartily indorsed and adopted by the directors of many of the leading Colleges and Seminaries for young women as a text-book, both for study and reading.

MINES, MILLS, AND FURNACES
of the Precious Metals of the United States.

BEING A COMPLETE EXPOSITION OF THE GENERAL METHODS EMPLOYED IN THE GREAT MINING INDUSTRIES OF AMERICA.

By ROSSITER W. RAYMOND, PH. D.,
U. S. Commissioner of Mining Statistics.

1 vol. 8vo. *With Plates.* Cloth, $3 50.

This is a very particular account of the condition of the mining interests, and the processes and mechanical appliances which are applicable to them, in California, Nevada, Oregon, Idaho, Montana, Utah, Arizona, Wyoming, Colorado, and New Mexico. It is the report of the Commissioner to the Secretary of the Treasury, and embodies all the information which official investigation and contributions from experts and residents of those regions can afford.

"The author is thorough in his subject, and has already published a work on our mines which commanded universal approval by its clearness of statement and breadth of views."—*Albany Argus.*

"His scientific ability, his practical knowledge of mines and mining, his unerring judgment, and, finally, the enthusiasm with which he enters upon his work, all combine to fit him for his position, and none could bring it to a greater degree of uprightness and fairness."—*Denver News.*

☞ Any of the above books will be sent to any address, post-paid, upon receipt of the price by the Publishers.

27 Park Place, and 24 & 26 Murray Street, New York.

Subscription Publications.

THE LIFE OF JESUS, THE CHRIST.

By HENRY WARD BEECHER.

PROFUSELY ILLUSTRATED, FROM DESIGNS AFTER NATURE, BY A. L. RAWSON, DRAWN ON WOOD BY HARRY FENN, AND ENGRAVED BY THE BROTHERS LINTON; WITH NUMEROUS MAPS; AND WITH A STEEL PLATE FRONTISPIECE, "HEAD OF CHRIST," COPIED FROM DA VINCI'S "LAST SUPPER," BY W. E. MARSHALL.

PART I.

Popular Edition. 1 vol. 8vo. Cloth, $3 50.
Imperial Edition. 1 vol. 4to. Cloth, $7 50.

It is rare to find in any one book so many attractions as this pretends, in the grandeur and interest of the subject, and the peculiar fitness of the author for its treatment both by native genius and careful preparation. Mr. Beecher has put his whole wonderful self into the writing of this book.

"The book which the masses of the Christian world have been waiting for."—REV. R. S. STORRS, D.D.

"He has neither thrown off his random thoughts nor strung together his best thoughts; but has brought all his powers, in the maturity of their strength, in the richness of their experience, and the largeness of their development, to produce a work that may fitly represent the results of his life."—REV. J. P. THOMPSON, *in the Independent.*

PART II. IN PREPARATION.

A LIBRARY OF POETRY AND SONG.

BEING CHOICE SELECTIONS FROM THE POETS.

WITH AN INTRODUCTION

By WILLIAM CULLEN BRYANT.

Illustrated with a Portrait on Steel of MR. BRYANT, twenty-six Autographic Fac-similes on Wood of Celebrated Poets, and sixteen full-page Wood Engravings by the best Artists

Popular Edition. 1 vol. 8vo. Cloth, $5 00.
Red-Line Edition. 1 vol. 8vo. Cloth, $7 50.

This book has been prepared with the aim of gathering into a single volume the largest practical compilation of the best poems of the English language, making it as nearly as possible the choicest and most complete general collection published.

"Good taste has ruled in the selections, and the compiler has performed his exceedingly difficult task with great success."—*Chicago Advance.*

"Bryant's Introduction to the volume is a most beautiful and comprehensive critical essay on poets and poetry, from the days of 'the father of English poetry' to the present time."—*Albany Evening Journal.*

"The frontispiece is an exquisite likeness of Mr. Bryant."—*New York Evening Post.*

𝔖𝔲𝔟𝔰𝔠𝔯𝔦𝔭𝔱𝔦𝔬𝔫 𝔓𝔲𝔟𝔩𝔦𝔠𝔞𝔱𝔦𝔬𝔫𝔰.—*Continued.*

A LIBRARY OF FAMOUS FICTION.

EMBRACING THE NINE STANDARD MASTERPIECES OF IMAGINATIVE LITERATURE.

WITH AN INTRODUCTION
By HARRIET BEECHER STOWE.

Illustrated with thirty-four Engravings on Wood.

1 vol. 8vo. Cloth, $5.

In this companion book to the "Library of Poetry and Song," the famous fictions which have delighted generations are offered to the public in an elegant and convenient form. Mrs. Stowe's Introtion is an admirable feature of the book.

"A fitting companion for the popular 'Library of Poetry and Song.'"—*Lyons (N. Y.) Republican.*

"All ages will delight in it—some because it presents the tales which charmed them in youth, and some because it will open to them the rich treasures of wildest fancy and most limitless imagination."—*Philadelphia Age.*

"Not a single one could be spared from this group."—*Rahway (N. Y.) Advocate and Times.*

"The book is a gathering of intellectual treasures, which all intelligent families must desire in *some* form to possess and preserve; and it is believed that this is the most convenient, interesting, and elegant form in which they have ever been presented to the public."—*Newburgh (N. Y.) Journal.*

THE NEW HOUSEKEEPER'S MANUAL.

Embracing "The American Woman's Home," and "The Handy Cook-Book."

By CATHARINE E. BEECHER and HARRIET BEECHER STOWE.

Profusely Illustrated.

1 vol. 8vo. Cloth, $3.

An eminently practical work, the result of long domestic experience, and thorough study of domestic needs. It deals with the foundation principles of successful housekeeping, besides being full of detailed directions. It gives the scientific and the common-sense *reason why*, which lies at the foundation of the operations of everyday life. It is also a complete Manual of Cookery.

"It is a book which, to country readers at least, must prove invaluable."—*N. Y. Tribune.*

"Young married women, if they will but read, may find many helps to pleasant and comfortable living in this volume."—*New York Times.*

"It treats *practically* of every subject relating to domestic life, from the woman's stand-point."—*Christian Advocate (N. Y.).*

"The reading of this work will tend to make better wives, mothers, and companions."—*Manford's Monthly (St. Louis.*

"The receipts, counsels, directions, hints, and experiences meet many of the little perplexities of a housekeeper's head."—*Northern Christian Advocate.*

27 Park Place, and 24 & 26 Murray Street, New York.

Printed in Great Britain
by Amazon